CHINESE RELIGION THROUGH HINDU EYES

CHINESE RELIGION
THROUGH
HINDU EYES

A STUDY IN THE TENDENCIES OF ASIATIC MENTALITY

BY

BENOY KUMAR SARKAR

Translator of Sukra-Mti (Hindu Economics and Politics), and Author of The Positive Background of Hindu Sociology, The Falk-Element in Hindu Culture, etc.

with an Introduction by

WU TING-FANG, LL.D.

Late Chinese Minister to U.S.A., Spain, Peru, Mexico and Cubs

GYAN

Published by

Gyan Publishing House
5, Ansari Road
Daryaganj, New Delhi-110002
Phone: 011-47034999, 9811692060
E-mail: books@gyanbooks.com

Distribution Network
gyanbooks.com
India, USA, Canada, UK, Australia, France

ISBN : 978-81-212-3239-5 (PB)
First Published, 1916

2nd Impression 2020

Printed at: Gyan Press, Delhi.

Chinese Religion Through Hindu Eyes
Author: Benoy Kumar Sarkar

CHINESE RELIGION

THROUGH

HINDU EYES

A STUDY IN THE TENDENCIES OF ASIATIC MENTALITY

BY

BENOY KUMAR SARKAR

Translator of *Sukra-nîti* (Hindu Economics and Politics), and Author of *The Positive Background of Hindu Sociology*, *The Folk-Element in Hindu Culture*, etc.

with an Introduction by

WU TING-FANG, LL.D.

Late Chinese Minister to U.S.A., Spain, Peru, Mexico and Cuba

SHANGHAI

THE COMMERCIAL PRESS, Ltd.

1916

DEDICATED TO THE SACRED MEMORY OF

KUMÂRA-JÎVA

(*c* A.D. 405)

A foremost Indian Educator of the age of Vikramâdityan Renaissance, who carried forward the missionising activity of Emperor Asoka the Great (begun with Western Asia and beyond) by bearing the torch of Hindu Thought to the Far Eastern Cathay and thus became instrumental in the establishment of Indian hegemony throughout the Orient;

HIUEN THSÂNG

(A.D. 602-664)

The great Chinese Master of Law, who, having studied Hindu Culture in Tienchu (or Heaven, *i.e.*, India) for 16 years (629-45) during one of the most brilliant epochs of Indian Imperialism under Harsha-vardhana and Pulakesin II., propagated it extensively in his native land under the patronage of the mighty Tâng Emperor Tai Tsung (627-50) and thus laid the foundations of a re-interpreted Confucianism;

and

KŌBŌ DAISHI

(A.D. 774—835)

The scholar-saint of Japan, who, inspired by the example of his illustrious predecessor, Prince Shōtoku Taishi (A.D. 573—621), devoted himself to Hindu *vidyâs* (sciences) for three years (804-6) in China, and became the first native pioneer to propagate *Indono Damashii* in the land of the *Kâmi*, thereby developing in manifold ways its infant civilisation;

By a Hindu Student of the institutions of
MEDIAEVAL ASIA

PREFACE

Neither historically nor philosophically does Asiatic mentality differ from the Eur-American. It is only after the brilliant successes of a fraction of mankind subsequent to the Industrial Revolution of the last century that the alleged difference between the two mentalities has been first stated and since then grossly exaggerated. At the present day science is being vitiated by pseudo-scientific theories or fancies regarding race, religion, and culture. Such theories were unknown to the world down to the second or third decade of the 19th century.

Comparative Chronology and Comparative History will show that man, as an economic, political and fighting animal, has displayed the same strength and weakness both on the Asian theatre as well as on the extra-Asian.

Comparative Literature and Comparative Art will show that man, as "lover, lunatic and poet", has worked upon the same gamut of passions from Homer to Mæterlinck as from the Pharaonic *Book of the Dead* down to *Gitânjali*.

Comparative Philosophy and Comparative Metaphysics will show that man, as positivist and mystic, has attacked the "problems of the sphinx" in the selfsame way and with almost similar results under the guidance of intellectuals from Confucius to Swâmi Vivek-ânanda as from Socrates to Bergson.

It has been held generally that the Orient is statical, and that the dynamic doctrine of Change is essentially non-Oriental. Thus, the following verses of Tennyson—

> "The old order changeth yielding place to new
> And God fulfils himself in many ways
> Lest one good custom should corrupt the world"

are supposed to embody exclusively the spirit of the Occident.

Let us, however, take a bit from the Mind of China, which is the proverbial representative of "the unchanging East," and which, besides, is known to be "sicklied o'er by the pale cast of the Confucian tradition." Even the Great Sage himself was an advocate of the "new order." The second article in what may be regarded as the

Educational Creed of Confucius is thus worded by Mr. Ku Hung-Ming in his recent translation of the classic *Ta Hsueh**:

"The object of a Higher Education is to make a new and better society (lit. people)."

An old commentary explains what 'to make a new and better society' means. The following is Mr. Ku's translation of the explanation:

1. "The Inscription on the Emperor Tâng's bath says: 'Be a new man each day, from day to day be a new man, every day be a new man.'

2. The Commission of Investiture to Prince Kâng says: 'Create a new Society.'

3. The *Book of Songs* says: 'Although the Royal House of Chow was on old state, a new mission was given to it.' "

The nature of the relation between Order and Progress was also well known to the Hindu thinkers of the *Mahâbhârata*-cycle. Their Messianic conception formulated in the *Gîtâ*-section (6th century B.C.—2nd century B.C.) of this literature is pre-eminently dynamic. The doctrine of *Yugântara*, i.e. "transformation of the age-spirit" or "revolution in *Zeitgeist*," is recorded in the following announcement of Lord Krishna regarding the occasions of His advent into the world of man:

"Whensoever into Order
Corruption creeps in, Bhârata,
And customs bad ascendant be,
— Then Myself do I embody.
For the advancement of the good
And miscreants to overthrow
And for setting up the Order
Do I appear age by age."

The Hindu Messiah is Revolution, Progress and Optimism personified. His was the message of Change and Hope. The idea of "God fulfilling himself in many ways" is thus neither an Occidental patent nor a modern discovery.

**Higher Education* (The Shanghai Mercury, Ltd., Shanghai, 1915). This is one of the four books in the Confucian Bible and has been called *The Great Learning* by Dr. Legge in his translation.

Comparative Anthropology and Comparative Psychology will show that man has everywhere and always been fundamentally a beast, and that beneath a superficial varnish of so-called culture "the ape and tiger" hold their majestic sway,—giving rise to superstitions, prejudices, *idolas* and *avidyâs* under different guises and conventions. The brute-in-man is a fact,—the *datum;* but the god-in-man is only an idea,—the ideal *to be* realised.

Comparative Religion and Comparative Mythology will show that man in his desire to have "something afar from the sphere of our sorrow" has everywhere had recourse to the same *modus operandi* and has achieved the same grand failure which in his vanity he always chooses to call success. It would be found that, after all, divinity is but an invention of human imagination, in fact, the first postulate taken for granted. And on a broad view of *all* the forces that have inspired and governed *elan* and activity, some of which are miscalled religion, and some not, man has ever been essentially a pluralist and an idolist.

If anywhere there have been people professing a so-called monotheism in religion, a study of their daily life would indicate that they have been polytheists with vengeance in every other sphere —indulging in thousand and one varieties, social, economic and political. These varieties which take away the monotony of life and give a zest to it, do not, "pragmatically" speaking, differ in the last analysis from the varied rites and practices underlying a so-called polytheistic faith. What the polytheists call religion, the monotheists call culture. Life demands variety; culture, therefore, is varied. If you abstract a millionth part of this *kultur*, *e.g.*, the unverifiable hypothesis of man about God, and choose to call it religion, every race can be proved to be monotheistic. But if you take the total inspiration of a human being or the chart of the whole life that a people lives, mankind has ever been polytheistic.

If, again, anywhere there have been people who have repudiated idols in religion, a study of their heart and feelings, their daily habits, their literary and artistic tastes, would indicate that they are paying the debt to "old Adam" in the shape of hero-worship, souvenir-cult, love-fetishes, "pathetic fallacy," mementos, memorials, relics, and what not. As formative principles of character, these "charms" are of the same genus as images erected in the temples by those who in their simplicity confess—"We do not understand, we love."

If there is superstition in the one form of pluralism and idolism there is equal superstition in the others. These are really "human, all too human." In fact, the greatest and most abiding of all superstitions in world's history has been the human demand for that ambiguous term Religion.

Superstition is nothing but *avidyâ* or *mâyâ*, *i.e.*, ignorance, rendered perceptible. Emancipation from this has been the highest ideal of man. The prayer of the most ancient Hindu *Rishis* or "seers" was—

A-sato mâ sad-gamaya,
Tamaso mâ jyotir-gamaya,
Mrityor mâ amritam-gamaya.

From the non-existent (*i.e.* transitory, unreal)
me to the ever-existent (*i.e.* permanent, truth, or reality) lead;
From darkness (*i.e.* ignorance)
me to light (*i.e.* knowledge) lead;
From death me to immortality lead.

This has been the prayer of mankind ever since. Knowledge is the only truth—the ever-existent reality—the light—immortality itself. Whether it be called religion or not, man has ever wanted this knowledge—*sat*, *jyoti*, *amritam*.

The modern world congratulates itself on the thought that the Bastille of ignorance was demolished with the Papal Doctrine of Infallibility. The flood of light that was being thrown on world-questions with the discovery of Sanskrit in the 18th century certainly heralded a new era. And the modern means of communication did really bring world-sense home to seekers of truth. Comparative philology, comparative mythology, and what Maxmuller hesitated to call comparative jurisprudence, were the first fruits,—the *Synthetic Philosophy* of Herbert Spencer, the *Philosophy of History* of Hegel, and Comte's *Positive Philosophy* were genuine attempts in the direction of *sat*, *jyoti* and *amritam*.

The holy quest of "enlightenment" is, however, always baffled by *Mâras* or Tempters. It is probably not given to man to have complete enlightenment at any stage of his history. He

"trusted God was love indeed
And love creation's final law."

But—"Nature, red in tooth and claw
With ravine, shriek'd against his creed."

The old *avidyâ* has only changed its guise. The guise of the modern *idola* or superstition has been the dogma: "Nothing succeeds like success." The successful races of the last three generations have been interpreting world-culture and human civilisation from the standpoint of a new "Infallibility." This is but the modern version of the mediæval Romanist theory.

The twentieth century demands a new synthesis,—a fresh "transvaluation of values," and, as prolegomena to that, a New Logic. A complete over-hauling of the whole apparatus of thinking is urgently needed to carry forward the tendencies initiated by the discovery of Kâlidâsa for world-literature and by the application of steam to the furtherance of human needs.

The work owes its origin to the first two chapters which were read before the Royal Asiatic Society (North China Branch) in October, 1915, as "First Impressions of Chinese Religion," more than which it does not claim to be. It was taken up at the kind suggestion of the Society's learned Secretary and Editor, the most unassuming sinologue, Rev. Samuel Couling.

A few chapters were read before the "International Institute" in connection with their studies in Comparative Religion. Rev. Dr. Gilbert Reid, Director-in-chief of the Institute, has placed me under great obligation by taking the trouble of interpreting the lectures in Chinese for those who did not understand English and also by publishing Chinese translations of the papers in the Institute Magazine.

I have made frequent use of the "Christian Literature Society's' Library, and take this opportunity of expressing my heart-felt thanks to the Director-Emeritus, Rev. Dr. Timothy Richard, who has been prominent in the Far East, as being, among other things, a keen student of Buddhism.

The Bibliography as well as the names of publications in the Index will indicate the nature and amount of my indebtedness, both direct and indirect. Footnotes with chapter and verse have, however, been avoided, as all interesting details, without which comparisons could not be instituted, have been given in full from the works of well-known authorities.

For the benefit of those to whom China with four hundred millions (?) and India with three hundred and fifty millions are still only geographical expressions learnt from school primers I venture here to single out two volumes:

1. *Descriptive Sociology: Chinese*—"compiled upon the plan organised by Herbert Spencer" by E.T.C. Werner,—H.I.B.M's Consul at Foochow, China (Williams and Norgate, London, 1910). It is really an Encyclopædia Sinica made up of extracts from about 200 English, French and German publications besides Journals, and from over 700 Chinese works.

2. *Early History of India* (B.C. 600—A.D. 1200) by Vincent A. Smith, late of the Indian Civil Service (Third Edition, Clarendon Press, Oxford, 1914). This is the only authoritative and systematic volume on "the political vicissitudes of the land." It is not a mere compilation but the work of one who has himself been one of the greatest figures in Indology.

A considerable portion of this work was published as articles in "The National Review" (Shanghai), "The Hindusthanee Student" (U.S.A.), and in the Indian periodicals, "The Hindustan Review" (Allahabad), "The Vedic Magazine" (Hardwar), "The Collegian" (Calcutta), and "The Modern Review" (Calcutta).

Dr. Wu Ting-fang, LL.D., late Chinese Minister to Washington, D.C. (U.S.A.), has kindly contributed his ideas on the Religion of the Chinese in the form of an Introduction to this work. The author is grateful for the favour thus accorded him by the veteran Confucianist scholar.

Shanghai, China,
March 9, 1916.

BENOY KUMAR SARKAR.

INTRODUCTION

We often have visitors coming to China from Europe and America on various missions ; some for scientific research ; some for economic investigation ; some for educational purpose, and others for art and general studies. It is the first time, if I am not mistaken, that a gentleman from India has come to China for such a purpose. Professor Benoy Kumar Sarkar is now on a visit to China to study the religion, literature and social institutions of the people, and the result of his earnest and laborious research extending over several months is seen in the following pages. Whether the reader will follow him and agree with all his views expressed in this book it must be conceded that he has not hastily come to his conclusions without personal study. The mass of facts collected by him and his views expressed thereon should afford the students of Sociology and Comparative Religion much food for thought and deserve their impartial consideration.

"What is the religion of your people?" This question has often been put to us Chinese. If the answer "Confucianism" is given, it will be most likely retorted that Confucianism is not a religion, it being a set of morals only. Now let us see what is Religion. Webster defines it as "the outward act or form by which men indicate their recognition of the existence of a god or gods having power over their destiny, to whom obedience, service, and honour are due." Then let us ascertain what Confucianism is. The doctrine of the founder is to teach the duty and relations of man, between the Sovereign and the subject, between the parent and the son, between elder and younger brothers, and between friends; the "four books" which practically constitute the canon of Confucian philosophy minutely describe the sayings and instructions of the great philosopher. His principal aim was to inculcate loyalty to the Chief of the State, filial piety to parents and sincerity amongst friends. It must be admitted that the result of his teaching has been on the whole eminently successful. That he did not expressly instruct his disciples to worship God as enjoined by other religions cannot be denied; but his tenets, if observed, would lead men to become good, for they are in many instances along similar lines to the teachings given by other religions. Take, for instance, the excellent rule laid down by Confucius:—"What you do not want done to yourself do not do to others." This is the golden rule only in a negative form. Thus it will be seen that a real Confucianist is just as good a man as a sincere Christian.

It is sometimes alleged that Confucius was an atheist or a materialist; this accusation is not just considering that he believed in the existence of a Supreme God. In the "Classics" there are many passages which prove this. On one occasion when he was very sick, one of his disciples asked leave to pray for him, he answered that it was scarcely necessary because he had been praying for a long time. On another occasion he exhorted his disciples to shew respect to spiritual beings; then again he declared that to offer sacrifice to spirits indiscriminately is flattery. In ancient times, as it was customary in every nation, the people were superstitious and naturally religious. Confucius, being brought up under these surroundings, could not help being influenced by them, but he had the sagacity to warn his disciples that while respecting spiritual beings they should keep aloof from them. He considered his mission was to make men morally good and he did not consider it his duty to interfere with spiritual and theological subjects. It may be asked that if he really believed in the existence of the Supreme God to whom obedience, service, and honour are due, how is it that in all his lectures to his disciples he did not touch upon the subject of religious piety and service to God? The reason is not far to seek. He was a staunch conservative and an ardent admirer of antiquity. In his dialogues he is seen expounding his views upon the duty of not only shewing obedience to parents and to ruler but also reverence for antiquity and strict adherence to the traditional usages of ceremony. The direct worship of God was confined in the ancient religion, as it has always been, to the Sovereign as the parent and priest of the people, so it was not a subject that he as one of the "governed" should touch upon. His silence on this point should not be construed that he was an atheist or a materialist.

About the same time, or a little before there arose a great figure who was a contemporary of Confucius and who founded the religion of what is called "Taoism." The founder was Lao Tan and generally known as Lao Tsze, and the book left behind by him which was his own composition, is well known as *Tao Teh King*. It contains only five thousand words but it is fully of gems. This work contains in substance his views on philosophy and expresses fully his doctrine. The author, it must be remembered, was a mystic, he expresses his views in symbolical and paradoxical language. His diction is simple but enigmatic in style. It is extremely difficult even for an earnest student to grasp his real meaning. It is generally supposed that his doctrine is Inaction, but this is not actually the case. He did not advise men to remain inert and do nothing, what he did advise was to purify the mind and cultivate a clear conscience. Its gist is reason and virtue, in other words, he exhorted men to distinguish between the real and the unreal and to perceive things in their proper light. His mode of teaching is different to that of Confucius. He holds that nature provides an ample lesson for man to study and he takes for instance the vegetable kingdom as his ideal. He advocates introspection for the purpose of self-reformation. He was opposed to the way of Confucius who was constantly on the move from one state to another with the view of inducing the chiefs of the state to employ him or to adopt his principles. In an interview sought by Confucius who praised reverence for the sages of antiquity he did not scruple to speak out his mind: "Those whom you talk about are dead, and their bones are mouldered to dust; only their words remain. When the superior man gets his time, he mounts aloft; but when the time is against him, he moves as if his feet were entangled. I have heard that a good merchant though he has rich treasures deeply stored, appears as if he were poor, and that the superior man whose virtue is complete is yet outwardly seeming stupid. Put away your proud air and many desires, your insinuating habit and will. These are of no advantage to you. This is all which I have to tell you." His deep and abstruse theory even Confucius was unable to understand, for soon after the celebrated interview he addressed his disciples, saying: "I know how birds can fly, how fishes can swim, and how animals can run. But the runner may be snared, the swimmer may be hocked, and the flier may be shot by the arrow. But there is the dragon. I cannot tell how he mounts on the wind through the clouds, and rises to heaven. To-day I have seen Lao Tsze, and can only compare him to the dragon." It is not strange that the deep doctrine of Lao Tsze has been misconstrued. The latitude allowed by the vagueness of his writings enabled and encouraged his disciples and adherents to graft upon the leading notions of his text, an entirely adventitious code of natural and physical philosophy which on the one hand expanded into a system of religious belief, and on the other became devoloped into a school of mysticism apparently founded upon the early secrets of healing and divination. Nevertheless, *Tao Teh King* is a marvellous and unique production of a Chinese philosopher who flourished twenty-six centuries ago. It has excited the admiration and appreciation of the oriental scholars who have studied his pages. Victor von Strauss says that it contains "a grasp of thought, a height of contemplation, and a purity of conception in the things of God such as we seek in vain anywhere in pre-Christian times except in the Jewish Scriptures." According to Dr. Paul Carus, "Lao Tsze was one of the greatest men that ever trod our earth, one of the most remarkable thinkers of mankind. The *Tao Teh King* is an indispensable book and no one who is interested in religion can afford to leave it unread." No wonder Lao Tsze is greatly revered in China and his doctrine has been accepted by a large majority of the Chinese.

Numerous European translations of the *Tao Teh King* have been made from time to time by eminent Oriental scholars. They must have spent much valuable time and mental labour in poring over this terse and obscure work and great credit is due to all of them. But to understand the mystic author and not to misinterpret his meaning, it requires a mystic translator and the publication of another translation by Mr. C. S. Medhurst who is well versed in mysticism is a welcome and valuable contribution.

There is another religion which must be mentioned although it is of foreign origin. Buddhism was imported to China in the year A.D. 61. It was done at the instance of the Emperor who had dreamt of a gigantic image of gold and had sent imperial messengers to India in search of this new religion. It is said by some that it was known in China before that time. The first century of its arrival was marked by numerous translations of Buddhistic works into Chinese. Under such favourable auspices it attracted universal attention in China; the people were eager to learn its tenets and many became proselytes. It was said that in the fourth century nine-tenths of the inhabitants of China were Buddhists. It is not surprising that this later religion has made such wonderful rapid progress in China. The principles of its doctrine are so grand that no earnest student could help being captivated by it. The teaching is suited to the *literati* and the illiterate, and the law of Karma and the hope of eternal bliss are so beautiful that nearly all the women of China are believers. The observance of formal rites and other external practices are contrary to the spirit of the doctrine.

Coming back to the original question, "What is the religion of the Chinese?" the answer can be given in a few words. Confucianism is acknowledged by almost every Chinese to be his creed. He is, however, practical and broadminded enough not to be opposed to, but most friendly to, any other religion which he thinks can be of benefit to him. It is therefore taken for granted that Confucianism, Taoism, and Buddhism form a combination of his religion. Let us take the case of an ordinary Chinese family. When the head of the family dies, the funeral services are conducted in a most cosmopolitan way, for the Taoist priests and the Buddhist monks as well as nuns are usually called in to recite prayers for the dead in addition to the performance of ceremonies in conformity with the Confucian rules of propriety. The general idea is that there are several ways of ascending to Heaven or the place of happiness; and if the deceased should not succeed by the Confucian ladder, he can take either of the other two.

The long existence of ancient China as a nation has generally been attributed by Christians to its obedience to one of God's ten commandments which is "Honour thy father and thy mother that thy days may be long in the land." I believe, however, that is not the only cause. Toleration of religious beliefs and the embracing of three religions have done much to keep China coherent and intact. This may appear to be paradoxical, but if I read the history of the world aright, a nation embracing one solitary religion, however excellent it might be, and prohibiting all others is not likely to exist permanently. The people of such a nation are naturally narrow-minded and bigoted, and believing that their religion is the best in the world, they are self-sufficient and intolerant, and will not condescend to hear or learn better religious truths. When the people are in such condition, their mental activity lies dormant and their minds are stagnant and instead of progressing they will degenerate, hence the downfall of the nation is natural.

It may be contended that the fact of a nation having a State Religion should induce its citizens to become more religious and orderly. This opens a big question which I do not wish to discuss at length. It may be conceded that a State Religion from some point of view may possess certain advantages; but if it is looked at in its larger aspect, it is open to grave doubt whether it works for the ultimate good of the nation. It confers special privileges such as eligibility for office; and people with no strict moral principles would not scruple to become members of the State Church for self-interest. It curbs freedom of thought and compels people to be subservient to the Church on religious matters, even against their better judgment.

It should be remembered that a religion cannot monopolize all the truth; at best it is like a spectrum presenting one side of it. The founder of every good religion promulgated certain portions of the truth to suit the conditions and habits of the people and it will be too presumptuous to assume that one religion contains whole truth. Truth is like light, men first used oil to light their houses and then they manufactured candles and used them. Recently gas was invented and we now have electric light. Should we still be contended with the light supplied by oil or candles and reject the brighter illumination furnished by gas or electricity? Light is open to all, so is truth. Truth cannot be exhausted: like a deep bottomless spring or well, the lower we go the more water we find. We cannot have enough of the truth, the more we investigate and discover, the better it is for mankind. The wise man will use the light he has to receive more light. He will constantly advance to the knowledge of the truth.

China, as it is well known, has been exceedingly conservative, but with respect to religion she has not been stubborn and exclusive, she has not waged war on account of any religious faith, and so far as I can remember, she has not spilt a drop of blood on that account.

In addition to three religions above mentioned, Muhammadanism has a firm hold in China; and many millions of her inhabitants are its believers. Then again, Christianity is not only tolerated but openly preached everywhere and Christian missionaries are found in every province of China. Toleration of every creed is her policy and we welcome all messengers of good religions who preach the eternal truth. We hope the day will soon come when the believers and adherents of all religions and creeds not only in China but in all other nations of the world will live in peace and concord without malice or hatred.

With these few words on the Religion of the Chinese I have great pleasure in introducing this Hindu *Study in the Tendencies of Asiatic Mentality* to the students of Chinese civilisation.

Shanghai,
Feb. 29, 1916.

伍廷芳

Wu Tingfang

CONTENTS

CHAPTER IV

The Religion of Empire-Building—Neutrality and Eclecticism

(B.C. 350—100 B.C.)

CHAPTER V

The God-lore of China and India under the First Emperors

(B.C. 350-100 B.C.)

CHAPTER VI

The Birth of Buddhism (B.C. 150—A.D. 100)

CHAPTER IX

The Augustan Age of Chinese Culture (A.D. 600-1250)

CHAPTER X

Japanese Religious Consciousness

CHAPTER XI

Sino-Japanese Buddhism and Neo-Hinduism

CHAPTER XII

Epilogue :

BIBLIOGRAPHY

Aston—*The Nihongi* (Kegan Paul, London, 1896)

—*Shintō the Way of the Gods* (Longmans, London, 1905)

Avalon—*Principles of Tantra* (Luzac & Co., London)

Bacon—*The Making of the New Testament* (Williams and Norgate, London)

Barnett—*The Heart of India* (Murray, London, 1908)

Bartholomew—(1) *A Literary and Historical Atlas of Asia* (Dent, London) (2) *An Atlas of Ancient and Classical Geography* (Dent, London) (3) *A Literary and Historical Atlas of Europe* (Dent, London)

Beal—*Buddhist Literature in China* (Trubner, London, 1882)

Bergen—*The Sages of Shantung* (Reprint from *Shantung*, C. L. S. Book Depot, Shanghai, 1913)

Bhândârkâr—*Vaishnavism, Shaivism and Minor Religious Systems of India* (Encyclopædia of Indo-Aryan Research, Strassburg, 1913)

Binyon—*Painting in the Far East* (Edward Arnold, London, 1908)

Broomhall—*Islam in China* (Morgan, London, 1910)

Chamberlain—*Kojiki* (Asiatic Society of Japan, Tokyo, 1906)

Chariar—*The Vaishnavite Reformers of India* (Madras)

Charles—*Between the Old and the New Testaments* (Williams and Norgate, London)

Coomâraswâmy—*The Arts and Crafts of India and Ceylon* (Foulis, London, 1913)

Cranmer-Byng—*A Lute of Jade*—Selection from the Classical Poets of China (Murray, London, 1913)

Douglas—*China* (The Story of Nations Series, 1912)

Edkins—*Chinese Buddhism* (Trubner, London, 1893)

Eitel—*Chinese Buddhism* (Trubner & Co., London, 1888)

Fenollosa—*Epochs of Chinese and Japanese Art* (Heinemann, London, 1913)

Getty Mrs.—*The Gods of Northern Buddhism* (Clarendon Press, Oxford, 1914)

Giles—*History of Chinese Literature* (Heinemann, London, 1901)
—*Religions of Ancient China* (London, 1905)
—*Confucianism and its Rivals* (Hibbert Lectures for 1914)
Govindâchâryya—*Life of Râmânuja* (Murthy, Madras)
Gowen—*Outline History of China* (Werner Lawrie, London)
Griffith—*Idylls from the Sanskrit* (Panini Office, Allahabad, 1912)
—*Specimens of Old Indian Poetry* (Panini Office, Allahabad, India, 1914)
Groot—*Religion in China* (Putnam's Sons, New York, 1912)
Growse—*The Râmâyana of Tulsidâs* (Government Press, Allahabad)
Grünwedel—*Buddhist Art in India* (Bernard Quaritch, London, 1901)
Hackmann—*Buddhism as a Religion* (Probsthain, London, 1910)
Harada—*The Faith of Japan* (Macmillan, 1914)
Hirth—*Ancient History of China* (Columbia University, New York, 1908)
Hirth and Rockhill—*Chau-Ju-Kua: His work on the Chinese and Arab Trade in the 12th and 13th centuries entitled "Chu-fan-chi."* (Imperial Academy of Sciences, Petrograd, 1911)
Hogarth—*Ancient East* (Williams and Norgate, London)
Holderness—*Peoples and Problems of India* (Williams and Norgate, London)
Howorth—*History of the Mongols* (Longmans, 1876)
Jackson—*Zoroaster, the Prophet of Ancient Iran* (Columbia University, New York, 1899)
Johnston—*Buddhist China* (Murray, London, 1913)
Journals—Asiatic Society of Bengal (Calcutta)
—Bangîya Sâhitya Parishat (Calcutta)
—China Review (Hongkong)
—Chinese Repository (Canton)
—The Modern Review (Calcutta)
—The Ostasiatische Zeitschrift (Berlin)
—Peking Oriental Society (Peking)
—Royal Asiatic Society of Great Britain and Ireland (London)
—Royal Asiatic Society (North China Branch, Shanghai)

Ku Hung-Ming—*The Universal Order* or *Conduct of Life* (Shanghai Mercury, Ltd., Shanghai, 1906)

—*The Spirit of the Chinese People* (Peking Daily News, Peking, 1915)

Law Narendra—*Ancient Hindu Polity* (Longmans, London, 1914)

Legge—*The Chinese Classics* (Trubner and Co., London, 1876)

—*The Religions of China* (Hodder and Stoughton, London, 1880)

—*Travels of Fa Hien* (A.D. 399-414) (Clarendon Press, Oxford 1886)

Lloyd—*The Creed of Half Japan* (Smith Elder and Co., London, 1911)

Macdonell and Keith—*Vedic Index* (1912).

Macnicol—*Indian Theism* (Oxford University Press, 1915)

Mookerji—*History of Indian Shipping* (Longmans, Green and Co., London, 1912)

Morrison—*The Jews under Roman Rule* (Fisher Unwin, London)

Moulton—*Early Religious Poetry of Persia* (University Press, Cambridge, 1911)

Nanjio Bunyiu—*A Catalogue of the Chinese Translation of the Buddhist Tripitaka, the Sacred Canon of the Buddhists in China and Japan* (Clarendon Press, Oxford, 1883)

Niveditâ—*Kâlî the Mother* (Udbodhana Office, Calcutta)

Niveditâ and Coomâraswâmy—*Myths of the Hindus and Buddhists* (Harrap, London, 1913)

Okakura—*Ideals of the East* (Murray, London, 1905)

Ōkumâ—*Fifty Years of New Japan* (Smith Elder and Co., London, 1909)

Parker—*Studies in Chinese Religion* (Chapman and Hall, London, 1910)

Ragozin—*Vedic India* (The Story of the Nations, Second Edition)

Ranade—*Rise of the Mârâthâ Power* (Bombay)

Rapson—*Ancient India* (Cambridge, 1914)

Ray Prafulla—*History of Hindu Chemistry* (Bengal Chemical and Pharmaceutical Works, Calcutta, 1909)

Rhys Davids—*Buddhist India* (The Story of the Nations, 1911)

,, ,, Mrs.—*Buddhism* (Williams and Norgate, London)

Richard—*The New Testament of Higher Buddhism* (T. and T. Clark, Edinburgh, 1910)

Sarkar B. K.—*Sukra-nîti* (English Translation, Panini Office, Allahabad, 1914)

—*The Positive Background of Hindu Sociology* (Panini Office)

Sarkar Jadunâth—*Chaitanya's Pilgrimages and Teachings* (Sarkar and Sons, Calcutta)

Seal Brajendranâth—*The Positive Sciences of the Ancient Hindus* (Longmans Green and Co., London, 1915)

Sen—*History of Bengali Language and Literature* (Calcutta University, 1909)

Sinha Nandalâl—*The Sâmkhya Philosophy* (English translation, Panini Office, Allahabad)

Smith Vincent—*A History of Fine Art in India and Ceylon* (Oxford University Press, 1911)

—*Early History of India* (Third Edition, 1914)

Stevenson Mrs.—*The Heart of Jainism* (Oxford University Press, 1915)

Suzuki—*History of Chinese Philosophy* (Probsthain and Co., London, 1914)

Tagore—*Kabîr's Poems* (Macmillan and Co. 1915)

Takakusu—*Itsing: Records of the Buddhist Religion* (A.D. 671-95) (Clarendon Press, Oxford, 1896)

Vasu Sris chandra—*The Chhândogya Upanishad* (English translation of the text and Madhva's commentary—Panini Office, Allahabad)

—*Yoga Philosophy* (Panini Office, Allahabad)

Vasu N.N.—Modern Buddhism (Probsthain, London, 1914)

Warren—*Buddhism in Translation* (Cambridge 1906)

Waterfield—*Indian Ballads* (Panini Office, Allahabad, 1913)

Werner—*Chinese Sociology* (Williams and Norgate, London, 1910)

Whitney and Lanman—*Atharvaveda* (Harvard Oriental Series, 1905)

Williams—*The Middle Kingdom* (Scribner's Sons, New York, 1907)

Writings, in Bengali language, of the following members of the "Bangîya Sâhitya Parishat" (Academy of Bengali Literature) of Calcutta:

1. Hirendranâth Datta (*Upanishads*, *Darsanas*, *Gîtâ*, etc.)
2. Haraprasâd Sâstri (Mahâyânism and Mediæval Buddhism)
3. Haridâs Pâlit (Folk-Religion in Bengal)
4. Ramâprasâd Chanda, and 5. Râkhâldâs Banerji (Archæology of Eastern and Northern India)

Wylie—*Notes on Chinese Literature* (London, 1867)

Yule—*Travels of Marco Polo* (Murray, London, 1903)

CHINESE RELIGION
THROUGH
HINDU EYES

CHAPTER I.

The Hypothesis

Prof. Dickinson, one of the latest English travellers in India has declared in his *Appearances* that the Hindus are the most religious people in the world. And Prof. Giles commences his Hibbert Lectures published just a few months ago under the title, *Confucianism and its Rivals*, with the statement popularised by more sinologue than one that the Chinese are not and have never been a religious people. According to one observer the genius of the Hindu race is essentially metaphysical and non-secular; according to the other the Chinese are a highly practical nation without any other-worldly leanings. The people of India are said to cultivate exclusively the thoughts and feelings based on the conceptions of the Eternal, the Infinite and the Hereafter; whereas with the people of China "the value of morality has completely overshadowed any claims of belief; duty towards one's neighbour has mostly taken precedence of duty towards God."

And yet the whole literature of Europe relating to foreign countries from Pliny to Tavernier, nay, from Megasthenes to Clive, bears unmistakable evidence of the secular achievements and material progress, and of the delight in the finite things of this world which the western travellers noticed among the people of Hindusthân. From their historic reports one knows really very little of the so-called transcendental and pessimistic beliefs which modern tourists seem to find in India. And as for the religious indifferentism of the Chinese and their tabooing of the unseen, the ideal and the supernatural, Giles' eight Lectures would bias the reader to a thoroughly contrary view; for it seems to me, a novice in things Chinese, that the whole work of the veteran Professor is intended to be a refutation of the paragraph with which he begins his interesting survey. Leaving aside for the moment the Taoistic, Buddhistic and post-Buddhistic strands of religious belief in China, one cannot but be impressed, if one were to follow Giles, with the vast amount of influence that the Super-natural and the Unknown have exerted on ancient Chinese life as manifested in pre-Confucian and Confucian literature.

In his third lecture Giles is his own critic and establishes the falsity of the universally recognised opinion when he remarks: "Confucianism has often been stigmatised as a mere philosophy, inadequate to the spiritual needs of man : the last words, however, of the above quotation go far to show that the cultivation of rectitude is, according to Confucian teachings, broad based upon the will of God."

The quotation is from Mencius : "He who brings all his intellect to bear on the subject will come to understand his own nature; he who understands his own nature will understand God. To preserve one's intellect, and to nourish one's nature—that is how to serve God. To waste no thoughts upon length of life, but to cultivate rectitude—that is to do the will of God."

This evidence from the Confucian camp about Chinese godlore is, however, not at all extraordinary. Giles himself has furnished numerous instances which go to prove that the agnostic or positivistic apotheosis of the actual, the practical and the worldly is not the exclusive feature of religious life and thought in China, but only one of the aspects or expressions of Chinese mentality, of which too much has been made by scholars. Rather, as one beginning the A. B. C. of a new subject, I am tempted to add to the stock of superficial analogies and parallelisms obtaining in the world of letters, with the hypothesis—

(1) That the trend of religious evolution in India the so-called land of mystics and China known to be the land of non-religious human beings has been since pre-historic times more or less along the same lines;

(2) That the importation of Buddhism (A.D. 67) into the land of Confucius from the country of 'western barbarians' did not create the cultural and socio-religious affinity between the two peoples for the first time, but simply helped forward and accelerated the already existing notions and practices along channels and through institutions which have since then borne Indian names;

and (3) That post-Buddhistic life and thought in both countries have been almost identical, so far as religious ideas are concerned,—and this in spite of differences in name, e.g., Vaishnavism, Shaivaism, Shâktaism, etc., in India, and neo-Confucianism, neo-Buddhism, neo-Taoism, etc., in China. And as the civilisation of Japan since the days of such pioneers as Shotoku Taishi and Kobo Daishi (7th-8th cent. A.D.) has been mainly an expansion of Indo-Chinese culture at Nara, Horiyuji, Kamakura and

Kyoto centres, the religious beliefs, practices and customs are fundamentally the same in *Sangoku* (or the three worlds, viz., India, China and Japan). What pass for Buddhism to-day in the lands of Confucius and Shinto cult are but varieties of the same faith that is known as Tântric and Paurânic Hinduism in modern *Tienchu* (Heaven) or *Tenjiku*, the land of Sâkya the *Buddha*.

Every case of analogy or parallelism and identity or uniformity during this comparatively recent period need not, however, be traced to the cultural, commercial or political intercourse between the three peoples during the Tang-Sung era of the Middle Kingdom (7th-13th cent. A.D.), the Augustan age of Chinese culture. This was synchronous with the epoch of Imperialism and benevolent 'Cæsaro-Papism' under such monarchs as Harshavardhana of upper India, Dharmapâla of Bengal and Râjendrachola of the Deccan. The unity in notions and conventions may as well be due to the sameness of mental outfit and psychical organism and the consequent uniformity of responses to the stimuli presented by the facts and phenomena of the objective world.

This is specially to be borne in mind while noticing the identities in earlier epochs. Take, for example, the idea of the hare in the moon in the poem called "God-questions" by Chu Ping who lived between 332 and 295 B.C:

> "What does the hare expect to get
> By sitting gazing in the body of the moon?"

Now in Sanskrit language some of the terms by which the moon is known imply the 'orb with the hare.' The Hindu idea is also very old; but probably, as Dr. Hirth suggests, the same notion has existed in the two countries prior to any intercourse between them. The researches of Sinologues and Indologists have not yet brought forth any positive proofs relating to Indo-Chinese relations before 3rd or 2nd century B.C.. So that identities or similarities in the cultural traits of the two peoples up till a century or two after Confucius and Sâkya have to be explained by other circumstances than facts of history, *e.g.*, the common psychological basis endowing the two races with the same outlook on the universe.

Mr. Ragozin in his *Vedic India* remarks about the impossibility of studying the ancient Hindus without reference to their western neighbours, the Iranians of Persia: "These two Asiatic branches of the Aryan race being so closely connected in their beginnings, the sap coursing through both being so evidently the same life-blood, that a study of the one necessarily involves a parallel study of the other." This cannot certainly be said with regard to the relations between ancient China and Hindusthân. And yet Indo-Iranian race-consciousness and Chinese race-consciousness seem to have been cast in the same mould.

CHAPTER II.

The Cult of World-Forces in Pre-Confucian China and Pre-Sâkyan India

(——B.C. 700)

(*a*) *Yajna* (SACRIFICE)

"Sacrificial service," says Prof. Hirth, "we may conclude from all we read in the *Shu-King* and other accounts relating to the Shang Dynasty, was the leading feature in the spiritual life of the Chinese, whether devoted to Shângti or God, or to what we may call the minor deities as being subordinate to the Supreme Ruler or to the spirits of their ancestors. That minuteness of detail which up to the present day governs the entire religious and social life of the Chinese gentleman, the more so the higher he is in the social, and most of all in the case of the emperor himself, had clearly commenced to affect public and private life long before the ascendency of the Chou Dynasty (12th cent. B.C.), under which rule it reached its highest development to serve as a pattern to future generations. The vessels preserved as living witnesses of that quasi-religious relation between man and the unseen powers supposed to influence his life are full of symbolic ornament."

Religious ceremonies are not described in detail in the Chinese Classics, but we can have an adequate idea from the incidental references in the *Book of History* (Shu-King) and She-King or *Book of Poetry*. Dr. Legge gives the following description which is "as much that of a feast as of a sacrifice." The "ceremonies at the sacrifices" "were preceded by fasting and various purifications on the part of the king and the parties who were to assist in the performance of them. There was a great concourse of feudal princes. * * * Libations of fragrant spirits were made to attract the spirits, and their presence was invoked by a functionary who took his place inside the principal gate. The principal victim, a red bull, was killed by the king himself. * * * Other victims were numerous, and II. vi. v describes all engaged in the service as greatly exhausted with what they had to do, flaying the carcases, boiling the flesh, roasting it, broiling it, arranging it on trays and stands, and setting it forth. Ladies from the harem are present, presiding and assisting, music peals: the cup goes round."

Pictures of such 'family re-unions where the dead and living met, eating and drinking together, where the living worshipped the dead, and the dead blessed the living' are constantly to be met with throughout Vedic Literature. For sacrifice or *Yaina* is the pivotal factor in Vedic Religion. This is noticed by Mr. Ragozin also, who remarks on "the immense extent of the subject, and its immense import not merely in the actual life, outer and inner, but in the evolution of the religious and philosophical thought of one of the world's greatest races." "The regular recurrence of the beneficient phenomena of nature—rain and light, the alternation of night and day, the coming of the dawn and the sun, of the moon and the stars"—all these came through the efficacy of sacrifice and prayer.

The following hymn to Agni the Fire-god translated by Griffith from the first Book of the *Rig Veda* would give an idea of the initial sacrificial rite, as well as the social and material well-being expected of the whole ceremony:

"Mighty Agni, we invite,
Him that perfecteth the rite;

O thou Messenger divine,
Agni! boundless wealth is thine.

* * *

Thou to whom the wood gives birth,
Thou that callest gods to earth!
Call them that we may adore them,
Sacred grass is ready for them.

Messenger of gods art thou—
Call them, Agni! call them now!
Fain our offerings would they taste,
Agni, bid them come in haste.

Brilliant Agni! lo, to thee
Pour we offerings of ghee;
O for this consume our foes
Who on demons' aid repose!

Praise him in the sacrifice,
Agni ever young and wise;
Glorious in his light is he,
Healer of all malady.

* * *

Agni! let the guerdon be
Riches, good and progeny!"

The music, dance, picnic, etc., attendant on Indian sacrifices have been described in my forthcoming work, *The Folk-Element in Hindu Culture*, under the chapter 'Socialisation and Secularisation of Hindu life.'

The Vedic Sacrifice is thus described by Ragozin (*Rig Veda*, I. 162): "When they lead by the bridle the richly adorned courser, the omniform goat is led, bleating, before him. * * * Pushan's allotted share; he will be welcomed by all the gods. Tvashtar will conduct him to high honours. When men lead the horse, according to custom, three times around (the place of sacrifice), the goat goes before (and is killed first) to announce the sacrifice to the gods. The priest, the assistant, the carver (who is to divide the carcass), he who lights the fire, he who works the pressing stones, and the inspired singer of hymns—will all fill their bellies with the flesh of this well-prepared offering. Those who fashion the post (to which the victim is to be bound), and those who bring it, and those who fashion the knob on top of it, and those who bring together the cooking vessels—may their friendly help also not be wanting. The sleek courser is now proceeding—my prayer goes with him—to the abodes of the gods, followed by the joyful songs of the priests; this banquet makes him one with the gods.''

It would thus appear that the *Rishis* of Vedic India could without the least difficulty incorporate the following verse from the *She-King* (Part IV. Book II. iv.) with their traditional lore:—

In autumn comes th' autumnal rite,
With bulls, whose horns in summer bright
Were capped with care;—one of them white
For the great duke of Chow designed;
One red, for all our princes shrined.
And see! they set the goblet full,
In figure fashion'd like a bull;
The dishes of bamboo and wood;
Sliced meat, roast pig, and pottage good;
And the large stand. Below the hall
There wheel and move the dancers all.

O filial prince, your Sires will bless,
And grant you glorious success.
Long life and goodness they will bestow
On you to hold the state of Loo,
And all the eastern land secure,
Like moon complete, like mountain sure,
No earthquake's shock, no flood's wild rage
Shall ever disturb your happy age.

In fact, all the thanksgiving verses in connection with husbandry and harvests as well as the whole Part IV of the *She-King* entitled *Odes of the Temple and the Altar* might be easily interpolated in his collection by *Veda Vyâsa*, the compiler of the Vedic texts.

Mr. Giles refers to the custom of human sacrifice obtaining among the Chinese and also the conditions under which it fell into desuetude. The *Satapatha Brâhmana* of the Vedists furnishes evidence from the Indian side:

"The gods at first took man as victim. Then the sacrificial virtue (*medha*) left him and went into the horse. They took the horse, but the *medha* went out of him also and into the steer. Soon it went from the steer into the sheep, from the sheep into the goat, from the goat into the earth. Then they dug the earth up, seeking for the *medha* and found it in rice and barley. Therefore as much virtue as there was in all those five animals, so much there now is in this sacrificial cake (*havis* made of rice and barley) i.e., for him who knows this. The ground grains answer to the hair, the water (with which the meal is mixed) to the skin, the mixing and stirring to the flesh, the hardened cake (in the baking) to the bones, the *ghee* with which it is anointed to the marrow. So the five component parts of the animal are contained in the *havis*."

(*b*) *Pitri*s (ANCESTORS)

In the Prolegomena to Dr. Legge's translation of *She-King* or the Book of Poetry we read:

"A belief in the continued existence of the dead in a spirit-state and in the duty of their descendants to maintain by religious worship a connection with them, have been characteristics of the Chinese people from their first appearance in history. The first and third Books of the last part of the *She* profess to consist of sacrificial odes used in the temple-services of the kings of Chow and Shang. Some of them are songs of praise and thanksgiving; some are songs of supplication; and others relate to the circumstances of the service, describing the occasion of it, or the parties present and engaging in it. The ancestors worshipped are invited to come and accept the homage and offerings presented."

The following is a picture of Chinese Shintoism or ancestor-worship ("She-King" Part IV. Book I Section ii. 7):

The helping princes stand around,
With reverent air, in concord fine.
The King, Heaven's son, with looks profound,
Thus prays before his fathers' shrine;—
"This noble bull I bring to thee,
And these assist me in the rite.
Father, august and great, on me,
Thy filial son, pour down the light!
All-sagely didst thou play the man,
Alike in peace and war a King.
Heaven rested in thee, O great Wan,
Who to thy sons still good dost bring.

The eye-brows of long life to me,
Great source of comfort, thou hast given.
Thou mak'st me great, for 'tis through these
Come all the other gifts of Heaven.
O thou my mysterious sire,
And thou in whose fond breast I lay,
With power and grace your son inspire
His reverent sacrifice to pay!"

The *Kojiki* and the *Nihongi*, the earliest records of Japanese Literature (7th-8th centuries A. D.) are the principal store-houses of information regarding the primitive *Kami*-myths. These contain Ancestor-cult supposed to be the original faith of the people in the Land of the Rising Sun.

Now if ancestor-worship be the characteristic feature of the 'sons of Han' and the people of the Yamato race, the Vedic Indians and even the present day Hindus are akin to the Chinese as well as the Japanese. Indian Shintoism is embodied in the following hymn to the *Pitris* or Fathers (domestic, tribal as well as racial) which has a place in the *Rig-Veda* (X. 15):

1. Let the Fathers arise, the upper, the lower and the middle, the offerers of Soma, they the kindly ones, versed in sacrificial lore, who have entered spirit life—let them be gracious to our invocation.
2. We will pay reverence to-day to the Fathers who departed in early times, and to those who followed later, to those who reside in the earth's aerial place and those that are with the races of the beautiful dwellings. * * *
3. Ye Fathers, who sit on the sacrificial grass, come to us with help; these oblations we have prepared for

you: partake of them; bring us health and blessings unmixed.

* * *

8. May Yama, rejoicing with our ancient Father, the best, the gracious, who have come to our Soma-oblations, drink his fill, eager, with the eager Vasisthas.

* * *

10. Come, O Agni, with the thousands of ancient and later Fathers, eaters and drinkers of oblations, who are reunited with Indra and the gods, who praise the gods in light.

In Vedic parlance the *pitri*s or ancestors are not only the deified heroes, *Rishi*s or 'inspired prophets' and eponymous culture-pioneers as we have in Homeric epics, Celtic legends and Scandinavian sagas, but often have the same rank as the elemental forces of the universe and the gods themselves. Ancestor-cult of the ancient and modern Hindus is essentially a branch of their god-lore, in fact, an aspect of their all-inclusive Nature-cult.

(*c*) *Sanâtanism* (ETERNAL ORDER)

Taoism is defined by Prof. De Groot in his *Religion in China* as the system whose "starting point is the *Tao*, which means the Road or Way, that is to say, the Road or way in which the Universe moves, its methods and its processes, its conduct and operation, the complex of phenomena regularly occurring in it, in short, the order of the World, Nature or Natural Order. It actually is in the main the annual rotation of the seasons producing the process of growth or renovation and decay; it may accordingly be called Time, the creator and destroyer."

The idea underlying this system of Tao is exactly what the Hindus are familiar with in the conception of *Sanâtana Dharma*, which, by the bye, is the term by which the people of India designate their own religion, the term *Hinduism* being an expression given by outsiders. *Sanâtana* means Eternal, Immutable, Changeless, and hence Universal. And the *Dharma i.e.* law, order or religion that is described by this expression points out the permanent realities or eternal verities of the universe, the truths which "having been must ever be," the ever-abiding laws that govern the world and its movements. *Sanâtanism* is thus the Indian cult of the *Tao*.

In the *Rig Veda* these immutable laws are in the custody of the god Varuna, and constitute the *Rita*—"originally the Cosmic Order." *Rita*, to quote Ragozin's *Vedic India*, "regulates the motions of the sun and moon and stars, the alternations of day and night, of the seasons, the gathering of the waters in clouds and their downpour in rain ; in short, the order that evolves harmony out of chaos."

This conception of the *Rita* or Eternal Law carries with it a moral and spiritual significance too. "*Rita* is holy, is one, is the right path, the Right itself, the Absolute Good. * * * There is a moral *Rita* as there is a material one, or rather the same *Rita* rules both worlds. What Law is in the physical, that Truth, Right is in the spiritual order, and both are *Rita*." The Chinese follower of *Rita* or *Sanâtana* Tao thinks exactly like his Hindu fellowman. "Should his act disagree with that almighty Tao, a conflict must necessarily ensue, in which he as the immensely weaker party must inevitably succumb. Such meditations have led him into the path of philosophy—to the study and discovery of the characteristics of the Tao, of the means of acquiring these for himself and of framing his conduct upon them." According to the Chinese system there is an attempt "to attract Nature's beneficial influences to the people and the government and to avert its detrimental influences." Likewise, the Vedic Hindu, when oppressed with the consciousness of wrong doing, and of sin, cried out for pardon and mercy to Varuna the Superintendent of the Tao.

(*d*) *Ekam* (The One Supreme Being)

According to Hirth, "from records of *Shu-King* we are bound to admit that the ancient Chinese were decided monotheists. *Shângti*, the Supreme Ruler, received as much veneration at the hands of his people as did God, under any name, from any contemporaneous nation." And we have the following from Dr. Legge's prolegomena to his translation of *Shu-King:* "The name by which God was designated was the 'Ruler,' the 'Supreme Ruler,' denoting emphatically his personality, supremacy and unity. By God kings were supposed to reign, and princes were required to decree justice. * * * Obedience is sure to receive His blessing; disobedience to be visited with His curse. * * * When they are doing wrong, God admonishes them by judgments, storms, famine and other calamities."

The ode vi. of Book I. Part II. in the *She-King* embodies the prayer and desire of the officers and guests at the end of an entertainment given by the King. The Chinese notion of the relation of God with human beings is very clearly set forth in the following lines:

Heaven shields and sets thee fast.
It round thee fair has cast
Thy virtue pure.
Thus richest joy is thine :—
Increase of corn and wine,

And every gift divine,
    Abundant, sure.

Heaven shields and sets thee fast.
  From it thou goodness hast;
    Right are thy ways.

Its choicest gifts 'twill pour,
  That last for evermore,
    Nor time exhaust the store
    Through endless days.

Heaven shields and sets thee fast,
  Makes thine endeavour last,
    And prosper well.

Like hills and mountains high,
  Whose masses touch the sky;
  Like stream aye surging by,
  Thine increase swell!

With rite and auspice fair,
  Thine offerings thou dost bear,
  And son-like give,

The seasons round from spring,
  To olden duke and King,
    Whose words to thee we bring:—
      "For ever live."

The following also is very interesting (*She*, Part IV. Book I, iii. 3) as describing the relation of man with God:

With reverence I will go
  Where duty's path is plain.

Heaven's will I clearly know;
  Its favour to retain
  Is hard. Let me not say
  Heaven is remote on high,

Nor notices men's way,
There in the starlit sky
It round about us moves
Inspecting all we do,
And daily disapproves
What is not just and true.

The angry mood of Heaven is expressed in the following verses (*She-king* Part III, ii. 10):

"Reversed is now the providence of God;—
The lower people groan beneath their load,
The words you speak,—how far from right are they!"

also in II. iv. 7:

With pestilence and death, Heaven aids disorder's sway;

* * *

O cruel heaven, that he such woes on all should bring.

* * *

O great unpitying Heaven, our troubles have no close.

further in II. iv. 10:

O vast and mighty heaven, why shrinks thy love?
Thy kindness erst so great, no more we prove.
Sent from above by thine afflicting hand,
Famine and death now stalk through the land.
O pitying Heaven, in terrors now arrayed,
No care, no forethought in thy course displayed,
Of criminals I do not think;—they bear
The suffering which their deeds of guilt prepare.
But there are many innocent of crime,
O'erwhelmed by ruin in this evil time!

The Vedic *Rishi* likewise cries unto Varuna, the god of gods:

Let me not yet, O Varuna, enter into the house of clay. Have mercy, almighty, have mercy!—If I go along, trembling like a cloud driven by the wind, have mercy, almighty, have mercy. Through want of strength, thou pure one, have I gone astray: have mercy, almighty, have mercy.*** Whenever we, being but men, O Varuna, commit an offence before the heavenly host, whenever we break thy law through thoughtlessness, have mercy, almighty, have mercy. (*Rig Veda* VII. 89).

The following, also quoted from Ragozin's *Vedic India*, illustrates the same attitude:

However we may transgress thy law, day by day, after the manner of men, O Varuna, do not deliver us unto death, nor to the blow of the furious, nor to the wrath of the spiteful (I. 25). * * Take from me my own misdeeds, nor let me pay, O King, for others' guilt (II. 28).

The attributes of the Chinese *Shângti* and Hindu *Varuna* are thus identical.

"Varuna was the dispenser of both light and darkness; when displeased with mortal man, he turned his face from him, and it was night. * * Disease was another of Varuna's fetters, and lastly death."

The conception of the Chinese Shâng-ti as Supreme Ruler is found in the following song of the Vedic Rishi (*Rig Veda* V. 85):

"Sing a hymn, pleasing to Varuna the King—to him who spread out the earth as a butcher lays out a steer's hide in the sun—He sent cool breezes through the woods, put mettle in the steed (the Sun), milk in the kine (clouds), wisdom in the heart, fire in the waters (lightning in the clouds), placed the sun in the heavens, the Soma in the mountains. He upset the cloud-barrels and let its waters flow on Heaven, Air and Earth, wetting the ground and the crops. He wets both Earth and Heaven, and soon as he wishes for these kine's milk, the mountains are wrapt in thunder-clouds and the strongest walkers are tired."

In *Rig* IV. 42 the Rishi makes Varuna declare his suzerainty to a fellow-god Indra:

"I am the king; mine is the lordship. All the gods are subject to me, the universal life-giver, and follow Varuna's ordinances. I rule in men's highest sanctuary.—I am king Varuna; my own are these primeval heavenly powers. * * * I, O Indra, am Varuna, and mine are the two wide deep blessed worlds. A wise maker, I created all the beings; Heaven and Earth are by me preserved.—I made the flowing waters to swell; I established in their sacred seat the heavens; I, the holy Aditya, spread out the tripartite Universe (Heaven, Earth and Atmosphere)."

The Hindu hymn (X. 121) which defines the notion of the One Creator of All is being reproduced below:

"In the beginning there arose the Golden Child. He was the one born lord of all that is. He established the earth and this sky: who is the god to whom we shall offer our sacrifice?

He who gives breath (*i.e.* life), He who gives strength; whose command all the gods revere; whose shadow is immortality, whose shadow is death. * * *

He who through his greatness is the one king of the breathing and awakening world; He who governs man and beast. * * *

He whose greatness the Himavat, the Samudra, the Rasa proclaim; He whose these regions are, as it were, his two arms. * * *

He through whom the sky is bright and the earth firm; He through whom the Heaven was established,—nay the highest heaven; He who measured out the ærial space.

* * *

May He not harm us, the Creator of this earth; who, ruling by fixed ordinances, created the heaven; who also created the bright and mighty water."

The following passage from Macnicol's *Indian Theism* describes the attributes of the Vedic *Shâng-ti*: "He sitteth on his thrône in the highest heaven and beholds the children of men; his thousand spies go fòrth to the world's end and bring report of men's doings. For with all those other tokens of preeminence he is specially a moral sovereign, and in his presence more than in that of any other Vedic god a sense of guilt awakens in his servants' hearts. His eyes behold and see the righteous and the wicked. The great guardian among the god sees as if from anear. * * * If two sit together and scheme, King Varuna is there as the third and knows it. * * * Whoso should flee beyond the heavens far away would yet not be free from King Varuna."

The student of Chinese Classics would find in this extract reminiscences from the *Book of Odes* and the *Book of History*.

(*e*) Pluralism in God-lore

The Chinese believed in the One Supreme Being, but they believed in His colleagues and assistants as well. Their universe of Gods and Higher Intelligences was a pluralistic one.

The following extract is quoted from *North-China Daily News* by Mr. Werner for his *Chinese Sociology* compiled upon the plan organised by Herbert Spencer: "The Chinese have the most profound belief in the existence of fairies. In their imagination, the hills and the mountains which are supposed to be the favourite resorts of these mysterious beings are all peopled with them, and from these they descend into the plains and * * * carry out their benevolent purpose in aiding the distressed and the forlorn."

According to Giles in *Historic China* "the first objects of religious veneration among the ancient Chinese were undoubtedly Heaven and Earth; they are the two greatest of the three great powers of Nature, and the progenitors of the third, which is Man."

We read the following in Legge's Prolegomena to his *She-King:* "While the ancient Chinese thus believed in God, and thus conceived of Him, they believed in other spirits under Him, some presiding over hills and rivers, and others dwelling in the heavenly bodies. In fact, there was no object to which a tutelary spirit might not at times be ascribed and no place where the approaches of spiritual beings might not be expected and ought not to be provided for by the careful keeping of the heart and ordering of the conduct. * * * King Woo is celebrated as having attracted and given repose to all Spiritual Beings, even to the spirit of the Ho and the highest mountains. Complaints are made against the host of heaven—the Milky Way, etc.,—as responsible for the sufferings caused by misgovernment and oppression. Mention is made * * * of the demon of drought; and we find sacrifices offered to the spirits of the ground and of the four quarters of the sky, to the Father of husbandry, the Father of war, and the Spirit of the path.''

The worship of Agni, the Fire-god, for which the Vedic hymn has been quoted above, has also been very old in China. We get the following in Lacouperie's *Western Origin* (P.161); ''Fire was looked upon since early times among the Chinese as a great purifier, and large state fires were kindled at the beginning of each season, to ward off the evil influences of the incoming period. Special wood-fuel was selected with that object. The management of these fires was in the hands of a Director of Fire. The first appointment of this kind dates from the reign of Ti Kuh Kao Sin (2160-2085 B.C.).

The worship of stars also was not unknown. And ''each district even had its protecting Spirit, and the Spirit of the ground was invoked at the solemnity which opened and terminated the agricultural labours of the year.'' Says Prof. Giles: ''Natural phenomena * * * have at all times entered very largely into the religious beliefs of the Chinese, and may be said to do so even at the present day when gongs and cymbals are still beaten to prevent a great dog from swallowing the Sun or Moon at eclipse time.''

This Chinese mentality as expressed in the pluralistic worship manifested itself equally if not more powerfully in the thousand and one '' Nature-myths'' of Vedic Literature. The following is the river-hymn of the *Rig Veda* (X. 75):

''O ye Gangâ, Yamunâ, Saraswati, Satadru, and Parusni, receive ye my prayers! O ye Marutbridhâ, joined by the Asikni, Vitastä and Arjikiyâ joined by the Susoma, hear ye my prayers!''

Mr. Griffith translates the Vedic Hymn to Morning thus:

Morning! Child of heaven, appear!
Dawn with wealth our hearts to cheer;
Thou that spreadest out the light
Dawn with food, and glad our sight;
Gracious goddess, hear our words,
Dawn with increase of our herds!

* * *

Morning! Answer graciously!
Boundless wealth we crave of thee.

* * *

All that live adore her light—
Pray to see the joyful sight;

* * *

Morning! Shine with joyful ray!
Drive the darkness far away—
Bring us blessings every day.

The French Vedic scholar Bernaigne gives the following account of the god Pushan, "pre-eminently a friend of men and whose career is one of almost homely usefulness":

"Pushan is, first of all, a pastoral and agricultural deity. He is reputed to direct the furrow; his hand is armed with the ox-goad; he is principally the guardian of cattle, who prevents them from straying, and finds them again when they get lost. He is, therefore, prayed to follow the cows, to look after them, to keep them from harm and to bring them home safe and sound. His care extends to all sorts of property, which he guards or finds again when lost. He is also the finder of hidden treasure—cows first on the list always. Lastly, Pushan guides men, not only in their search for lost or hidden things, but on all their ways generally. In a word he is the god of wayfarers as well as of husbandmen and herdsmen. He is called the Lord of the Path, he is prayed to 'lay out the road,' to remove from them foes and hindrances, to guide his worshippers by the safest roads, as knowing all the abodes."

Pushan is thus the Chinese "God of the road, invoked for safe journeys" mentioned by Giles.

The following hymn to Parjanya (*Rig Veda*, V. 83) illustrates the same tendency to have a god for, and deify, everything:

"Sing unto the strong with these songs, laud Parjanya, with praise worship him. Loud bellows the Bull; he lays down the seed and fruit in the herbs.

He cleaves the trees asunder, he slays the Râkshasas; all living creatures fear the wearer of the mighty bolt. Even the sinless trembles before him, the giver of rain, for Parjanya, thundering, slays the evil-doers.

As a driver who urges his horses with his whip, he makes the rainy messengers appear. From far arises the roar of the lion when Parjanya makes the cloud full of rain.

The winds rage, the lightnings shoot through the air, the herbs sprout forth from the ground, the heavens overflow, refreshment is borne to all creatures, when Parjanya blesses the earth with rain. * * * ."

Hymns like these are the spontaneous outcome of a religious conciousness which is exhibited materially in sacrifices and prayers for rain, good harvests, health and general well-being; and these constituted a great part of the socio-religious life of both Celestials and Hindus.

(*f*) Folk-Religion

The pluralistic universe of the Chinese gods includes not only the *Shângti*, Heaven, Earth, "the six honoured ones," the stars, ancestors, spirits, hills and rivers, etc., but is wide enough to embrace almost anything. Thus animals, reptiles, birds, fishes, insects and plants were regarded as abodes of spirits and were worshipped. Mr. Werner gives the following bibliography: "On Zo-anthropy generally see De Groot iv. 156-63, and on the different classes of animals (were-tigers, wolves, dogs, foxes, bears, stags, monkeys, rats, horses, donkeys, cows, bucks, swine, etc.) pp. 163-212. On were-reptiles ("tortoise worship may be said to have a somewhat extensive literature of its own, and dates back as far as 2900 B.C."—Balfour, *Leaves from my Chinese Scrap-book* 151-2), birds, fishes and insects, De Groot iv. 212-43, on plant-spirits pp. 272-324, on Dendrology and Sorcery vol. v., and on the war against spectres vol. vi."

Miss Simcox remarks that the "Chinese rendered quasi-divine honours to cats and tigers because they devoured the rats, mice and boars of the fields," and they "offered also to the ancient inventors of dykes and water-channels; (all these were) provisions for husbandry."

The demonocracy, witchcraft, incantations, charms, amulets, sorcery, divination by tortoise-shell or stalks of the plant, shamanism, fetichism, totemism, exorcism, and sentiments regarding eclipses, droughts, famines, floods, locusts, diseases, earthquakes, etc., mentioned by every observer of ancient Chinese socio-religious life have their parallels or duplicates in Vedic texts as well. The desire to enjoy the good things of this earth and ward off the hydra-headed evil inspired the people of India as well as of China to have recourse to the same rites and practices. One has only to go through the table of contents and index of such a work as the Englished *Atharva Veda* (in Harvard Series) to be convinced of the common mentality and attitude towards Nature, Man and God, that characterised the two races in spite of their divergence in physiognomy and language, and the absence of intercourse during the period under review. As far as I am aware, students of Comparative Philology and Somatology or Physical Anthropology have not yet been able to trace any connexion between these two peoples. Nor have Archaeologists been successful in proving beyond doubt the existence of intercourse between them prior to 2nd or 3rd century B.C. But I venture to think that the data of Psycho-Social or Cultural Anthropology are copious and varied enough to attract sinologues to the study of Indology as a subsidiary branch of their special subject.

In this connexion may be quoted the following remarks of Dr. Wilhelm in his paper '*On the sources of Chinese Taoism*'—in the Journal of the North China Branch of the Royal Asiatic Society, vol. XIV:

"The suggestion lies near that Taoism and pre-Buddhist Brahmanism may have something in common. It seems that many Brahmanic gods have found their way into Taoism even more easily than into Buddhism. Even the central notions of Taoism, *Tao* and *Te*, have an analogue in Brahma and Atman. So we venture the suggestion that the affinity of Buddhism and Taoism may have for its reason certain Brahmanic influences on Taoism."

"Taoism was not founded by Lao-Tzu, neither was Confucianism founded by Confucius. Both of them have their footing on Chinese antiquity. From that antiquity the foundations of the religious life of China have come down. * * The religious teachings common to early Taoism and

Confucianism can be traced in the scriptures of the *literati* as well as in the Taoist works;"—as well as, it may be added, in the earliest Hindu texts.

Even in *Rig Veda* we have the following hymn to a herb which would be quite intelligible to the Chinese mind :

"Hundred-fold are your ways, thousand-fold your growth, endowed with hundred various powers; make me this sick man well. * * * Give me victory as to a prize-winning mare. * * For I must have cattle, horses and clothes. * * * You will be worth much to me if you make my sick man well. * * * When I, O ye simples, grasp you sternly in my hands, sickness flees away, as a criminal who fears the grip of the law. * * * Flee then, sickness, flee away—with magpies and with hawks; flee on the pinions of the winds, nay of the whirlwinds."

In *Rig* X. 145, we read also of a woman, who digs up a plant of which to make a love potion and succeeds in getting rid of her rival in her husband's affections.

The Chinese conception of the Dragon, the serpent which typifies immortality and the Infinite and has its abode in the sky or cloudland is also very old in India. Thus Indra the Vedic thunder-god is celebrated as the fighter of *Ahi* the cloud-serpent. Hirth quotes an article by Prof. Chavannes in the *Journal Asiatique* (1896, P. 533) in which we read: "The dragon itself could well be related to the Nâgas of India."

The following is the hymn sung by Visvâmitra for the increase of barley (*Atharva Veda*—Harvard, P. 387):

1. Rise up, become abundant with thine own greatness, O barley, and ruin all receptacles, let not the bolt from heaven smite thee.

2. Where we appeal unto thee, the divine barley that listens, there rise up like the sky; be unexhausted like the ocean.

3. Unexhausted be thine attendants, unexhausted thy heaps, thy bestowers be unexhausted; thy eaters be unexhausted.

In the *Atharva Veda* we read of the amulet of *udumvara* (*Ficus glomerata*) plant as conferring various blessings :

"Rich in manure, rich in fruit, *swadhâ* and cheer in our house--prosperity let Dhâtar assign to me through the keenness of the amulet of *udumvara*. * * * I have seized all the prosperity of cattle, of quadrupeds, of bipeds, and what grain (there is); the milk of cattle, the sap of herbs, may Brihaspati, may Savitar confirm to me. * * * As in the beginning, Thou, O forest-tree, wast born together with prosperity, so let Saraswati assign to me fatness of riches."

Again, "Since thou, O off-wiper, hast grown with reverted fruit, mayest thou repel from me all curses very far from here."

In the *Atharva Veda* X. 10 we have an extollation of the cow and in IX. 7 of the ox. The following is a specimen :

"The draft-ox sustains earth and sky; the draft-ox sustains the wide atmosphere; the draft-ox sustains the six wide directions; the draft-ox hath entered into all existence * * * With his feet treading down debility, with his thighs extracting refreshing drink—with weariness go the draft-ox and the plowman unto sweet drink."

About the goat we read:

"With milk, with ghee, I anoint the goat, the heavenly eagle, milky great; by it may we go to the world of the well-done, ascending the heaven, unto the highest firmament."

Like plant-amulets we have also jewel-amulets in Vedic literature. The following is from Macdonell and Keith's *Vedic Index* Vol. II: "Mani is the name in the Rig Veda and later of a jewel used as an amulet against all kinds of evil." And we have the following testimony from the *Atharva Veda* in Harvard Series: "The bit of Hindu folklore about the origin of pearls by the transformation of rain drops falling into the sea * * * is at least ten centuries old. Born in the sky, ocean-born, brought hither out of the river, this gold-born shell is for us a life-prolonging amulet." Amulets of gold, lead, and of three metals are also mentioned in *Atharva Veda*.

(*g*) IDEALISM AS A PHASE OF SPIRITUALITY.

The forefathers of the Chinese and the Hindus were not without their intellectuals who tried to probe the mysteries of the universe. The results of their metaphysical investigation, though not quite systematised on a regular plan, we have in such works as the Heraclitean *Yi-King* (Book of Changes), the Taoist legends and *Upanishadic* lore. Neither the Chinese classics nor the Vedic texts are complete without these speculative discourses. To look upon these as separate from the classics is to misunderstand the earliest encyclopædias of the two peoples.

The *Book of Changes*, the most difficult of Chinese classics, is probably also the oldest work. As for Taoist doctrines, though they get methodised in a presentable shape about the 6th cent. B.C. or later, there is no doubt that they have been coeval with Chinese civilisation as floating literature. And the *Upanishads* which embody Hindu Taoism have existed ever since the *Rigs* have been recited and the *Sâmas* chanted at the sacrificial ceremonies. They are integral parts of the Vedas according to Indian tradition. Thus *pari passu* with the development of the ancestor-cult, *Shângti*-cult, demonology, etc., we notice the dualistic conception of the *Yang* and *Yin*, *Purusha* and *Prakriti*, heaven and earth, male and female, as well as the monistic pantheism and mysticism of the unconditioned, absolute and transcendent Reality. The parallelism between Chinese and Hindu religious consciousnesses up till about 8th-7th century B.C. is as great in ritualism and naturalism as in idealism and supernaturalism.

We notice this parallelism pervading every side of the spiritual life of the two peoples. Thus even before there was any intercourse between them we get pictures of asceticism, *Yoga*, retirement from life etc., in both China and India. De Groot begins his chapter on 'Holiness by means of asceticism and retirement' thus: "A study of the text, which I have quoted in the two preceding chapters from the ancient classics and the writings of the early patriarchs of Taoism, necessarily leads us to the conclusion that there has prevailed, in the long pre-Christian period which produced those books, a strong leaning towards stoicism and asceticism. Perfection, holiness, or divinity were indeed exclusively obtainable by "dispassion," apathy, will-lessness, unconcernedness about the pleasures and pains of life, quietism or *wu-wei*."

Again, "Chwangtsze boldly refers Taoist asceticism to China's most ancient times. He represents the mythical Emperor Hwangti as having retired for three months, in order to prepare himself for receiving the Tao from one Kwang Shentsze, an ascetic who practised quietism, freedom from mental agitation, deafness and blindness to the material world, and so on. Retirement from the busy world is frequently mentioned in the Classics and other ancient writings by such terms as *tun*, *t'un*, *Yih* and *Yin*."

This phase of religious activity manifested itself in India also. Mr. Macnicol speaks about the 6th century B.C.:

"The passionate quest of all awakened spirits, whether they were mendicants or kings, was for immortality, for deliverance from that bondage which was life itself. The orthodox * * * pursued it along the 'road of works,' the way of rite and oblation. * * * The intellectuals * * * sought the same goal along the 'road of knowledge,' reaching it at last by the intuition that perceives the spirit within to be one with the spirit that is ultimate and alone. The devout worshipped in loving faith the god of their devotion, believing that his grace would save them in the midst of a world of a *samsára*. But the most earnest among all these * * * would take the staff of the mendicant and go forth as seekers, *Sramanas*, *Yogis*, *Munis*, *Yatis*—labouring to reach by self-torture or by mental exercises the goal of deliverance so passionately desired."

It would thus appear that the passion for *Mukti* (Salvation) is as old in China as in India.

(*h*) "THROUGH NATURE UP TO NATURE'S GOD"

The Japanese scholar Suzuki in his historical treatment of the Chinese intellect during the period we have been considering lays special stress on a fact which, according to him, "must be borne in mind when we investigate the history of Chinese philosophy". The remark which has been made by almost every sinologue is thus worded: "The philosophy of the Chinese has always been practical and most intimately associated with human affairs. No ontological speculation, no cosmogonical hypothesis, no abstract ethical theory seemed worthy of their serious contemplation, unless it had a direct bearing upon practical morality. They did, indeed, speculate in order to reach the ultimate ground of existence; but as they conceived it, it did not cover so wide a realm as we commonly understand it, for to them it meant not the universe generally, with all its innumerable relations, but only a particular portion of it—that is, human affairs—and these only so far as they were concerned with this present mundane life, political and social. Thus, we do not have in China so much of pure philosophy as of moral sayings."

Sinologues must certainly be accused of 'crying for the moon' when they are disappointed in not finding among the Celestials a Spencerian *Synthetic Philosophy* or a Hegellian *Dialectic* and a Bergsonian *Creative Evolution*. They seem to forget that the Chinese of the Chou, Shang and previous Dynasties were contemporaries, if not of the builders of the Pyramids, at least of the precursors of the bards of the *Iliad* and the *Odyssey* and of the *Rishis* who were just contemplating the founding of a superb civilisation on 'the banks of the seven rivers.' To understand Chinese intellect in its proper perspective we have to take a cross-section of world-culture, say, about 8th-7th century B.C., the period which prepared the advent of a Confucius, a Sâkyasimha, a Zarathustra and a Pythagoras. The ancient Egyptians and Assyrians, the Ægeans of Crete who formed the connecting link between the land of the Nile and the Isles of Greece, the Achæans and Ionians of the Homeric and Hesiodic eras, and the Hindus of the Vedic age would all be found to be equally wanting in the capacity for philosophical speculation or methodical intellectual work, if one were to judge of their achievements by the standard of to-day. The Hindus and Hellenes are often mentioned as pre-eminently speculative races, and the Chinese placed in a miserable light by their side; but what specimens of Indo-Aryan intellectuality do we come across during the period synchronous with the first half of the Chou Dynasty (1122-249 B.C.), not to speak of the previous two milleniums during which the Chinese people have lived in history? Indeed, all the great races of men who have pioneered human civilisation have in their initial stages been mainly concerned with the problems of bread and butter, and subsidiarily or incidentally with the 'problems of the sphinx,' 'pure philosophy,' 'speculative systems,' methodology, and all those topics with which we are familiar in modern times.

There is another pitfall into which we moderns are apt to be led by our temptation to read into old world life the facts and ideas of the present day. Scholars have their own theories about the ideally best form of religion, as they have also their own ideas of the ideally best form of government. Sinologues as well as Indologists are, therefore, ever anxious to know what was the formula or catchword by which the ancient Chinese as well as Vedic Hindus tried to express their religious notions. Was it polytheistic, monotheistic, pantheistic, henotheistic, anthropomorphic, naturalistic, animistic or what? Probably those pioneers of world's culture did not care for any formula at all.

It is a matter of common experience that there is no one word which can explain all the multifarious thoughts and activities of even a small group of human beings whom we can watch everyday. Strictly speaking, in this world of ours there is no purely republican or purely despotic state just as there is no purely monotheistic or purely polytheistic people. In every field we meet with cases of 'mixed systems,' toleration of diversities, reconciliation of opposites, and choice of the 'lesser evil.' So that in matters of religion as of politics people are compelled for all practical purposes to accept for their guidance the dictum of Alexander Pope:

> " For forms of government let fools contest,
> Whatever is best administer'd is best."

The Celestials like their contemporaries of Vedic India were essentially the worshippers of Nature. What they cared for most was Life, and what they feared most was the enemy of Life, both physical and human. The chief inspiration in all their activities was the desire to equip themselves for the 'struggle for existence.' They made use of anything that was likely to promote and advance the interests of life; and therefore, all the World-Forces, taken collectively in their totality, as well as individually and singly, attracted their attention. They wanted to harness the energies of Nature as best as they could to the production of the necessaries, comforts and luxuries of life. These natural benefactors of the human race were personified in their imagination, and they became the deities, the spirits, the fairies and the *Shângti* or *Ekam*. Furthermore, the example of predecessors is a great help to subsequent generations especially when they are bent on an arduous task. So the ancestor-cult has had a prominent place in the comprehensive cult of world-forces ever since the dawn of Chinese and Indian history, the heroified fathers being as great beneficent agencies as the planets, the earth, fire and wind.

Nature or Universe, considered materially, gave to these pioneers of civilisation the primitive sciences and primitive arts. Nature or Universe, considered animistically, gave them the higher personalities or transcendent Beings who, like Prometheus, were the discoverers and custodians of all these instruments of human culture. They began that "quest of the Holy Grail," both intellectual and spiritual, which mankind is pursuing still and will continue to pursue for ever under the guidance of myriads of Sir Galahads.

We have read Charles Lamb's famous "Dissertation on Roast Pig" in his *Essays of Elia*. The humorous account of the Chinese invention of the art of cooking through cumbrous processes that we have in this most delightful of mock-anthropological essays is, after all, a serious chapter in the origins of civilisation. This was the kind of things the Celestials and Vedic Hindus were doing—discovering the rudiments of every desirable knowledge. And in the process of discovery they 'postulated' or took for granted the spiritual Being and Beings—(has not the 'God' of every race, at best, been only a postulate?)—who are above the ordinary mortals and who are capable of helping them in their need. They were thus looking "through Nature up to Nature's God." Their religion was fundamentally the handmaid of Life and hence coincided fully with what we call *Kultur*.

There are, however, certain contrasts which must not be overlooked by the student of Comparative Religion:

1. The form in which Vedic Literature has come down to us is quite different from that in which we have the Chinese Classics.

2. Vedic religion is more martial than that embodied in *Shu-King* and *She-King*. Earliest Hindu Rishis seem to have been burning with the passion for extirpating the enemies.

3. The tone of Vedic texts is more naturalistic than that of Chinese classics; but the actual socio-economic life as described in the *Liki* would indicate that planetary and natural phenomena had equal if not more influence among the Celestials.

4. Neither the Celestials nor the Vedists knew of any icons or images, unless the personifications and metaphors necessarily involved in the use of language as a medium of expression be regarded as images, as, strictly speaking, they should. But while we read of temples in ancient China, we have only open-air altars in the 'land of seven rivers.'

5. The sacrificial service was the monopoly and prerogative of the king, the "son of Heaven" in the Middle Kingdom, but it was the function of the people or at any rate their sacerdotal delegates in Hindusthân.

If we neglect these and other minor differences we may state that the socio-religious world into which Sâkya was born was identical with that in which Confucius was to work. The two great Sages found in their respective compatriots the same mental biases and spiritual attitudes, and, as we shall see, preached to their disciples almost the selfsame gospel.

CHAPTER III

Confucius the historian and Sâkyasimha the philosopher

Section I.

Aufklarüng in Asia—the Age of Encyclopædists

(7th-5th Cent. B.C.)

Matthew Arnold in his Introduction to Johnson's *Lives of the Poets* remarks on the 18th century as being in England pre-eminently an age of prose. This remark can apply to the whole Europe of the 18th century and to every department of its thought. Prose is the instrument of reason, science, criticism and philosophy. The eighteenth century was thus the era of rationalism, discussion, summing-up, stock-taking, paraphrasing, explanation, *aufklarüng*. It was the epoch of French encyclopædists, English deists and German classicists.

It witnessed the production of the Cuvierian *System of Natural History*, Hume's *Essay on the Human Understanding* and the Kantian *Critique of Pure Reason*. It was a time when rulers and statesmen were apostles of "Enlightenment" and came to their work equipped with philosophical theories as to the common weal; when poets and artists were archæologists, philologists, folklorists, botanists and art-critics, and when the title of a poetical work could be *The Essay on Man*. Truly, the sway of the Muses was held in abeyance, and the "sad Nine * * * left their Parnassus" to the tender mercies of the prophets of 'the philosophy of history,' 'the proper study of mankind,' and 'the rights of man.'"

Corresponding to the systole and diastole in every living organism we have to recognise an epoch of expansion and creative originality as well as an epoch of concentration and interpretative criticism in social organisms. An epoch of concentration was the 18th century. Another such epoch in European history was the 15th century prior to the discoveries which initiated a 'new learning,' a new religion, a new state-system as well as a new industrial and commercial era. And yet another such age of criticism and concentration was the 4th century B.C. which summed up the whole history and philosophy of classical Hellas. The close of that epoch heralded the birth of altogether new conceptions of life under the auspices of Alexander, the mighty son of the "barbarian" conqueror of the disunited Greek city-states, and witnessed the inauguration of a new world for which Professor Mahaffy coins the term "Hellenistic" as contrasted with Hellenic.

The fourth century B.C. was essentially an age of prose and discussion. The dramatists like Euripides and Aristophanes thought in terms of the Periclean demagogues and mobocrats, and wrote for an audience every second person in which was a sophist. Unfortunately, the term 'sophist' has not yet been able to shake off the degraded sense associated with it in spite of the monumental apology offered by Grote in his celebrated *History of Greece*. It is, however, the sophists who represent the best products of Athenian culture in the most flourishing period of the Hellenic race. In the 4th century B.C. Athens was the "school of Hellas," and the most prominent men of the day were the sophists, those peripatetic pedagogues and apostles of encyclopædic culture to whom the world owes Greek physics, Greek logic,

Greek psychology, Greek politics, and Greek ethics. Socrates was the prince of sophists, Plato was the disciple of that Christ of Hellas, and Aristotle, the *guru* or "guide, philosopher, friend" of Alexander, "drank deep of the pierian spring" at Plato's Academy. The whole age was dominated by questionings and answerings, criticism and counter-criticism, mass-meetings and street-corner talks, doubts and explanations regarding the individual, the family, the city, the state and the universe. In one word, it was the first epoch of *sturm und drang* in the history of Europe.

Asiatic History also furnishes several such ages of 'storm and stress,' criticism, interpretation, explanation, *aufklarüng*. The sixth century B.C. was probably the first epoch of this kind. During this epoch the whole humanity of the Orient was passing through a period of interpretative criticism. We notice this both in China and India as well as in Persia. All Asia was stirred to her depths by thousand and one questionings, intellectual, moral and spiritual. In the near East, middle East and the far East, there could be seen plentiful as blackberries the Paracelsuses and Fausts, the seekers after truth, beauty and good, brain-workers with their methods for solving the doubts, the spiritual doctors with their philosophical recipes, moralists with their systems of diagnosis, and healers of the "Sorrows of Werter." This all-round stir and turmoil was characterised by literary efforts which led to the collection, compilation and codification of the ancient traditions, legends and songs; the best intellectuals of the times became the systematisers and conservers of their race-culture. Every work that has been handed down to us from this age is a summing up of the previous ages; every person on whom we can definitely lay our hands at this age is an all-round sophist, an encyclopædist who has tried all methods and who has mastered all available facts. Like Plato and Aristotle, the Asiatic master-minds of the sixth century B.C. thus represent the sunset of an old system rather than the dawn of a new.

The last word of classical Europe was being taught in the schools of Academy and Lyceum. The last word of primitive Asia was being preached by Zarathustra (B.C. 660-583), Sâkyasimha (B.C. 563-483) and Confucius (B.C. 551-479). The next epoch was created by Alexander (B.C. 330) the unifier of the East and the West, Chandragupta Maurya (B.C. 330) the first Emperor of United India, and Shi-Hwangti (B.C. 220) the first "Son of Heaven" to rule the whole Celestial Empire. The problems of these Empire-builders were too far beyond the ken of a Greek sophist, a Hindu philosopher and a Chinese historian. Sâkyasimha, Confucius, and Plato were anachronisms in that new age with novel problems which required another Socratic method and another *Novum Organum.*

It was not the conventional and orthodox Greek philosophy of man as 'a political animal,' but the un-Greek individualism and cosmo-politanism or universalism of the Stoics and Epicureans (with their doctrines of the "Law of Nature," "Law of Reason," etc, anticipating the *jus gentium* and "Law of Nations" of the Romans) that expressed the ideals of the post-Alexandrian Ptolemies and Seleucidæ who in their daily lives were bringing about a *rapprochement* between diverse races and diverse sentiments. This new age is, therefore, signalised by Shi Hwangti's order for the wholesale burning of the Confucian texts and massacre of the Confucian pedantocrats,—the most emphatic protest against fossils ever recorded in history. It is certainly an allegory of the method followed by those who have the "shortest way" with old *idolas*. And in Hindusthân the Finance Minister of Chandragupta is not a yellow-robed monk of Sâkyasimha's monastery, but Kautilya, the Machiavelli and Bismarck of Indian politicians. All the world over, the "old order" changed "yielding place to new." But as yet we have to see something of this old order as conserved by the Asiatic Encyclopædists of the 6th century B.C..

SECTION 2.

Confucius and Sâkyasimha in Contemporary Asia

(*a*) "HIGHER CRITICISM"

Besides Zarathustra four men of Asia living in the sixth century B.C. have been honoured as the founders of four new cults: Lao-tsze the prophet of *Taoism*, and Confucius the teacher of *Propriety*, in China; and Sâkyasimha the propounder of *Nirvânism*, and Mahâvira the founder of *Jainism*, in India. Of these four, one in each country towers above his rival and the rest of his compatriots into solitary greatness. They are Confucius and Sâkyasimha.

Mankind is so obsessed by the current notions and superstitions about such ancestors as have been fortunately canonised and heroified by the verdict of subsequent history that it is impossible for scientific purposes to get an exact idea of what those men of flesh and blood were like. This is all the more difficult in the case of prophets and seers whose worshippers number in present day life by hundreds of millions. The instruments of Higher Criticism, the Doctrine of Relativity, and Comparative-Historical Method have got a place in sociologists' laboratories only recently. It may sometimes, therefore, be worth one's while to listen to the opinion of a cynic and satirist, if not for anything else, at least to get a fresh view-point.

Let us see what Anatole France, the pupil of Ernest Renan, says about the *man* Jesus in relation to his brother-Jews and their masters the Romans. "Wherever in modern poetry or art the figure of Jesus is treated, no matter in what spirit—let it be by Paul Heyse, by Sadakichi Hartmann the Japanese, or Edward Soderberg the Dane—He is the principal figure of His day, occupying the thoughts of all. France, in his story, *Judaeus Procurator*, has, in an extremely clever manner, indicated the place occupied by Jesus in the consciousness of the contemporary Roman. To any one who can read, the fact that the life and death of Jesus interested only a little band of humble people in Jerusalem, is sufficiently established by the circumstance that Josephus, who knows everything that happens in the Palestine of his day, does not so much as name Him. The man who argues that such an event as the Crucifixion must have made some impression forgets what a common and unheeded incident a crucifixion was in troublous times. During the Jewish war of the year 70 in the course of which 13,000 Jews were killed at Skythopolis, 50,000 in Alexandria, 40,000 at Jotapata—1,100,000 in all—Titus crucified on an average 500 Jews every day. When, impelled by hunger, they crept under the walls of Jerusalem, they were captured, tortured and crucified. At last there was no more wood for crosses left in Palestine."

The above extract is from Dr. Georg Brandes the Danish critic's work on Anatole France in "Contemporary Men of Letters Series." The following rather long account is also from the same: "As his principal character, France has taken the Titus Ælius Lamia, * * * a gay young Roman who * * * is banished, * * * goes to

Palestine and meets with a friendly reception in the house of Pontius Pilate. Forty years pass; Ælius Lamia has long been back in Italy, he is at Baiae, taking the baths, and is sitting one day by a path * * * when in the occupant of a litter * * * it seems to him that he recognises his old host, Pilate.

"And it really is Pilate. * * * They talk of old days —of all the trouble Pontius had with those wretched Jews, who refused to do homage to the image of the Emperor on the banners and allowed themselves to be flogged to death rather than worship it. * * * He recalls an evening on which he saw one of them (Jewesses) dancing. * * * She had heavy red hair, this girl, whose charms enticed the young Roman to follow her everywhere. 'But she ran away from me,' he continued, 'when the young lay preacher and miracle-worker came from Galilee to Jerusalem. She became inseparable from him and joined the little band of men and women who were always with him. You remember him of course?' 'No,' replies Pilate. 'His name was Jesus, I think; he was from Nazareth.' 'I do not remember him,' reaffirms Pilate. 'You were obliged to have him crucified.' 'Jesus—' mutters Pilate, 'from Nazareth—I have no recollection of it.'"

This is how "values" are "transvalued" by a cynic. Anatole France makes even Pilate forget Jesus and Lamia remember him only because of Magdalene! But as a countryman of mine, Professor Seal, has well put it in his introductory note to Mookerji's *Indian Shipping*: "To explode the Mosaic authorship is not to explode Moses in culture-history." Christ, the "strong Son of God, Immortal Love" lives in human imagination though the man Jesus is forgotten. It should, therefore, be a most natural thing if we do not find the historic persons Confucius and Sâkyasimha to be the sole luminaries of their age which the reverent and pious imagination of future generations of devotees have made out of them as the Eternal Sage and the god *Buddha*.

(*b*) The Peers of Confucius

Indeed in the China of the 6th century B.C. there was no place for Dictator in any field. It was a period of feudalism or political disruption, and there was no one centre of gravity in the socio-economic or socio-political system. Decentralisation in politics necessarily brought with it the establishment of culture-centres throughout the length and breadth of the country. In the history of civilisation feudalistic disintegration thus serves a very useful purpose in so far as it leads to diffusion and popularisation of ideas through the rivalry of contending states. This is what happened in mediæval Europe under the regime of the Barons, Markgrafs and Dukes, guilds and city-states. Every barony or duchy had its own *minnesinger*, *châran*a, minstrel, *volksdichter*, *wanderlehrer*, *troubadour* and *trouvere*. It is extremely difficult for even an extraordinary genius to get more than a parochial fame under conditions which foster local patriotism, unless there be special circumstances calculated to break the barriers between centre and centre and create a common standard of culture.

The following account of Legge about the manner in which the *Book of Odes* could be compiled is interesting as showing how cultural unity is possible even under feudal conditions: "The feudal states were modelled after the pattern of the royal state. They also had their music-masters, musicians, and their historio-graphers. The Kings in their progresses did not visit each particular state. * * * They met, at well-known points, the marquises, earls, barons of the different quarters of the kingdom. * * * We are obliged to suppose that the princes would be attended to the places of rendezvous by their music-masters, carrying with them the poetical compositions collected in their several regions, to present them to their superior of the royal court." It was the *Durbars* or Imperial conferences that supplied the connecting link between state and state in feudal China. But though such gatherings might be good opportunities for minstrels to get a hearing beyond their little platoon, it is very much to be doubted if they furnished facilities for scholars and thinkers to reach their peers throughout an entire continent. In disintegrated Germany, on the other hand, culture could be unified and the first-class thinkers could acquire an all-German reputation because, according to Merz in the *History of European Thought*, "the migration of students as well as eminent Professors from one university to another was one of the most important features of German academic life." The condition of the Celestial kingdoms during the Chou Period cannot, however, be compared to that of the German states of the 18th century.

Professor Gowen gives the general character of the Chou Dynasty which ruled over China from B.C. 1122 to 249: "The period as a whole reveals a gradual weakening of the central authority by reason of the increase of power in the vassal and confederate states. The number of these at one time was as many as a hundred and twenty-five, and even in the time of Confucius there were fifty-two."

About the middle of the 8th cent. B.C., to quote again from Gowen's *Outline History of China*, "the vassal princes became more and more powerful and therewith more and more independent. They began to take possession of entire provinces and to govern them without reference to the decrees of the Emperors." And "the history of the next century *i.e.* from B.C. 685 to 591 has been entitled the period of *Five Leaders* because it exhibits the rise in succession to power of the five states." The disunion and struggle for hegemony went on till B.C. 249.

Professor Hirth also remarks: "If we glance at a historical map of Germany during the Thirty Years' War, and if we recall the changes it underwent before and after that period within the space of about two centuries and a half, corresponding in duration to the *Chun-tsin* period (B.C. 722-481) we may comprehend the difficulty, not to say impossibility, of furnishing a synoptic view of the numerous states constantly at war with each other, falling under the nominal sway of the Chou Dynasty."

Each feudal lord certainly considered himself to be a son of Heaven, and the royal court was everywhere organised on the same plan fully described in the *Chou-li*, the Text-Book of Politics compiled in the 12th century B.C.. Regarding this work Hirth says: "As an educator of the nation the *Chou-li* has probably not its like among the literatures of the world, not excepting even the Bible. This remark refers especially to its minute details of public and social life. * * * The most rigid religious ceremonial regulates the daily life of the Emperor, government officers and feudatory lords."

According to the stereotyped constitution set forth in the *Chou-li*, every state had to maintain six departments of government, each under a Mandarin. Unfortunately, we know very little of the names of the persons who, like the Great Sage and his rival Lao-tsze, filled those posts, and of the kind of work they actually did. But it is evident that scattered throughout the Middle Kingdom there were born during the long period of the Chou Dynasty men of mark in statesmanship, education, philosophy, and warfare. As it is, we have the names only of Laotsze the keeper of archives at the Imperial capital, and Confucius the Judge and Librarian at a provincial city, both belonging to the sixth century B.C., and of Kuantzi the Prime Minister of a small state towards the beginning of the seventh century B.C.. About this statesman-philosopher Hirth remarks: "The advice given by Kuantzi has become the prototype of governmental prudence for Chinese official life. Thus Kuantzi * * * has become the father of institutions of the utmost importance to the whole empire during its later economic development; for example, in regard to the iron and salt monopolies. If we consider that his life-time lay in the early days of regal Rome, and that the work of his life was done before Solon the Athenian was born, Kuantzi may be regarded as having furnished the very type of a statesman in the modern sense by collecting facts for the purposes of governmental administration; further by endeavouring to describe such facts in the shape of a numerical formula, he may be regarded as the oldest statistician of all nations.''

In the present state of Sinology we have only vague references to the ancient sages and professors of Taoism in connexion with Laotsze, and to previous collectors, compilers and editors in connexion with Confucius. If the fame of Confucius depends mainly on his work as editor, he has certainly been usurping the meed due to others, since neither the *Book of History* nor the *Book of Odes*, the two most important, nor the *Book of Changes*, the most ancient and abstruse, of Chinese Classics, owe their compilation to him. In any case it is clear that Confucius was only one of the many intellectuals who applied their brains to the problems associated by posterity exclusively with his name. His life, we know, was not a success. He was not confident even of his posthumous fame. He is said to have remarked about himself: "My principles do not make way in the world; how shall I make myself known to future ages?" He retired from public life in despair and died broken-hearted. He declared himself to be a failure—"The great mountain must crumble, the strong beam must break, the wise man withers away like a plant."

This was the historic person Confucius. He had not to renounce royalty like a Sâkya or suffer martyrdom like a Jesus. He was not a successful nation-maker like the Prophet of Mecca, nor did he experience the ecstasy of a Chaitanya of Bengal. Yet, in the words of von der Gablentz, "even at the present day, after the lapse of more than two thousand years, the moral, social, and political life of about one third of mankind continues to be under the full influence of his mind." It was under the Han Dynasty *i.e.* over 300 years after his death, that Confucius was made Duke and Earl. The Chinese Herodotus, the historian Suma-chien (2nd-1st centuries B.C.) calls him "the divinest of men." And he was made "Perfect Sage" in the 5th century A.D. *i.e.* a whole millenium after he was dead and gone. Surely, "distance lends enchantment to the ear!"

In the sixth century B.C. Confucius was only a mortal among mortals. But the age itself was an extraordinary one. Says Prof. Suzuki: "What a glorious age this was for early thinkers of China can be seen from the fact that several writers and historians of the day made attempts to classify them according to their doctrines, the number of which had become confusingly large. To quote only one of these historians, Panku, author of the History of the Han Dynasty, divides the ante-Chin (Chou dynasty) thinkers into ten classes: (1) Scholars (Confucians), (2) Taoists, (3) Astrologers and Geomancers (4) Jurists, (5) Logicians or Sophists, (6) Followers of Mutze, (7) Diplomatists, (8) Miscellaneous writers, (9) Agriculturists, (10) Story writers."

Confucius may be great, but China is greater. Regarding the general stir and turmoil of the period Suzuki remarks: "The Chinese mind may have developed later a higher power of reasoning, and made a deeper study of consciousness; but its range of intellectual activities was never surpassed in any other period. * * * During the ante-Chin period Confucianism was not yet firmly established, and there were many rival doctrines struggling for ascendency and recognition."

Confucius is not China. We have been misunderstanding the Celestial People by taking it as but Confucius "writ large." To understand the Middle Kingdom of the time of Confucius it is desirable to have the fresh standpoint of an Anatole France with regard to the age of Jesus. The so-called Confucian classics must not be allowed to cover our whole mental horizon. They should rather be awarded a place neither superior nor inferior to, but alongside of, the works of the class of *Chou-li* and the Taoist lore compiled by the Great Sage's senior and no less great rival. And to have a complete picture of the intellectual atmosphere one would have to familiarize oneself with numerous other forms of literature which unfortunately seem to have been neglected and not given their due by sinologues. Much useful work remains to be done in the culture-history of pre-Confucian China covering, as it does, a period of over 3000 years.

The only original work done by Confucius is the compilation of the history of the state in which he was born from the court documents. It is called "Spring and Autumn Annals," the dullest of the five classics, and generally recognised to be unreadable except for the notes added by a subsequent disciple. As for the other four, his position is that of the Hindu *Vyâsa* (lit. the compiler of ancient texts), to whom we owe the *Vedas* and *Mahâbhârata* in their present forms. Not even that, because there had been other Chinese Vyâsas before him; and it is to them that the credit should be given.

(c) THE PEERS OF SÂKYASIMHA

Similarly in painting the intellectual and spiritual India of the sixth century B.C. the artist should not cover the whole canvas with the huge portrait of a Sâkyasimha. Sâkyasimha is surely a giant, but his peers were as great giants as himself. It was, in fact, an age of giants, to be compared with any Augustan era in world's history. The compatriots and immediate precursors as well as juniors of Sâkyasimha counted among them the Protagorases, the Anaxagorases, the Socrateses, the Platos and the Aristotles of Hindusthân—that band of *Vyâsas*, sophists and encyclopædists to whom we owe in a systematic form the earliest specimens of Indo-Aryan medicine, chemistry, botany, zoology, philology, logic, metaphysics, and sociology.

It was an age of *Parishats* or academies, permanent forest-universities, periodical forest-conferences of the master-minds, itinerant preachers, Socratic questioners, closet-recluses, and researchers and investigators into everything from sexual science to salvation. Sâkyasimha was only one of the numberless "stormers and stressers" in that epoch of *sturm und drang*.

Like the China of those days India also was in the feudal stage. So much of the country as had received the light of the Vedic Rishis was divided into a number of royalties, chieftaincies, and even clan-republics. It was not till about 150 years after Sâkyasimha that the people of entire Hindusthân were to realise and achieve their political unity under the organising genius of the Maurya Monarch. But as yet the fact that Sâkya was born not on the banks of the sacred Indus or in chief cities like Benares and Pâtaliputra but in a *markgrafate*, the debatable border-land *between Bengal and Nepal (certainly, to a great extent, the *ultima thule* of the enlightened people of those days), indicates that Aryan culture was not confined only to the metropolis and well-established centres of influence but was gradually bringing "fresh fields and pastures new" under its sway. Feudal India in the age of Sâkyasimha witnessed the diffusion and expansion of culture, which, to quote Merz's remarks about the progress of thought in Feudal Germany, was "not a stationary power, but continually on the move from south to north, from west to east, to and fro, exchanging and recruiting its forces, bringing heterogeneous elements into close contact, spreading everywhere the seed of new ideas and discoveries, and preparing new land for still more extended cultivation."

To mention only a few names among the master-minds of Sâkyasimha's age. There were the grammarians of the Pânini cycle, whose comprehensive work on Sanskrit language stands the most rigorous test of modern philologists as a monument of logical insight and thorough-going research. There were the chemists, botanists and zoologists of the

*A non-Aryan sphere of influence, according to Pandit H. P. Sâstri of Calcutta.

Charaka-school whose encyclopædic work on *Âyurveda* (The Science of Life) continues to be the basis of Hindu medical practitioners even to-day. Then there were the sociologists who, following the lead of the eponymous culture-hero Manu, were the compilers of *Dharma Sâstras*, *Smriti Sâstras*, *Nîti Sâstras*, etc., each of which is at once the Hindu *Yi-king*, and *Li-king* and partially also the *Shu-king*. It was out of this class of literature that about 150 years after Sâkya-simha, Kautilya the Finance Minister of the Maurya Emperor derived materials for the Hindu *Chou-li*, called the *Artha Sâstra*, the Imperial Gazetteer of India in the 4th-3rd centuries B.C..

Besides, the students of *Upanishads* and *Darsanas*, those systems of psychology, logic and metaphysics, were a legion. Add to these the scholiasts who took as their master Vedà-Vyâsa, or the famous compiler of Vedic Literature, and we get an idea of the all-round intellectual activity that characterised the life of the people during the age of Sâkya. Nor is this all. There were innumerable 'orders' or corporate bodies of wanderers or hermits. Says Prof. Rhys Davids in *Buddhist India:* "In a note to Pânini IV. 3,110 there are mentioned two Brahmin orders, the Karmandinas and the Pârâsârinas. * * * In the *Majjhima* (3, 298), the opinions of a certain Pârâsâriya, a Brahmin teacher, are discussed by the Buddha." Rhys Davids also mentions several Orders older than the Sâkyan. Also, "the Jains have remained as an organised community * * * from before the rise of Buddhism." All these Orders equally "claimed to be pure as regards means of livelihood, * * * to be unfettered * * * to be friends; * * * were all mendicants."

The chapters, "Mahavira's predecessors and disciples' and "Introduction to Jaina philosophy" in Mrs. Stevenson's *Heart of Jainism* furnish also from a new angle an account of the thought-forces that had been moving in the Indian mind during the 6th century B.C..

There were thus other *Nirvânists* (Quellers of Misery) and salvationists, spiritual doctors and moralisers, self-torturists and *moksha*-seekers, renunciationists and "path"-finders, theists and non-theists, as well as positivists, humanitarians, and teachers of the 'whole duty of man' besides Sâkyasimha. His were no new-fangled ideas, and he was not branded as the 'corrupter of youths;' the topics of his talk were all in the air, the man in the street was equally at home with those problems and probably also with some of the solutions. If his contemporaries had reasons to find fault with him they had equal reasons to find fault with thousand others. Nor was Pâli, the language or dialect in which Sâkya's *Analects* or discourses, sayings and dialogues have been preserved, his own improvisation. It had been growing as the medium of communication all through upper India especially among the *wanderlehrers*, *paribbâjakas*, the peripatetic sophists, itinerant monks, etc., as Prof. Rhys Davids has carefully pointed out. Naturally, therefore, like Confucius, Sâkya also could not be regarded as a god, a prophet or even an extraordinary saint in his life-time. He was only a man among men, not even a demi-god, at best, the founder of an Order (or *Samgha*).

Section 3

Development of Traditional Socio-Religious Life

(*a*) Relativity of Religion to Environment

The historic Jesus of Nazareth is said to have advised his compatriots to follow the doctrine of Non-Resistance:

"Render unto Cæsar the things that are Cæsar's." Another such quietistic and passivistic announcement was made by him when he declared: "My Kingdom is not of this world."

The Bible is the gospel of political *Nirvânism* (annihilation) and non-secular other-worldlyism, what in latest phraseology is called Pessimism. It is strange, therefore, that Schopenhauer, whom nature and the discouraging circumstances in the national outlook of Young Germany cooperated to make the arch-prophet of Pessimism in modern Europe, should try to have his views confirmed by a few passages from the Indian *Upanishads* and *Dhammapada*. His authority was nearer home, and he might have well remarked of the anti-military and anti-political verses of the Bible what he said about the *Upanishads:* "They have given me solace in life, and they will give me solace in death." But the pessimistic character of the teachings of Jesus has been pointed out by another philosopher who has been recently much in vogue. Nietzsche finds in the Hindu sociologist Manu's Code a rational system of social "values," whereas he condemns the Bible as preaching the "slave-morality," as teaching exactly the thing which the quietist Schopenhauer would have appreciated.

Political indifferentism and desire to escape from the troubles and difficulties of this world into the convenient other-world of spiritual bliss were characteristics of the Apocalyptists of the 2nd-1st centuries B.C., who contributed to the building up of the Bible story. This has been noticed by historians also. Prof. Dunning of Columbia University in his *History of Political Theories* has dealt with the subject from the rational standpoint of evolutionary sociology. He accounts for the quietistic pessimism in the declarations of Jesus by reference to the economico-political subjection of the Jews to the Roman Cæsars.

A subject race can have no politics. The Jews had no scope for advancement in this world. It was out of the question for them to successfully resist the Romans. "To render unto Cæsar the things that are Cæsar's" was a "virtue of a necessity." As the mediæval Shylock put it in Shakespeare's language: "Sufferance is the badge of all our tribe." To this might be appended:—"And non-resistance is the creed of all our *Rishis.*" A persecuted and suffering tribe can evolve out of its inner consciousness not the philosophy of energism but only the metaphysics embodied in such *sutras* as "My Kingdom is not of this world," or "the Kingdom of God is within you."

This Historical Method of criticism applied to the interpretation of the Bible may be one-sided to a certain extent. But it throws light from a new angle and hence requires to be applied to the study of all the culture-systems of the world.

It is, however, a very new method even in Europe and America. It goes without saying that Asiatic Sociology has not been attacked with this weapon. For as yet sinologues, indologists, assyriologists and egyptologists have been interested in their sciences mainly as archæologists, palæontologists and necrologists, i.e., as students of interesting curios, specimens of fossils, bones of dead organisms, etc. A real Biological study of these phenomena as specimens of living human culture, as expressions of growing vital force will commence after the pioneers have done their work.

To whom is Plato's *Republic* intelligible without the mass of facts bearing on the whole *milieu* of Hellenic city-states out of which it grew? What would be the appreciation of Dante's *Divine Comedy* and Milton's *Paradise Lost* without reference to the Catholicism of mediæval Europe and all that Puritan England implies? It must be admitted that as yet neither Confucius nor Sâkyasimha, in fact, none of the philosophers, poets and religious leaders of the Orient have been placed in their proper historic perspective, i.e., their socio-economic and political background. We try to understand Asia from single passages, or single books, or single individuals, or single institutions or single movements!

The difficulty of understanding the religious consciousness or the whole mentality and intellectuality of peoples who have been extinct or are in very unfavourable position in modern times would be apparent if we take a simple instance from successful specimens of to-day. Suppose one has to interpret England or English mentality or the religious consciousness of the English people in the year 1915. Applying the conventional method of interpreting Asia by such catchwords as "changeless East," "pessimistic Orient," and "non-aggressive Asiatics" or by single individuals as when we use the equation "Confucius=China," and the like, we ask—"Who or what is England? Is it Stopford Brooke or Frederick Harrison or Bernard Shaw or Kitchener?—or Is it the Manchester capitalists or the University undergraduates or Slum-landlords or Labour-Unions?—or Is it the Times Book Club or Armstrong & Co., or the British Museum or Trafalgar Square?—Or rather is it the Bible or the Encyclopædia Britannica?" The question itself seems to be absurd. And yet we have to be satisfied with answers to absurd questions regarding Asia.

China is greater than Confucius as India is greater than Sâkyasimha. The religious sentiments and spiritual activity of the people of both these continents are, therefore, more than what can be found in the writings, compilations, sayings or dialogues of these two men.

(*b*) CHINESE RELIGION IN THE AGE OF CONFUCIUS

As contributing to the picture of Chinese religion in the 6th century B.C., it is interesting to know of the legend that Confucius came to Laotsze to interrogate the great Taoist sage about the laws and rites of social life. Says Prof. De Groot—"Although Confucius was evidently no adherent of the Taoist discipline in its rigorous form, and certainly no hermit, yet we are not entitled to admit that he was not a good Taoist. The fact that he piously visited Laotsze in his retirement is significant; moreover, according to two Classics, he explicitly mentioned Taoist retirement and indifferentism with high praise."

"The very wise and virtuous man," said Confucius, "acts and behaves according to the Tao; * * * but it is only the holy man who can withdraw from the world and conceal his wisdom without spite. * * * Those who with earnest faith, wish to learn the Tao of natural goodness, which protects against death, neither enter a state which is in danger nor stay in a state where disorder reigns."

"After reading these classical passages," says De Groot, "we may look with less distrust at a page in Chwang's writings which represents Confucius as a most ardent apostle of Taoism, urging a prominent disciple of his own towards the cultivation of indifferentism about his own person and the things around him, and also to the practice of 'inaction.'"

Whatever be the value of the Taoist teachers' story about the historic Confucius having studied and practised their teachings, there is no denying the fact that these were as powerful in his days as in classic times. The mysticism of the Taoists must not be ignored if we are to get a full view of Chinese religious ideas. Thus in the classic *Book of Rites*, as De Groot points out, we read of ascetic practices as being traditional. "In the month of midsummer the growth of the days reaches the ultimate point, and the Yin and the Yang commence their annual struggle so that the principles of death and production separate. Men eminent for virtue and wisdom then fast; they conceal themselves somewhere in their dwellings, where their desires are stilled, where they do nothing with precipitation, and banish music and lust. Nobody may enter there; they must take the smallest possible quantity of savoury food, and have no well-tasting mixtures brought to them. They must put their sexual desires in the background, and set their minds at rest."

Not only did mysticism prevail as of old; but the classical socio-religious life seems to have remained entire. According to Giles "the reeds and the tortoise shell were still employed, * * we find allusions to fasting. * * * It appears that fasting and purification were practised for about ten days before the performance of the sacrifices took place."

The deities of the earliest Chou Dynasty continued to receive worship and sacrifices in Confucius' and Laotsze's time. The pantheon still consisted of the Shângti, heaven, earth, ancestors, mountains, rivers, elements, planets, etc. Nor was there anything to counteract the perpetuation of fetichism, shamanism, demonolatry, charms, etc., observed by the Celestials of the classic age. The Vedic Indians could still live and move easily with the Chinese, and also with the great Confucius.

For Confucius was not the founder of any new school, religious or moral or educational. Probably his method was Socratic, and he had pupils, disciples, admirers, and followers. "Sometimes," it is said, to quote Rev. Bergen's *The Sages of Shantung*, "his followers numbered 3,000. It is not to be assumed that this number was instructed at any one time, but there were crowds competing to get within the sound of his voice, and be regarded as attendants on his lecture."

He was a man of encyclopædic culture. So the topics of his lectures were diverse. "It is said that he taught literary criticism, and history. Practical ethics, faithfulness, honesty, music and poetry were discussed and studied. Theories of governments, and even metaphysics were amongst his favourite themes."

His reputation with posterity depends on the Classics alleged to have been edited by him. His literary work is that of a historian, not of a philosopher. But as historian, his chief object was moral. He may be compared to Plutarch who wrote the *Parallel Lives* of Greek and Roman celebrities to inculcate moral lessons. Confucius cared to chronicle the history of his own state as well as to set his seal upon the storehouses of information regarding the classic past because his practical object was to educate the princes and statesmen by warning as well as by example. But unlike Plutarch, the Chinese Vyâsa did not take the Carlylean view of history as a "biography of great men."

Prof. Hirth says:—"To reform the social life of his native land, to lead his contemporaries to adopt a certain standard of morality as exhibited in their daily doings, was the main ambition of his work. This standard he endeavoured to derive from the records of the past."

So far as religion was concerned, the Celestials of Confucius' age were not at all affected by what he did; because he had nothing new to give. Rather, his editorship placed before them as fixed codes the Bibles they had been traditionally following. His work was not creative in any sense, but conservative. The old cult of Nature-forces thus continued to persist in its entirety. And if to future generations of Chinese, Confucianism has meant simply the study of the classics, religion in China may be supposed to have been the same after as before Confucius and also in his own age.

Nor did the personal life of Confucius contribute any new factor to the traditional religion. In the third lecture Giles has shown that the sage followed in *toto* everything that was done by his contemporaries. He had no ideas of reform as to the conceptions or practices governing the socio-religious life of his countrymen. "He believed firmly in a higher power—the God of his fathers. * * * Not only did he believe in the existence of this Deity * * * but he was conscious, and expressed his consciousness openly, that in his teachings he was working under divine guidance."

Confucius once said: "If my doctrines are to prevail, it is so ordered of God; if they are to fail, it is so ordered of God." Yet Confucius has been known to be an atheist and a positivist, and the Chinese who follow him as a non-religious people!

Giles remarks further: "Although he would not discuss in a familiar way the *pros* and *cons* of belief in an unseen world, probably because of the solemnity of the subject, he did not hesitate to use the name of the Deity in any suitable connexion." As for the Supernatural world, the following opinion of Confucius is recorded in *Confucianism and its Rivals*: "How abundantly do spiritual beings make their presence manifest among us! We look for them but do not see them, we listen to them, but do not hear them; yet they enter into all things, and there is nowhere they are not. They cause all the people in the world to fast, and to put on their best clothes, in order to take part in the sacrifices." What more do we find in the religious beliefs of Vedic or modern Hindus? Surely, if the Indians of any age are religious, so too was Confucius, so too are all those who call themselves Confucianists.

Confucius believed in sacrifices, and in the existence and presence of the spirits of the departed dead. He also sacrificed to his dead ancestors and to spirits in general. All his life was thus perfectly in accord with the prevailing religious customs. Both by writings and practice Confucius was conserving the past. If the Vedist could appreciate easily the sentiments and tendencies of the Chinese of the 12th century B.C., he could certainly be quite at home among the audience of Confucius.

Under these circumstances it seems absurd to ask the question: "Is Confucianism a religion or simply a system of morals?" The proper question rather is: "Should the Chinese religion of the classic age or of the age of Confucius be called Confucianism? What is the contribution of Confucius to the making of this religion?" It would have been clear that Confucianism as a title applied to Chinese religion down to the 6th century B.C. is a misnomer. Following the Chinese example, the Hindus would have called their ancient religion Vyâsic simply because Vyâsa happened to be the compiler and editor of the Vedic texts! The best name for the cult of World-Forces like those in ancient India and China is *Sanâtanism* as devised by the

Hindus and *Taoism* as known to the Celestials—both implying the idea of Eternal Order or Permanent Way.

The Chinese like the Hindus have ever been prolific in the invention of gods and goddesses. There are facts to indicate that the classical Nature-cult did not remain stationary but passed through various stages of development. Even the unchanging Chinese change—and they knew how to change and adapt themselves according to the *Zeitgeist* millenniums before the so-called "opening up of China."

The following extracts from the *China Review* (XIII. 416-18) are quoted to show that deities unknown to people of the first three or four hundred years of the Chou Dynasty have been introduced in subsequent periods:

"The worship of the gods of the five elements * * * appears first in the seventh century before Christ and in northwestern China, in a region at that time only recently admitted to China proper. This worship spread afterwards to other parts of the country. * * *

"In the sixth century before Christ there can be no doubt that in the countries of Sung and Tsin the brighter stars of these groups (Scorpio and Orion) were worshipped. * * *

"It is then (6th century B.C.) that we find stars worshipped in particular cities and that the twelve signs of the Zodiac were believed to control the destinies of states. Particular stars and groups of stars were worshipped in the supposed causes of fires and such like calamities. * * * In B.C. 540 there is a more detailed account of the same worship in the *Tso chwen*, and at about the same time, in the *Kwo Yü*, we find abundant proof that the Chinese then believed that the various baronies of China were all controlled by particular stars."

The writer goes on to say that "fresh legends unknown to Confucius were growing up in his time on the Shantung coast which greatly extended classical records of Chinese primitive history." So, after all, the poet's dictum—"Better fifty years of Europe than a cycle of Cathay"—should not be the starting hypothesis of the sober historian.

Terrien De La Couperies' *Western Origin* is quoted by Werner for his *Chinese Sociology*. In this we get evidence of the additions to, and modifications in, the classical pantheon of the World-Forces.

"Fire-worship, connected with Astrology, was established in the state of Sung, some time before B.C. 564. Various new notions about fire appeared in the 6th century B.C. * * * Among other innovations were: "A state sacrifice every year at the vernal equinox for the renewal of fire; all fire had to be extinguished three days previously and food taken cold. The rule was established for the first time in Tsin (Shansi) by the Marquis Wen (B.C. 636-27)."

It may be remarked by the bye that this is a custom observed in India even to-day.

Further, "We hear of a new worship of a deity of fire named *Hwei-luh*, and of a deity of water named *Hiuen Ming* in B.C. 524 in Tcheng (S. Honan)—once only, as if it were a local affair. * * * The worship of the fire-goddess *Hwei-luh* * * * has become the worship of the spirit of the hearth, the household fire-god, commonly called the kitchen-god. It was sacrificed to for the first time by Hia Futchi, keeper of the ancestral temple of the state of Lu about B.C. 600. * * * This worship was not yet an ancient institution at the time of Confucius."

The following history of the fire-deity is also interesting: "In B.C. 533 it existed in E. Honan, and in the third century B.C. it was also flourishing in Kiangsu and Shansi. It was adopted by the Emperor himself under the Han dynasty (B.C. 133); at present it has become the most extensively worshipped divinity of China, the various names given to it show the successive and different aspects under which it was considered."

These and many other facts point inevitably to the analogy and parallelism between Chinese and Hindu religious developments as we shall show presently. In the mean time the remarks of Rhys Davids about the elasticity, flexibility and adaptability of the Hindu genius may be deduced from the history of Chinese religion: "The old gods, *i.e.* the old ideas, when they have survived, have been so much changed; so many of them have not survived at all, so many new ones have sprung into vigorous life and wide-reaching influence, that one conclusion is inevitable. The common view that the Indians were very different from the other folk in similar stages of development, that to that difference was due the stolid, not to say, the stupid, conservatism of their religious cenceptions, that they were more given to superstition, less intellectual than, for instance, the Greeks and Romans, must be given up. * * * The real facts lead to the opposite view—they show a constant progress from Vedic times onwards. * * * But whatever the facts, and whatever the reasons for them, we are not likely to cease from hearing that parrot-cry of self-complacent ignorance, 'The immovable East'—the implied sop to vanity is too sweet to be neglected."

This is the greatest "idola" of the 19th and 20th centuries, for every age has its own *idola*. The sooner this superstition of the modern West regarding the Orient be given up, the easier would be the solution of the "Inter-Racial Problems," and the better would it be for the science of Sociology. The world is in need of a Bacon equipped with the *organon* of the Historico-Comparative Method to demolish the unthinking vanities and obstinate mediævalisms of the so-called "superior races" in this the most enlightened age of Culture-History.

(c) Indian Religion in the age of Sâkyasimha

Sâkyasimha was preëminently a philosopher and metaphysician. Confucius was mainly a historian and sociologist. The intellect of Confucius was not vigorous enough to come out of the struggle with the 'eternal questions' quite unscathed. He, therefore, considered it prudent to leave them "open" but did not, as we have seen, disbelieve or demolish them. He was not in any sense an agnostic like Mill or Huxley. He accommodated himself rather to the floating notions of the age.

These questions, however, were not left unattacked by the Chinese mind. Where Confucius dared not enter, some of his contemporaries were quite at home. Thus, to quote Suzuki, "there were people who believed that the cycle of birth and death is an irrevocable ordeal of nature. This life is merely a temporary abode, and not the true one. Life means lodging, or sojourning or tenanting, and death means coming back to its true abode. Life cannot be said to be better than death or death than life. Life and death, existence and non-existence, creation and annihilation, are the inherent law of nature, and the world must be said to be revolving on an eternal wheel. The wise man remains serene and unconcerned in the midst of this revolution; he lives as if not living."

These metaphysical ideas were the common ingredients in the intellectual solution of both China and India, and could not be ignored by anybody. Confucius as a weaker intellectual calmly took them for granted, but Sâkyasimha boldly set out like Laotsze and Mahâvira and thousand other Chinese and Hindu thinkers to contribute his own quota to the untying of the Gordian knot.

It has been pointed out by every scholar, Hindu as well as foreign, that there was nothing original in either the methodology or the achievement of a Sâkyasimha or a Mahâvira; they differed from the existing metaphysicians (e.g., those of *Chhândogya Upanishad* and *Sânkhya Darsana*), if at all, only in the emphasis laid on certain incidents.

Thus, as Mrs. Stevenson says, "the Jaina, in common with the Buddhists, seem to have accepted as the ground work of their belief the philosophy of the Brahman Sannyâsin. They incorporated into their faith the doctrines of transmigration and *Karma* without putting a special stamp on either, but the doctrine of non-killing (*ahimsâ*), which they also borrowed, they exalted to a position of primary importance, and they laid an entirely new emphasis on the value of austerity both inward and outward. * * * The Jaina hold that the six schools of philosophy are part and parcel of an organic whole."

We have already seen how the idea of the sacredness of sentient beings as embodied in the doctrine of *ahimsâ* was getting hold of the Hindu mind in the *Satapatha Brâhmana*. It is difficult, therefore, to believe that the founder of what has been known as Jainism ever contemplated or actually effected any revolt from the socio-religious order of the day. It is doubtful if Mahâvira was a Protestant in his metaphysics or theology.

This would be all the clearer from MacNicols' *Indian Theism*. Jainism and Buddhism are generally regarded as atheistic and agnostic, but the author points out the theistic element in both. "And yet a closer examination reveals the fact that genuine elements of the theistic tradition were present specially in Buddhism from its very inception, and that with the development of the religion these discovered themselves more and more fully. It is natural indeed that this should be the case; for those new religions did not, any more than other religions elsewhere, spring full-grown from the brains of their founders, nor are they out of organic relation to the speculation and the devotion that precede them. * * * Both Jainism and Buddhism are, after all, phases of the long Hindu development, absorbing elements from its complexity and responding to certain demands of the spirit it expresses."

The story that Sâkyasimha began his spiritual quest with lessons from the philosophers of his time and found the whole encyclopædia of contemporary Hindu culture inadequate to the hunger of his soul, points emphatically to the intimate connexion with his age. It is like the legend of Confucius' interview with Laotsze. The following account of Mahâvira's initiation is also interesting as showing the general trend of Indian thought in the sixth century B.C.: "Jainism, though it denies the existence of a creator and of the three gods of the Indian trimurti, Brahmâ, Visnu and Siva, has never shaken itself free from the belief in many of the minor gods of the Hindu pantheon. It gives these gods, it is true, a very secondary position as servants or tempters of the great Jaina saints, but their existence is accepted as undoubted; accordingly, in the account of Mahâvira's initiation we shall find many of the old Hindu gods represented as being present."

We have seen that among the Celestials their classical mentality and religious consciousness expressed themselves in their entirety in the sixth century B.C.. We have examined also some of the materials which enable us to get an idea of the modifications or changes in emphasis that must have been accomplished through the age-long evolution. So in Hindusthân the religious consciousness which was exhibited in the Vedas is apparent to students of Hindu mentality in the sixth century B.C.. The continuity of the traditional metaphysics was not broken. Rather it was the age when the whole philosophic culture of the race got systematised and codified as "Schools." These schools, therefore, as embodying the past, constitute the landmarks of an old life.

Confucius believed in the god-lore of his contemporaries and subscribed unhesitatingly to the whole theological apparatus and religious laboratory of the time. Sâkyasimha, Mahâvira, and some others probably did not believe in the traditional god-lore. But the god-lore itself remained entire. It was neither demolished nor got atrophied. On the other hand, the whole Vedic Mythology came down in a more concrete and personified form. The vague became distinct, the metaphors became organisms, the words became facts. In certain cases the names of the deities changed, in others their functions changed, while a few new names were added to the list, and there was a readjustment in the position and importance of the members of the Pantheon. All this was due to the impact of history, race, place, and the people. It is exactly these modifications in Chinese religion due to the folk-element and place-element that one would like to know. We have noted some of these in the previous Subsection (b).

The stage of development attained by the Nature-cult of the Vedists about the sixth century B.C. is thus described by Rhys Davids.

"Siri, the goddess of luck, was already a popular deity in Buddha's time. * * *

"Our two poets are naturally anxious to include in their lists all the various beliefs which had most weight with those whom they would fain persuade. The poet of the *Mahâsamaya* (the Great Concourse) enumerates first the spirits of the Earth and of the great Mountains. Then the Four Great Kings, the guardians of the four quarters, East and South and West and North. * * *

"Then come the Gandharvas, heavenly musicians, supposed to preside over child-bearing and birth. * * *

"Then come the Nâgas, the Siren-serpents, whose worship has been so important a factor in the folklore, superstition, and poetry of India from the earliest times down to to-day. * * *

"Then come the Garulas or Garudas, the Indian counterpart of the harpy and griffin, half man, half bird. * * *

"Then come a goodly crowd of Titans and sixty kinds of gods. * * * First we have the gods of kindly nature and good character, then the souls or spirits supposed to animate and reside in the moon and the sun, * * * in the wind, the cloud, the summer heat; then the gods of light, then a curious list of gods, personifications of various mental qualities; then the spirits in the thunder and the rain, and lastly the great gods who dwell in the highest heavens. * * *

"In neither of these two lists is Indra, the great god of the Veda, even mentioned. * * *

"In the period we are considering had Sakka in his turn almost ousted Indra. * * *

"It is the same, but in each case in different degrees, with other Vedic gods. * * * Isâna, the vigorous and youthful form of the dread Siva of the future, is already on a level with Soma and Varuna. And Prajâpati and Brahmâ will soon come to be considered as co-partners with Sakka in the over-lordship of the gods. * * * The worship of Agni is scoffed at. Vâyu the wind-god * * * will soon also be the laughing stock of the story-teller. Varuna is still a power. * * * And Vishnu * * * has scarcely as yet appeared above the horizon. Pajjunna is still the rain-god in the Suttântas. * * *

"I know of no other Vedic gods mentioned in this literature. Dyaus, Mitra and Savitri, Pushan, the Adityas, the Aswins, and the Maruts, Aditi and Diti, and Urvasi, and many more are all departed."

Prof. Rhys Davids in his *Buddhist India* gives the following account of the folk-religion in the sixth century B.C., which is nothing but a continuation of what we found recorded in the *Atharva Veda* and affords a striking parallelism to the classical and contemporary religious practices in China.

"We are told of palmistry, divination of all sorts, auguries drawn from the celestial phenomena, prognostication of dreams, auguries drawn from marks on cloth gnawed by mice, sacrifices to Agni, * * * oblations of various sorts to gods, determining lucky sites, repeating charms, laying ghosts, snake charming, using similar arts on other beasts and birds, astrology, the power of prophecy, incantations, oracles, consulting gods through a girl possessed or by means of mirrors, worshipping the great one, invoking Siri (the goddess of luck), vowing vows to gods, muttering charms to cause virility or impotence, consecrating sites, and more of the same kind."

All these superstitions, or "religions of the feeble minds," or primitive sciences and primitive arts, have existed both in China and India from time immemorial and are not yet extinct in either. It may be interesting to note that "determining lucky sites," "consecrating sites," etc., form the topics of a special branch of Chinese literature called *Fung Shui*, "the science of building houses, graves, and temples under the beneficial influence of the universe." We find these ideas in later Sanskrit literature as well, *e.g.* in Varâhamihira's *Brihat Samhitâ* (6th century A.D.). Dr. Edkins in his *Chinese Buddhism*, and Professor De Groot in his *Religion in China* have devoted special chapters to this branch of learning dealing with *fung* (*i.e.* wind) and *shui* (*i.e.* water). The term is exactly equivalent to the Hindu conception of climate as *Jala* (water) and *Vâyu* (wind).

From the accounts of Edkins and De Groot it would appear that *Fung-shui* is really a primitive science of climatology applied to the interests of social welfare. Thus as De Groot remarks: "The influence which Heaven and its phenomena, in particular *fung shui* or 'wind and rain' exercise upon Earth is greatly modified by the configuration of the earth. This simple truth has given birth to the geomantic doctrine that hills may prevent noxious winds from striking buildings or tombs. * * * Windings and bends of rivers and brooks are objects of studious care." Students of sociology may thus be interested in *Fung-shui* as representing the primitive and mediæval Indo-Chinese conceptions relating to the Influence of Geography on History which in modern times have been made into a science in such works as Montesquieu's *Spirit of Laws*, Hegel's *Philosophy of History*, Buckle's *History of Civilisation* and Bagehot's *Physics and Politics.*

Georg Bühler's *Indian Studies* is quoted by Rhys Davids to indicate that the *Jâtaka Stories* also point to the continuation of Vedic cult in the age of Sâkyasimha and Mahâvira: "Just as the Three Vedas are the basis of the higher instruction, so the prevalent religion is that of the path of works with its ceremonies and sacrifices, among which several, like the Vâjapeya and the Râjasuya, are specially and repeatedly mentioned. Side by side with these appear popular festivals, celebrated with general merry-makings and copious libations of *Surâ*, as well as the worship of demons and trees, all of which go back to the earliest times. Nor are the hermits in the woods and the wandering ascetics unknown."

The Celestial and the Hindu of the sixth century B.C. lived in the same world of morals, manners and sentiments. If the Chinese happened to be in India they would not feel any distance from the natives except only in language. And if the Hindus happened to be in China they would enter into the spirit of the Chinese people in spite of the language-barrier.

Section 4.

Asiatic Positivism

"The whole duty of man" has been preached in every age and every clime; and conceptions of moral obligations found in all literatures are almost the same. What we in modern times are likely to regard as moral truisms or copy-book maxims abound in every holy book as the "Eightfold

Path" or "Ten Commandments" or "The Five Duties." It is certainly unhistorical and unphilosophical to make any such formula or *sutra* the standard by which to test the worth of the other moral systems of the world. Nor is it strictly scientific to call a doctrine "positivism" on the strength of a few moral passages or sayings only.

Unfortunately, this has been done with regard to the teachings of Confucius in the *Analects* and the other works about him compiled by his disciples. If the term be applied to any inculcation of humanitarian principles or social duties and the like, every religion is surely positivistic and every human being has been a positivist.

If every instance of moral teaching were to be placed in the category of Positivism, the following Decalogue, quoted from *Sukrâniti*, a mediæval Sanskrit work, is an embodiment of Positivism:

1. Thou must not forsake your own duty in life.
2. Thou must not tell lies.
3. Thou must not commit adultery.
4. Thou must not bear false witness.
5. Thou must not forge.
6. Thou must not accept bribes.
7. Thou must not extort more than what is due unto you.
8. Thou must not steal.
9. Thou must not oppress (commit violence).
10. Thou must not rebel (commit perfidy).

Sukrâniti I. 613-616.

Such instances of positivistic cult are to be met with here and there and everywhere in Hindu Literature.

We have seen that Confucius the historian and sociologist took the classical metaphysics for granted, but Sâkyasimha actively contributed to the fund of traditional metaphysics according to his findings. Further, Confucius accepted the theology of his people as he found it. Sâkyasimha probably did not accept his contemporary theology at all; but neither did he argue it out of existence. The old cult of World-Forces thus continued its sway in both China and India, unhampered as of yore, but certainly modified according to local and tribal conditions.

Strictly speaking, Confucius the man and the historian was not an atheist or agnostic. And Sâkyasimha the philosopher and mystic was probably an agnostic, though theistic ideas may be traced even in him. But whatever technical term be applied to the life or writings or sayings of these men, that term would not be the label for the socio-religious tendency of their contemporaries; for neither of them represents his country entirely. Theism, atheism, mysticism, naturalism, monotheism, polytheism, in fact, every *ism*, existed side by side.

In spite of Confucius' faith in God, he has been wrongly classed with Positivists. His Positivism is deduced from the Socratic Dialogues illustrative of his views on all matters.

In his *Religion of China* Dr. Legge states that Confucius' "greatest achievement in the inculcation of morality was his formulating the golden rule, which is not found in its condensed expression in the old classics. The credit of it is his own. We find it repeatedly in the *Analects*, the *Doctrine of the Mean*, and the *Great Learning*. Tsze Kung once asked him if there were one word which would serve as a rule of conduct for all the life; and he replied, "Is not reciprocity such a word? What you do not want done to yourself, do not do to others."

As has been previously stated, Confucius left the abstruse questions open. That he himself felt the importance of

> "Those obstinate questionings
> Of sense and outward things,
> Fallings from us, vanishings,"

is apparent from his life as well as conversations. But he did not care much to vouchsafe an answer to queries on those things. The record of his sayings, therefore, must not be regarded as a complete biography or auto-biography.

As it is, we get his moral creed in the following quotation from Ku Hung Ming's translation of the classic called by him "The Universal Order or Conduct of Life" (known as *Doctrine of the Mean* in Legge's versions):

"When a man carries out the principles of conscientiousness and reciprocity he is not far from the moral law. What you do not wish others should do unto you, do not do unto them."

"There are four things in the moral life of a man, not one of which have I been able to carry out in my life. To serve my father as I would expect my son to serve me: that I have not been able to do. To serve my sovereign as I would expect a minister to serve me: that I have not been able to do. To act towards my elder brother as I would expect my younger brother to act towards me: that I have not been able to do. To be the first to behave towards friends as I would expect them to behave towards me: that I have not been able to do."

"The duties of universal obligation are five, and the moral qualities by which they are carried out are three.

The duties are those between ruler and subject; between father and son; between husband and wife; between elder brother and younger; and those in the intercourse between friends. These are the five duties of universal obligation. Intelligence, moral character and courage: these are the three universally recognised moral qualities of man."

This is the so-called Positivism of Confucius who never repudiated God or Divinity as an idea or ideal. However, we get here a picture of the code of morals which prevailed among the Celestials of the sixth century B.C. and has become stereotyped for all generations. This has been called by some as the Cult of "Propriety" or Good Manners. Mr. Ku Hung Ming calls it the "religion of good citizenship" in his *Spirit of the Chinese People.*

It is interesting to note that the word *Sila* in Buddhist literature is the exact equivalent of "Propriety," and that the "Eight-fold Path" described in the *Digha-Nikâya* (Sutta 22) contains some of the rules embodied in the Confucian Catechism. Says Hackmann in *Buddhism as a Religion*: "He who wants to get at the details of these duties may turn to writings such as *Mangala Sutta*, the *Dhammapada*, and the *Sigâlawâda.* They set forth the duties of parent and child, of teacher and pupil, of husband and wife, of friend and friend, of master and servant, of laymen toward the religious institutions."

Besides, it is also remarkable that in the age when *Nirvâna*, renunciation, other-worldlyism, were being preached by the followers of more than one Sâkyasimha and one Mahâvira, such humanitarian ethics and secular or non-mystical morality as we find in the Edicts of Asoka (3rd century B.C.) should have been predominant. But such a phenomenon should not strike as strange to those who would take the synthetic view of socio-religious life. History does not furnish data as to the immediate influence of *Nirvânistic* teachings on the contemporaries of Sâkya. But what we do get, after the lapse of two hundred years, is the strong centralised Imperialism of a Chandragupta, the worshipper of Nature-Forces, and the "enlightened" Cæsaro-Papism of his grand son Asoka. Surely the Sâkyasimhans had not extinguished or enervated the political and military genius of the Hindu race.

The following has been summarized from some of the Edicts of Asoka by Rhys Davids for his *Buddhist India:*

1. No animal may be slaughtered for sacrifice.
2. Tribal feasts in high places are not to be celebrated.
3. Docility to parents is good.
4. Liberality to friends, acquaintances and relatives, and to Brahmins and recluses is good.
5. Not to injure living beings is good.
6. Economy in expenditure, and avoiding disputes is good.

7. Self-mastery 8. Purity of heart 9. Gratitude 10. Fidelity	are always possible and excellent even for the man who is too poor to be able to give largely.

11. People perform rites or ceremonies for luck on occasion of sickness, weddings, childbirth, on starting on a journey—corrupt and worthless ceremonies. Now there is a lucky ceremony that may be performed—not worthless like those, but full of fruit—the lucky ceremony of the *Dhamma*. And there is included right conduct towards slaves and servants, honour towards teachers, self-restraint towards living things, liberality to Brahmins and recluses. These things and others such as these are the lucky

ceremony according to the Dhamma. Therefore should one —whether father or son or brother or master—interfere and say: "So is right. Thus should the ceremony be done to lasting profit." People say liberality is good. But no gift, no aid is so good as giving to others the gift of the Dhamma, as aiding others to gain the Dhamma.

12. Toleration. Honours should be paid to all, laymen and recluses alike, belonging to other sects. No one should disparage other sects to exalt his own. Self-restraint in word is the right thing. And let a man seek rather after the growth in his own sect of the essence of the matter.

13. The Dhamma is good. But what is the Dhamma? The having but little, in one's own mind, of the Intoxications, doing many benefits to others; compassion, liberality; truth; purity.

14. Man sees but his good deeds, saying: "This good act have I done." Man sees not at all his evil deeds, saying: "That bad act have I done, that act is corruption." Such self-examination is hard. Yet must a man watch over himself, saying: "Such and such acts lead to corruption, —such as brutality, cruelty, anger and pride. I will zealously see to it that I slander not out of envy. That will be to my advantage in this world; to my advantage, verily, in the world to come."

The greatest and most renowned devotee of the so-called arch-pessimist of the world was also the most pronounced positivist! As Hackmann remarks: "It is so much the more interesting, to see how Buddhism works through a gifted and influential layman, full of character. All the King's inscriptions prove that he draws from his religion a strengthening of moral effort, a consciousness of duty, a devotion to public welfare." I need only point out that the religion or morality of good citizenship, social service and humanitarianism has been in India along with, in spite of, and even in and through, every so-called *ism*. One word *Nirvâna*—does not explain three thousand years of Hindu culture.

Further, it requires to be stated that Sâkyasimha's teachings were not meant for ascetics and Rosicrucians alone. He catered for the spiritual needs of the householders and citizens as well. Such anti-domestic and anti-social statements as have been fathered upon Jesus are never recorded among the sayings of the Hindu *Nirvânist* (Queller of Misery). He came to show the path to the extinction (*Nirvâna*) of pain but did not make a *forte* of the so-called "escape from life."

The Syrian Saviour announced emphatically:

"He that loveth father or mother more than Me is not worthy of Me" (Matt. 10: 37).

"If any man cometh unto Me, and hateth not his father and mother and wife and children, he cannot be My disciple." (Luke 14: 26).

On the other hand, the Hindu Saviour taught the *Eightfold Path*. The *Digha Nikâya* (Sutta 22) in Pâli language describes the "noble truth of the path leading to the cessation of misery." Warren in his *Buddhism in Translations* has given the eight terms as right belief, right resolve, right speech, right behaviour, right occupation, right effort, right contemplation, and right concentration. And all this as much for husbands and wives, as for monks and nuns.

CHAPTER IV.

The Religion of Empire-Building—Neutrality and Eclecticism

(B.C. 350—100 B.C.)

SECTION 1.

The Political Milieu

(*a*) IMPERIALISM AND *Laisser faire*

Confucius died in B.C. 479. The political history of China for the next two centuries and a half repeats the previous tale of feudalistic disintegration. It is the period of "contending states," as Hirth calls it, like the Heptarchy in England; and nothing of political importance can be observed till the establishment of the hegemony of Tsin state in B.C. 249. Shi Hwang Ti, the "first Emperor" of all China, began his reign in B.C. 221, which lasted only for ten years. The Tsin dynasty was succeeded by the House of Han (B.C. 210-A.D. 220) which lasted for four centuries. The sixth Emperor of this dynasty was Wu Ti who reigned for fifty-four years (B.C. 140-87), one of the most illustrious among the rulers of China.

In India Sâkyasimha died in B.C. 483. The political history of India for the next century and a half may be supposed to repeat the story of the old struggle for over-lordship, though documentary evidences are wanting. But by B.C. 322, the hegemony of Magadha state is established and Chandragupta is found to be at its helm. He reigns from B.C. 322 to 298, and his grandson Asoka from 270 to 230 as the contemporary of the First Chinese Emperor.

The period is characterised by one and the same idea in both the countries. It is the epoch of nationalism, of a strong unified rule, and of a vast Imperialistic organisation. The land of the Celestial people gets a common name 'China' from the Tsin state which is instrumental in this unification; and "for the first time in the history of India there is one authority from Afghanistan across the continent eastward to Bengal, and from the Himâlayas down to the Central Provinces." The boundaries of this Indian Empire are further extended by Asoka so as to include the whole of Southern India excepting the extreme south which remains feudatory.

In external relations, also, the two countries present a striking parallelism. For the Chinese Napoleon commences at once the completion of the Great Wall to defend his empire against the inroads of the 'barbarian' Tartars or Mongols. And the Indian Napoleon commences his life-work by vanquishing the vanity of the barbarian Seleukos, the ruler of the Hellenistic Syria, who had invaded India.

The Year No. I of Chandragupta's Imperialism is his brilliant victory over this *mlechchha* (foreigner). It is with this fact that Indian political history, of which records have been preserved, really begins.

Referring to Greek invasion, however, Matthew Arnold started the superstition, now common to every westerner:

> " The East bowed low before the blast
> In patient, deep disdain;
> She let the legions thunder past,
> And plunged in thought again."

Even Mr. Vincent Smith, who is generally very sober, devotes a disproportionately large space to Alexander's campaign in his *Early History of India.* Strictly speaking, these researches should be incorporated with the investigations of Professors Mahaffy and Bury and have no place in a textbook of Indian history. The account of Alexander's expedition may loom large to students of Greece as a World-Power but is an incubus on the students of Indian civilisation. Besides, Mr. Smith himself admits that Alexander's enterprise did not leave any impression on India.

India did not "plunge in thought again." Says Rhys Davids: "At the end of the fourth century B.C., Seleukos Nikator, then at the height of his power, attempted to rival Alexander by invading India. But he met with a very different foe. * * * Seleukos found the consolidated and organised empire of Magadha against which all his efforts were in vain. After an unsuccessful campaign he was glad to escape by ceding all his provinces west of the Indus, including Gedrosia and Arachosia (about equal to the Afghanistan of to-day), and by giving his daughter in marriage to the victorious Emperor of India in exchange for five hundred elephants of war."

Nirvânism of the Sâkyasimhas did not militate against the establishment of the Indian Empire and the triumph over a foreign foe. About B.C. 300 India was not only a first-class power but the first power of the world, and Pâtaliputra, the capital, was the centre of gravity of the international system. The Hindus maintained this position unrivalled for a full century. It was only towards its close that Chinese Imperialism began to share with the Indian the same importance as a World-Power. Roman Imperialism was not yet conceived. Neither Sianfu, nor any of the Alexandrias, nor Rome, could thus vie with Pâtaliputra in its political prestige and diplomatic importance.

A natural concomitant of Imperialism both in China and India was the spirit of eclecticism and *laisser faire* in matters religious. It may seem to be a paradox to say that Shi Hwang Ti, the 'Burner of the Books,' was not possessed by a Papal doctrine of "Infallibility," and that he was not a bigot but a tolerant monarch. It is true, however, that this destroyer of Confucian literature was not a despiser of the Confucian morality and theology. He was a Confucianist of Confucianists for he respected the Classical gods and also added some to their list. He was really an enemy of the *literati*, those obscurantists, whose "words, words, words" stood in the way of his mission. A nation-maker cannot afford to be a dogmatist, a strict follower of the letter, for it is the "letter that killeth." The Chinese Napoleon, therefore, abolished the Confucian dogma, but preserved its spirit, viz., the Cult of World-Forces. The Confucian pedantocracy represents, as I have said, the last link of an old chain, not the first of a new.

The first link of the new chain could be forged by a man who, like Alexander, knew how to harmonize the folk-customs and traditions with all the speculative tendencies of his time, and harness them all to the great work of Empire-building. The burner of the classics was himself a Classicist and also a Taoist. It is thus a far cry from Confucius to Shi Hwang Ti. The *Zeitgeist* of the 3rd century B.C. was represented not by the "Perfect Sage" but by the "First Emperor." This spirit of toleration and synthesis was noticeable also in the Han Emperor Wu Ti who was at once a patron of Confucianists as well as of Taoists.

Professor Fenollosa in his *Epochs of Chinese and Japanese Art* draws almost a similar picture of the first Chinese Imperialist: "He brought the past consciously to an end, because he wished to rebuild with new stones; thus causing the burning of all past books, especially those which dealt with the endless disputations of the Confucian and Taoist philosophers. If there were any philosophy at all in this brief meteoric career, it was a sort of Nietzscheism backing raw freedom and force against formalism."

In fact, like the European and American of to-day addressing the Chinaman, Shi Hwangti may be imagined as having addressed the manes of the Great Sage thus:

"There are more things in heaven and earth, Confucius,
Than are dreamt of in your philosophy."

The same tendency is observable in India also. The great monarchs Chandragupta and Asoka were no hidebound pedants. Whatever their personal faiths, they knew that their function was not to advocate one or other of the prevailing *isms*, but to elaborate a new Imperialistic creed which should be quite independent of all. Their mission was not to be fulfilled by making the State subordinate to one or other of the speculative systems of the age. The *Zeitgeist* was therefore represented not by *Nirvânism*, or *Yogaism* or *Upanishadism*, or *Jainism*, but by the policy of let-alone and non-intervention so far as the people's views were concerned. The State cared solely for the systematic carrying out of a propaganda according to the financial, economic, political and militaristic teachings recorded in the *Arthasâstra** of Kautilya.

* This difficult Sanskrit work has been translated into English by Mr. R. Shamashastri for the Mysore Government and its materials utilised by Mr. Naren Law in his *Hindu Polity*.

(*b*). HINDU *Bushidō* AND *Indono Damashii.*

We do not know exactly what was the personal faith of Chandragupta. The followers of Mahâvira claim him for a Jaina. According to Hackmann in *Buddhism as a Religion*, "Chandragupta himself was not a Buddhist; he was on far more friendly terms with the Brahmans, and it was the same with his son Bindusâra." And those modern scholars, who take their cue from a Schopenhauer, a Matthew Arnold and a Kipling in trying to understand India, need note that Megasthenes, the Head of the Hellenistic Embassy at Pâtaliputra, observed nothing of the so-called Nirvânism, quietism and pessimism. Says Hackmann: "From the fragments of them * * we learn as to matters of importance very little about Buddhism. Megasthenes names the Buddhists as 'Sramanai,' and says that they were opposed to the 'Brahmanai.' But his description of their mode of life is vague, and he seems to mix the Buddhists up with other Indian sects."

This was perfectly natural, because Megasthenes came with his eyes open. He was not obsessed by any preconceived theory. He had not also the hypothesis of his own race as being superior. Rather he knew that he was living as a guest of the first power of the world. By the test of war Megasthenes the Greek belonged to an inferior race—he was the ambassador from a humiliated second-class power.

So in Pâtaliputra, the city of the East, this representative of the West noticed not the predominance of any non-secular and transcendental speculation but the apotheosis of Imperialism and all-round Eclecticism. The morality of the age can be expressed in the terms of *Sukranîti*, which, though a later compilation, does really represent the *Niti* or rules of life that have been prevalent since the age of Kautilya. The following is a translation from the Sanskrit texts edited by Gustav Oppert for the Government of Madras:

"Even Brahmanas should fight if there have been aggressions on women and priests or there has been a killing of cows. * * * (IV. vii. 599.)

The man who runs away from battle is surely killed by the gods. * * * (IV. vii. 601).

The life of even the Brahman who fights when attacked is praised in this world, for the virtue of a Kshatriya is derived also from Brahmâ. (IV. vii. 606-7).

The death of Kshatriyas in the bed is a sin. The man who gets death with an unhurt body by excreting cough and biles and crying aloud is not a Kshatriya. Men learned in ancient history do not praise such a state of things. Death in the home except in a fight is not laudable. Cowardice is a miserable sin. (IV. vii. 606-13).

The Kshatriya who retreats with a bleeding body after sustaining defeat in battles and is encircled by family-members deserves death. (IV. vii. 614-15).

Kings who valorously fight and kill each other in battles are sure to attain heaven. He also gets eternal bliss who fights for his master at the head of the army and does not shrink through fear. (IV. vii. 616-19).

People should not regret the death of the brave man who is killed in battles. The man is purged and delivered of all sins and attains heaven. (IV. vii. 620-21).

The fairies of the other world vie with each other in reaching the warrior who is killed in battles in the hope that he be their husband. (IV. vii. 622-23).

The great position that is attained by the sages after long and tedious penances is immediately reached by warriors who meet death in warfare. (IV. vii. 624-25.)

The rascal who flies from a fight to save his life is really dead though alive, and endures the sins of the whole people. (IV. vii. 656-7).

When the Kshatriyas have become effete, and the people are being oppressed by lower orders of men, the Brahmans should fight and extirpate them (IV. vii. 666-7)."

This *Kshatriyaism* is *Bushidō* according to Japanese notions, Chivalry in mediæval European phraseology, militarism in modern parlance. You may call this the spirit of Sparta, or if you like, Prussianism.

Another aspect of Hindu Chivalry is being described from the authoritative *Laws* of Manu, the Moses of India. This work is generally recognised as older than Chandragupta and may be as old as Sâkya (though, in its present form, probably as late as fourth century A.D.):

"Let the soldier, good in battle, never guilefully conceal
(Wherewithal to smite the unwary) in his staff the treacherous steel;
Let him scorn to barb his javelin—let the valiant never anoint
With fell-poison juice his arrows, never put fire upon the point.
In his car or on his war-horse, should he chance his foe to meet,
Let him smite not if he find him lighted down upon his feet.

Let him spare one standing suppliant, with his closed
hands raised on high,
Spare him whom his long hair loosen'd blinds and
hinders from to fly,—
Spare him if he sink exhausted; spare if he for life
crave;
Spare him crying out for mercy, 'Take me, for I am
thy slave.'
Still remembering his duty, never let the soldier smite
One unarm'd, defenceless, mourning for one fallen in
the fight;
Never strike the sadly wounded—never let the brave
attack
One by sudden terror smitten, turning in base flight
his back;
He, that flying from battle, by his foe is slaughter'd
there,
All the burthen of his captain's sin hereafter shall he
bear."

The translation is by Griffith. In these declarations by the Hindu International legists of Manu's School at least 2500 years ago we seem to be reading the latest resolutions of the 'Concert of Europe' at their Hague Conferences and the pious wishes of Peace-apostles like Carnegie.

As with Chandragupta, so with Asoka the contemporary of Shi Hwang-Ti. It is a far cry from the dogma of the historic Sâkyasimha to the *Dhamma* proclaimed by Asoka. Besides, Asoka was a nationalist, i.e., an Imperialist first, and a follower of *Dhamma* afterwards.

Imperialists must necessarily be neutral in religious policy and eclectic in personal life unless they choose to fail like a Philip II of Spain, a Louis XIV of France, an Aurangzib of India, or a James II of England. Asoka's Edicts are therefore neither the fiery fulminations of ban and anathema and a Bull of excommunication;—nor the autocratic proclamations of a so-called state-religion such as was embodied in the Inquisition, the Revocation of the Edict of Nantes, the Re-imposition of the Jizya, or the arbitrary Declaration of Indulgence. They are the sober and sedate expressions of a social-service-propaganda and a universal moral sense to which nobody in the world could object. Like his Chinese contemporary, Asoka was harsh towards pedants, e.g., the Brahmans, and did not like their sacrifices, but had no objection to Brahmans as such. Rather, he made toleration an important article of his faith.

Such religious neutrality, toleration and eclecticism have been exhibited by the Asoka of Modern Asia. Mutshuito the Great of Japan is inspired by the same sanity of good sense and liberalism in his formulation of the Educational Rescript which characterises the "Meiji" Era or Epoch of "Enlightenment" in *Dai Nippon*. Like the "enlightened despot" of the third century B.C. the Mikado assumes the position of a schoolmaster. The picture is that of an Emperor, with a *ferula* in hand, administering to the whole empire as to an elementary school homœopathic doses of common-sense morality. The Proclamation is in the right patriarchal style,—comparable in its austere dignity and earnestness with the historic edicts of the Indian Emperor, and breathes the simple eloquence of the "Ten Commandments" though there is no mention of God in it:

"Know ye, Our subjects,

Our Imperial Ancestors have founded our Empire on a basis broad and everlasting and have deeply and firmly implanted virtue; our subjects ever united in loyalty and filial piety have from generation to generation illustrated the beauty thereof. This is the glory of the fundamental character of our Empire, and herein also lies the source of our Education. Ye, our subjects, be filial to your parents, affectionate to your brothers and sisters; as husbands and wives be harmonious, as friends true; bear yourselves in modesty and moderation; extend your benevolence to all; pursue learning and cultivate arts, and thereby develop intellectual faculties and perfect moral powers; furthermore advance public good and promote common interests; always respect the constitution and observe the laws; should emergency arise, offer yourselves courageously to the state; and thus guard and maintain the prosperity of Our Imperial Throne coeval with heaven and earth. So shall ye not only be our good and faithful subjects, but render illustrious the best traditions of your forefathers.

The Way here set forth is indeed the teaching bequeathed by our Imperial Ancestors, to be observed alike by their descendants and the subjects, infallible for all ages and true in all places. It is Our wish to lay it to heart in all reverence, in common with you, our subjects, that we may all thus attain to the same virtue."

This Imperial *Michi*, i.e., "Way" or *Tao* or *Magga* is neither Shintōism nor Confucianism, nor Buddhism, nor Christianity, and yet in a sense it is all. In fact, here is *Yamato Damashii*, the spirit of Japan. So also the *Dhamma* of Asoka embodies *Indono Damashii*, the spirit of Hindusthân rather than any *ism*. It is not necessary to connect or identify Asoka's creed or "way" with any of the isms of his day. Like one of his illustrious successors, Akbar the Great, he may be credited with having founded a new faith. Philosophically speaking, it was a practical morality evolved eclectically out of the thousand and one isms floating in the air. Historically, it may be traced to the positivistic element of Sâkyasimha's teachings or to the same element in others' teachings as well. Rhys Davids observes: "The doctrine, as an ideal, must have been already widely accepted. * * * But how sane the grasp of things most difficult to grasp! How simple, how true, how tolerant, his view of conduct and life! How free from all the superstitions that dominated so many minds, then as now, in East and West alike!"

In personal life Asoka may have been a daily reciter of Pâli Tripitaka and a monk of the Sâkyan Order. But the statecraft enunciated in his *Dhamma* was not Sâkyaism. The Dhamma was a distinctively new force meant to govern the life and thought of the day. To ignore this is to ignore the laws of social evolution and ignore the philosophy of history.

It is absurd to suppose that Shintōism or Buddhism explains modern Japan. It is absurd to believe that the primitive Christian doctrine, e.g., "The Kingdom of God is within you," had any significance in Mediæval Europe when Guelphs and Ghibellins were flying at each others' throats in every city and every state. It is childish to think that modern Germany can be understood solely on the strength of such terms as the Classicism of a Goethe, the Idealism and Romanticism of a Fichte and a Pestalozzi, or the *Zollverein* of a Frederick List, without reference to all that the name Bismarck connotes. It is equally absurd to try to explain China and India of the third century B.C. and after by ignoring the Napoleonism of Shi Hwangti and the Machiavellism of Kautilya and the *Dhamma* of Asoka.

Chandragupta, Asoka, Shi Hwangti and Wu Ti are at least as powerful names in culture-history as Sâkyasimha, Mahâvira, Confucius and Laotsze. They were, in fact, the great protagonists in the drama of contemporary life, having pushed every other character into the back-ground. The old super-annuated doctrines were given the go-by in the *denouement;* so that to the post-Mauryan Hindus and the later Hans the "new sun rose bringing the new year." There was no longer a Sâkya the moralist, but a Buddha the god, one of those whom Sâkya had most probably repudiated. No longer a Confucius the librarian-sage of Loo, but a Confucius the god, a colleague of Shângti.

Section 2.

Internationalism

(*a*) Western Asia and India

A most striking feature of this epoch both for China and India is its pre-eminently international and cosmopolitan character. The origin of this internationalism is, however, due neither to the Hindus nor to the Chinese, nor even to their western colleagues the Hellenes, but to one who was a "barbarian" to all these peoples. This was the Macedonian Alexander.

The ever-fighting city-states of Greece could not protect their freedom against the monarchical resources of Alexander's father, nor did they present a united front against him. So Alexander succeeded Philip to a rich conquest. With him the old spirit of Hellas had no charm. He had no Hellenic traditions. He began his life-work, therefore, by abolishing, first, the republican form of government, and secondly, the parochial nationalisms of the people. Then he started on a world-conquest which was as much intellectual as physical. To students of science his expedition looks like the campaign of modern anthropologists, archæologists and naturalists. The pupil of Aristotle had mastered his comparative, historical and inductive methods quite well, though he rejected his system of city-states. So throughout his expedition he never forgot to bring about social and marital alliances between East and West, and to facilitate comparisons between facts of the same order by founding libraries, museums, gardens, etc. The whole route began to be dotted with Alexandrias, the nucleuses of race-mixture, culture-fusion, and wedlock between Asia and Europe, the ganglionic centres of an all-round eclecticism.

Alexander with his world-sense was altogether a new phenomenon in history. This conscious internationalism was a new force and left its stamp on Western Asia, Egypt, and Greece, the principal field of its application, and to a certain extent on India and China. For centuries after the premature death of Alexander in B.C. 320 the spirit of Alexander dominated every part of Asia and Europe. Signs of the bridging of the gulf attempted and partially achieved by this greatest of idealists need be read (though with great caution) in every important item of world's pre-Christian Culture.

It seems that Chandragupta had caught something of the great conqueror's internationalism, while a mere adventurer in the Punjab. Hence his acceptance of the daughter of Seleukos as wife. The marriage of a Hindu monarch with a Greek princess was an epoch-making event in Indian history like the expulsion of the foreigner. But such marriages were not few and far between in those days. It was probably an epoch of inter-racial marriages.

Metropolitan life, e.g., at Pâtaliputra, was intensely international. Its position as the diplomatic centre of the world naturally made it the headquarters of foreign Embassies. Rhys Davids suggests the following picture: "And with the princess and her suite, and the ambassador and his, not to speak of the Greek artists and artisans employed at the court, there must have been quite a considerable Greek community, about B.C. 300, at the distant city on the southern bank of the Ganges." Mr. Vincent Smith remarks in his *Early History of India* that "the Maurya Empire in the 3rd century B.C. was in constant intercourse with foreign states, and that large numbers of strangers visited the capital on business." Further, "all foreigners were closely watched by officials who provided suitable lodgings, escorts, and in case of need, medical attendance." According to this scholar, Hindu intercourse with Persians was greater than that with Greeks.

Internationalism inaugurated by Chandragupta continued under his successors. According to Lloyd in *The Creed of Half Japan*, while Bindusâra (B.C. 297-272) "was on the throne, the king of Egypt sent an embassy, under a certain Dionysus, to Pâtaliputra; and on one occasion he wrote a letter to Antiochus, king of Syria, asking to have a professor of Greek sent to him. Greek writers speak of him * * * that he adopted the Sanskrit title *Amitraghâti*, the slayer of his foes."

Asoka also was a great internationalist. He cherished the ambition of being a world-monarch. In the 13th edict we read of his embassies to the kings of Syria, Egypt, Macedonia, Epirus, and Kyrene, to the Cholas and Pandyas in South India, to Ceylon and to the peoples dwelling on the borders of his empire. The missionaries sent out by him to various parts of the world were as much secular as religious—at once the St. Augustines, Alcuins and Sir Thomas Roes of Hindusthân. Himself combining the functions of a Cæsar and a Pope, Asoka's 'legates,' those 'hands and eyes,' were necessarily the plenipotentiaries and consul-generals for his empire.

Mr. Lloyd gives a detailed account of Asoka's missionary activity. "These sovereigns and peoples Asoka addresses mainly on two subjects—care for the health and welfare of the people, and 'true conquest' over themselves and their passions." He refers to the "Greek merchants trading and travelling in India, whose votive inscriptions have been found in ancient Buddhist temples in the peninsula."

We read:—"It was to Antiochus I. (of Syria) that Asoka had applied for assistance as to medicinal herbs. * * * In the wars which Antiochus I. waged against the Gauls and Celts * * * he had used elephants which he, like his contemporary, Pyrrhus of Epirus, had obtained from Asoka's father, Bindusâra. * * *

Macedonia must have been full of men who had been in Central Asia and India in those days of constant coming and going, and there must have been a great interest taken in things Indian. * * *

Among the dialogues of Aristippus the founder of the Cyrenaic School of Philosophy, there was one which bore the name of Porus, a name well known among Indian kings. * * *

Alexandria was connected with India by at least three routes. A certain amount of the overland traffic from China came into Alexandria *via* Palestine (which was in the

Egyptian sphere of influence), and even the superior attractions of Antioch could not kill this commerce, which was, however, more Central and Eastern Asian than Indian. A further contingent of caravans brought in Indian goods *via* the Persian Gulf, Palmyra (later) and Palestine. The Egyptian ports in the Red Sea had direct communication, without any serious rivals, with the Indian ports at the mouth of the Indus."

Internationalism must have continued during the post-Asokan times also. For Sewell remarks in *The Imperial Gazetteer of India*, Vol, II. on the commerce of the period from B.C. 200 to A.D. 250: "There was trade both overland and by sea with Western Asia, Greece, Rome and Egypt, as well as with China and the East. * * Pliny mentions vast quantities of specie that found its way every year from Rome to India." And for the same period in Northwestern India there was great intercourse with Rome during the ascendency of the Kushans.

(*b*) CENTRAL ASIA AND CHINA.

The early history of the intercourse of China with foreigners is not yet clear. Scholars like Lacouperie have been assiduous in proving the connexion of the Celestials with the Hindus, Persians and Babylonians from pre-Sâkyan and pre-Confucian times. Astrological notions, totemistic practices and some of the superstitions, as well as the whole Taoistic metaphysics and 'hocuspocus' have been traced to foreign sources. Even the theory has been started that the first Emperor Shi Hwang Ti, the contemporary of Asoka, "was in some way connected" with the Maurya Dynasty of India. And there is a tradition that Buddhism first came to China about B.C. 217.

Incontestable evidences are not forthcoming. Hence Hirth, the great authority on the ancient period of Chinese history, is sceptical about any foreign relations of China before Wu Ti's time. And yet he is compelled to criticise himself thus:

"We possess the most plausible arguments for the introduction of foreign influences in Chinese culture at the time when relations with Western Asia were opened under the Emperor Wu Ti at the end of the second century B.C.; but if we examine numerous facts still on record as referring to times immediately preceding the Wu Ti period we are bound to notice that changes of a different kind had come over the Chinese of this as compared with those of the Confucian and pre-Confucian periods. The growing influence of foreign elements from Tsin in the west, Chau in the north, and Chu in the south may account for this. * * * Lau-tzi, as a native of the state of Chu, was born and probably brought up among the southern barbarians."

Further:—"Altogether, readers of the history of Chau, as represented in Ssima-Tsien's account, will receive the impression that it contains various prognostics of that important change in cultural life which became dominant in the age of Tsin Shi Hwang Ti; namely a Tartarised China, the traditional Confucian views of life having been supplanted by Tartar, Scythian, Hunnic or Turkish elements, elements that, whatever name we may give them, had grown out of the national life of Central Asiatic foreigners."

Just as Western Asia plays an important part in Indian history of the 3rd century B.C., so Central Asia, *i.e.*, the regions to the west of China, plays an important part in her history of the period. And Central Asia is also the connecting link between India and China. Wu Ti formed an alliance with the Yueh Chi or Indo-Scythians against the common enemy, the Huns. Later, to quote Gowen, "the great generals carried the arms of China into Western Asia, caused the banners of Eastern Empire to meet the banners of Rome on the shores of the Caspian, and made a way for the merchants of China to carry their silk and iron into the markets of Europe."

The following is from Parker's *China:* "A great revolution in thought took place about two centuries before our era; the time coincides with the conquests of the Parthians, and it is possible that Græko-Roman civilisation was affected by the same wave that influenced China—whatever it was. At all events, there was a general movement and a simultaneous expansion in the world all the way from Rome to Corea. The result was that China now first heard of India, Buddhism, and the Parthians."

Eitel's *Buddhism* also may be quoted; "Chinese armies had been fighting a series of campaigns in Central Asia and had repeatedly come into contact with Buddhism established there. Repeatedly it happened that Chinese generals, engaged in that war, had occasion to refer, in their reports to the throne, to the influence of Buddhism.

Laurence Binyon in his *Painting in the Far East* speaks of the same foreign intercourse in the following terms:

"In B.C. 200 the Chinese seeking markets for their silk opened communication with Western Asia. A century later the Emperor Wu Ti sent a mission to the same regions. Greek designs appear on the earliest metal mirrors of China. It is possible that in the Chinese fable of the Paradise of the West the myths of the Greeks may be reflected.''

The whole epoch beginning with Alexander's accession to the Greek throne and extending for at least three centuries may be presumed to have been one in which race-boundaries were being obliterated, cultural angularities were being rounded off, people's intellectual horizon was being enlarged, and the sense of universal humanity generated. It was a time when the Aristotelians, Platonists, ''Cynics'' and Stoics were likely to meet the Apocalyptists, Zoroastrians, Confucianists, Taoists, *Nirvânists* and Yogaists on a common platform,—when the grammarians and logicians of Alexandria were probably comparing notes with the *Pâninians* and *Darsanists* of India, when the herbalists of Asia Minor could hold debates with the Charakan Âyurvedists of Hindusthân, when, in one word, culture was being developed not from national angles but from one international view-point and placed as far as possible on a universal basis. The courses of instruction offered at the great Universities of the world, e.g., those at Honanfu, Taxila, and Pâtaliputra, the Alexandrias, and Athens, comprehended the whole encyclopædia of arts and sciences known to both Asia and Europe.

The *literati*, *bhikshus*, magi and *sanyâsins* of the East met the mystics, sophists, gnostics and peripatetics of the West at out-of-the-way inns or caravanserais or at the recognised academies and seats of learning. 'Universal-Races-Congresses' and International Conferences of Scientists may have been matters of course, and every man who was of any importance—Hindu, Chinese, Persian, Egyptian, Greek—

was necessarily a student of world-culture and a citizen of the world. This intellectual expansion influenced the social systems also in every part of the civilised world. Inter-racial marriages may be believed to have been things of common occurrence, and everywhere there was a *rapprochement* in ideals of life and thought. The world was fast approaching a common consciousness, a common conscience and a common standard of civilisation.

A picture of this fusion of cultures though for a subsequent period is given by Laurence Binyon in his chapter on *Early Art Traditions in Asia:*

"What then do we find in this little, remote kingdom in the heart of Asia? We find sculpture and paintings, we find heaps of letters on tablets of wood; odds and ends of woven stuffs and furniture; and police notices on strips of bamboo. * * * The police notices are in Chinese. The letters are written in a form of Sanskrit. But the string with which the wooden tablets are tied is sealed with a clay seal; and in most cases the seal is a Greek seal, the image of an Athena or a Heracles. Here, then, we touch three great civilisations at once: India, Greece, China. * * *

If we ask ourselves what affinities these paintings reveal, with what art we can connect them, * * * we are reminded of features in Indian, Persian, Chinese and Japanese Painting. * * *

Will the sculptures tell us more? They at once remind us of other sculpture. * * * We see what seems a Greek Apollo; and then little by little the Greek features become more Indian; Apollo transforms himself into a Buddha."

The marriage of Asia with Europe—that meeting of "the twain" which is never to be—was thus an accomplished fact in every department of human culture at least 2200 years ago!

SECTION 3.

General Culture

(a) PHYSICAL AND POSITIVE SCIENCES

The intellectual turmoil of the period, in which there was no monopoly of any one system of thought, is thus described by Hirth in his *Ancient History of China*: "That unsteadiness characteristic of political life in the fourth century B.C., which knew of no equilibrium among the contesting powers and which caused even conservative minds to become accustomed to the most unexpected changes in politics, was coupled with a hitherto unprecedented freedom of thought in the ranks of thinkers and writers. The most heretical views on state and private life were advanced and gained public adherence."

According to the "Complete Edition of the Philosophers that lived prior to the Tsin Dynasty" compiled during the Ming Dynasty about A.D. 1600, "the minor philosophers are divided into Confucianists, Taoists, writers on government, Mihists (adherents of Moti, the philosopher of universal love), criss-cross philosophers, *i.e.*, those who teach the dialectic art of defending opposite views in politics, and miscellaneous celebrities."

These accounts should make one cautious about trying to sum up the whole age by any convenient term. Among the master-minds of the age, Hirth mentions the pessimist Yang Chu "one of the most original thinkers China has produced,'' Moti, "whose teachings are diametrically opposed to those of Yang Chu," who, besides, represents the *Zeitgeist* in his "revolutionary independence of old Chinese tradition," Mencius, who upholds the teachings of Confucius against the upstarts and expands them by applying them to economic and political problems, and Chuangtzi, the greatest mystic exponent of Taoism and arch-enemy of the Confucianists.

Mr. Giles observes in his *Chuangtzi, Mystic, Moralist and Social Reformer:* "Against these hard and worldly utterances, Chuangtzi raised a powerful cry. The idealism of Laotsze had seized upon his poetic soul, and he determined to stem the tide of materialism in which men were being fast rolled to perdition."

The literary activity of India also during this period shows a remarkable versatility. It was not an epoch of mere prose, if there was ever any exclusively prosaic age in India, nor was it one in which cold philosophical intellectualism prevailed. Neither did it produce solely the so-called religious literature—nor was it swamped by the publications of Sâkyasimhañ moral tracts. The literature of the age was a perfect mirror of its many-sided enterprise and exhibited the eclecticism and comprehensiveness of its social *milieu.*

In the *Kâmasûtra*, a Sanskrit work on Erotics by Bâtsâyana of the second century B.C., there is an enumeration of 32 *vidyâs* or sciences and 64 *kalâs* or practical arts known to the Hindus. It need hardly be said that during the period we have been considering all these were pursued. The 32 branches of learning are enumerated below:

1. Vedas 4
2. Upa-vedas (science of life, archery, music and science of divination, totemism, sorcery, etc.).... 4
3. Vedângas (Phonetics, Philology, Rituals, Etymology, Astronomy and Prosody) 6
4. Darsanas (Systems of Philosophy) 6
5. Itihâsa (History) 1
6. Purâna, dealing with cosmogony, history of the ruling dynasties, etc. 1
7. Smriti (Socio-legal, Socio-economic and Socio-religious treatises).... 1
8. Scepticism ("Rationalism which advocates the origin of all things from Nature [not from God] and repudiates the authority of the Vedas") 1
9. Arthasâstra (Economics and Politics) ... 1
10. Kâma Sâstra ("which describes the marks of living beings both male and female, *e.g.*, of men according to their physical character, and of women according to external and internal characteristics) 1
1. Silpa Sâstra ("which treats of the construction of palaces, images, parks, houses, canals and other works").... 1
12. Alankâra (Rhetoric) 1
13. Kâvya (Poetry) 1
14. Deshabhâshâ (vernacular language) 1
15. Avasarokti ("which teaches the proper use of words at the proper time") 1

16. *Yavana* philosophy ("foreign" systems of thought, "which recognise God as the invisible creator of this universe, and recognise virtue and vice without reference to the Vedas and post-Vedic classics, and which believe that the Vedas embody a separate religious system.") 1

The above list gives a schedule of the courses of instruction offered at the Imperial Universities of India in those days. It need be remarked that the botany, zoology, physiology, chemistry, mathematics, astronomy, etc., of the Hindus of the pre-Christian era compare favourably with the researches of Theophrastus and his fellow-Aristotelians and the Alexandrian investigators. The physical sciences of the Hindus were not surpassed by the European scientists of even a very late age, *e.g.* Vesalius, Stahl, Brunfels, etc.. The contributions of the ancient and mediæval Hindus to physical science must be a fascinating subject to students of the history of world-culture. Learned monographs on the subject have been issued by Professors Roy and Seal of Calcutta.

Along with the physical sciences in which medicine and chemistry occupied the lion's share, the scholars of India certainly continued the compilation, editing and annotation of the philological and philosophical classics. The workers in all these fields of investigation were Brahmanical, Jaina as well as Sâkyan, and the seats of learning were the *Parishats*, academies, monasteries or *vihâras*. The chemists, physiologists, logicians and grammarians came from all sects.

At least three special classes of moral and theological literature must have necessarily grown up to cater for the needs of the people following the three prominent systems of metaphysics. It is said that the Jaina Canon was fixed at Pâtaliputra by a council of monks convened by Sthulabhadra early in the 3rd century B.C..

Mrs. Stevenson remarks: "The council fixed the canon of the Jaina Sacred literature, consisting of the eleven *Anga* and the fourteen *Parva.* It seems likely that the books were not committed to writing at this time, but were still preserved in the memories of the monks. The action of the council would thus be limited to settling what treatises were authoritative."

The dialect used by the Jainas for their sacred texts was *Prâkrit*, the language spoken by Mahâvira and his monks. Sanskrit came to be in vogue later. So also during this period the Sâkyasimhans used for their sacred writings the Pâli dialect, very much allied to the Jaina. But Sanskrit was the language adopted by those who founded Buddhism or the Buddha-cult in subsequent times.

The following verses on the Duty of Kings are translated by Griffith from Manu's *Laws*, a Sanskrit work popular during the period under review:

"He that ruleth should endeavour with his might and main to be
Like the Powers of God around him, in his strength and majesty:
Like the Rain-God in due season sendeth showers from above,
He should shed upon his kingdom equal favour, gracious love;

As the sun draws up the water with his fiery rays of might,
Thus let him from his own kingdom claim his revenue and right;
As the mighty wind unhinder'd bloweth freely where he will,
Let the monarch, ever present with his spies all places fill;
Like as in the judgment Yama punisheth both friends and foes,
Let him judge and punish duly rebels who his might oppose.
As the moon's unclouded rising bringeth peace and calm delight,
Let his gracious presence ever gladden all his people's sight;
Let the king consume the wicked—burn the guilty in his ire,
Bright in glory, fierce in anger, like the mighty God of Fire,
As the General Mother feedeth all to whom she giveth birth,
Let the king support his subjects, like the kindly fostering Earth."

These lines describe the divine attributes that the king possesses, for the king, according to statesmen of Manu-cycle is a "great god in human form." The Chinese and Shintō conceptions of the king being 'a son of Heaven' have their counterpart in Hindu tradition as well.

(b) Metaphysical Thought

We find in *Confucianism and its Rivals*: "One point specially to be noticed is the persistence, even where cobwebs of mysticism hang most thickly, of the old ideas of a personal if not anthropomorphic god."

The ideas of Chwangtsze, the most brilliant Taoist, the contemporary of Mencius, are thus described by Suzuki: "When we come to Chuangtsze the world of relativity was felt like a big pen; he left it behind him in his ascent to the realm of the Infinite, and there he wished to sleep an absolutely quiescent dreamless sleep. This was his ideal. He was, therefore, more radical than Laotsze in his transcendental idealism."

Chinese mentality approaches the Hindu so much that Gowen is led to remark about this transcendentalist: "He plainly reflects in his writings, which have much charm, an Indian influence, as in the closing lines of his poem on *Peaceful Old Age:*

"Thus strong in faith I wait and long to be
One with the pulsings of Eternity."

This "Eternity" of Chuangtsze is thus described in Giles' *Confucianism:* "We are sometimes confronted with a psychological unity instead of a concrete personality. With Chuang-tsze all things are one, and that One is God, in whose obliterating unity we are embraced. * * * Therefore, we are advised to take no heed of time, nor of right and wrong, but passing into the realm of the Infinite, *i.e.* of God, to take our final rest therein. Contraries, he explains, cannot but exist, but they should exist independently of each other, without antagonism. Such a condition is found only in the all-embracing unity of God; in other words, of the Infinite Absolute."

The *Tao-te-ching*, the most famous mystical work of this period, may be regarded as a Chinese *Gîtâ*. The following Chinese sayings could be illustrated by parallel passages from Sanskrit:

1. Keep behind and you shall be in front. Keep out and you shall be kept in.

2. Mighty is he who conquers himself.

3. Do nothing, and all things will be done. I do nothing, and my people become good of their own accord.

4. He who is content has enough.

5. He who is conscious of being strong is content to be weak.

Such Taoistic mysticism was imported to England by Carlyle from German Transcendentalists with the celebrated preamble: "Close thy Byron, open thy Goethe." His advice, "Make thy numerator zero, and the quotient will be infinite," is Taoism!

The following declaration of Chuangtse about the method of finding the "real nature of things" could be equally made by a contemporary Hindu: "Be free yourself from subjective ignorance and individual peculiarities, find the universal Tao in your own being, and you will be able to find it in others, too, because the Tao cannot be one in one thing and another in another. The Tao must be the same in every existence, because 'I' and the 'ten thousand beings' grow from the selfsame source, and in this oneness of things we can bury all our opinions and contradictions."

Taoism of the period under discussion has such remarkable features in its doctrine, that, as says Suzuki, "a foreign origin has been suspected, which claim satisfactorily solves the question of its striking resemblance to Hindu philosophy. They even go so far as to suggest the Brahmin descendency of the Yellow Emperor Laotsze and other unknown Taoist thinkers."

In any case it is clear that both in India and China the environments were getting closer and closer to each other.

The *Tao-te-ching* supposed to contain the sayings of Laotsze is generally believed by sinologues to be a compilation of the second century B.C.. The Celestials of that age could therefore easily interpolate the Hindu *Gitâ* in their literature. The following verses translated from Sanskrit by Griffith would be at once recognised as Taoistic:

"Mourn not for them, O Arjun! for the Wise
Grieve for none living, weep for none that dies;
Nor thou, nor yonder princes were not,
For ever have they been, though changed their lot,
So shall their being through all time extend,
Without beginning, and without an end.
The vital spirit in this mortal clay
Lives on through youth, from childhood to decay;
And then new forms the fleeting souls receive—
Why for these changes should the hero grieve?
Know that what is can never cease to be,
What is not can be never—they who see
The mystic Truth, the Wise, alone can tell
The nature of the things they study well,
And be thou sure the mighty boundless soul,
The Eternal Essence, that pervades this whole,
Can never perish—never waste away,
The Indestructible knows not decay.
Frail though its shrine, undimm'd it lasts for ever,
The bodies perish—That can perish never;
Up then, and conquer! in thy might arise!
Fear not to slay it, for it never dies."

Thus the most highly mystical syllogism is led up to the most practical climax—that of slaying the enemies. This is the "Natural Supernaturalism" of Carlyle crystallised in the formula: "Always do the Duty that lies nearest thee." It may be remarked, by the bye, that the whole *Gîtâ*, known to be the abstrusest and most other-worldly treatise in Hindu literature, was delivered by the Lord Himself on the battlefield of Kurukshetra, the greatest Armageddon conceived in world's literature. This certainly is Positivism and Secularism with vengeance.

(*c*) Idealism and Supernaturalism in Literature

Literature of the age (Tsin and Han) bears evidence of the idealistic tendency of the Chinese mind. According to Giles' *History of Chinese Literature*, "the poetry which is representative of the period between the death of Confucius and the second century B.C. is a thing apart. There is nothing like it in the whole range of Chinese literature. * * * Poetry has been defined by the Chinese as 'emotion expressed in words.' * * * Poetry, they say, knows no law. And again, 'the men of old reckoned it the highest excellence in poetry that the meaning should lie beyond the words.' "

Mr. Werner quotes the following from the *Journal of the Peking Oriental Society* from which it would appear that the Confucian age of prose was followed by an era of romanticism: "The Confucian age produced no poetry brilliant enough to be preserved. * * * The *literati* did not encourage it. * * *

From B.C. 312 onward much poetry was written and an unbroken succession of poets maintained a position of influence in the literary firmament. * * * Chu Yuan * * took pleasure in adding Taoist ideas which then prevailed in that part of China where he lived.''

Further, ''the mythology and supernaturalism of the times after Confucius were a powerful factor in originating the school of poetry which Chu Yuan and his fellow poets of the third century B.C. united to establish. It operated on their minds as it did on the minds of Chuantszi in prose. * * * Our poet gave himself up to be under the control of legend and fancy, and at the same time, was swayed by the most sincere and deeply laid loyalty and love of country. His fondness for vigorous conceptions, the rapidity of his transitions, his luxuriant imagery, the evident pleasure felt by him in personification of the elements, the agreeable balance of his sentences, the impetuosity of his style, and the richness of his vocabulary are features that command our literary admiration, while his depth of sincerity and patriotic eagerness ensure our moral sympathy.''

The following lines of Chu Yuan on 'the land of exile' in his *Li Sao* ("Falling into Trouble") are quoted from Cranmer-Byng's *Lute of Jade*:

> "Methinks there's a genius roams in the mountains,
> Girdled with ivy and robed in wisteria,
> Lips ever smiling, of noble demeanour,
> Driving the yellow pard, tiger-attended,
> Couched in a chariot with banners of cassia,
> Cloaked with the orchid, and crowned with azaleas;
> Culling the perfume of sweet flowers, he leaves
> In the heart a dream-blossom, memory-haunting.
> But dark is the forest where now is my dwelling,
> Never the light of day reaches its shadow.

Thither a perilous pathway meanders.
Lonely I stand on the lonelier hill top,
Cloudland beneath me, and cloudland around me.
Softly the wind bloweth, softly the rain falls,
Joy like a mist blots the thought of my home out;
There none would honour me, fallen from honours.
I gather the larkspur over the hillside,
Blown mid the chaos of boulder and bell-bine;
Hating the tyrant who made me an outcast,
Who of his leisure now spares me no moment:
Drinking the mountain spring, shading at noon day
Under the cypress my limbs from the sun glare.
What though he summon me back to his palace,
I cannot fall to the level of princes.
Now rolls the thunder deep, down the cloud valley,
And the gibbons around me howl in the long night.
The gale through the moaning trees fitfully rushes.
Lonely and sleepless I think of my thankless
Master, and vainly would cradle my sorrow."

Thus, neither in Confucius' time nor since has China been only Confucius 'writ large.' To understand the Chinese people of any age we must not allow ourselves to be possessed by Confucian pedants.

It is unfortunate that we have very few fragments of earliest Jaina literature, but specimens of earliest Pali literature are copious. Some of these may be regarded as the common storehouse of ballads, legends, sayings, and myths out of which Buddhist, Jaina, Vaishnava, and Shaiva epics, dramas and story-books were built up. The following remark of Rhys Davids opens up the Maurya age before our minds' eye very vividly: "It is interesting to notice that, just as we have evidence at this period of first steps having been taken towards a future epic, so we have evidence of the first steps towards a future drama—the production before a tribal concourse on fixed feast-days of shows with scenery, music and dancing. There is ample evidence in the Buddhist and Jaina record, and in Asokan inscriptions, of the existence of these *Samajjas*, as they were called, as a regular institution:"

During this period Sanskrit, however, was not neglected. It remained the language of scholarship and of the traditional Brâhmanists and Upanishadists and was destined to be the language of the adherents of the two new orders also. In the meanwhile it became the vehicle of high class poetry, which, according to the Hindus, is "impassioned speech" (*Kâvyam rasâtmakam vâkyam*). This Wordsworthian idea is shared with them by the Chinese.

The following verses about the birth of Râma illustrate the influence that the supernatural was exerting on the people's mind at the time. The translator is Griffith.

"With costly sacrifice, with praise and prayer,
Ayodhyâ's King had claimed from Heaven an heir;
When from the shrine, where burnt the holy flame,
Scaring the priests, a glorious angel came,
With arms that trembled as they scarce could hold
A flood of nectar in a vase of gold:
A weight too vast for even him to bear,
For Vishnu's self, the first of Gods was there.
With reverent awe the Lord of Kosal's land
Received the rectar from the angel's hand,
As erst Lord Indra from a milky wave
Took the sweet drink that troubled ocean gave.

Soon as the queens had shared that mystic bowl,
Hope, sure and steadfast, filled each lady's soul.
They saw, in dreams, a glorious host who kept
Their watch around them, as they sweetly slept.

* * *

Proud waxed the monarch, as each happy queen
Told the bright visions that her eyes had seen :

* * *

As many a river lends its silver breast
Where the calm image of the moon may rest,
So in the bosom of each lady lay
That God, divided, who is one for aye.

* * *

The babes were born: then sin and sorrow fled,
And joy and virtue reigned supreme instead.
For Vishnu's self disdained not mortal birth,
And heaven came with him as he came to earth.
Once more the regions, where each guardian lord
Had quailed before the giant he abhorred,
Were cheered with breezes pure from dust and stain,
And freed from terror hailed a gentler reign.
The fire was dimmed by cloudy smoke no more,
And the sun shone untroubled as before."

Students of Biblical literature would notice in these old Hindu verses the Messianic conception that was crystallising itself about the first century B.C. into a definite shape in the *Psalms of Solomon* (XVII. 23-25):

"Behold, O Lord, and raise up unto them
    Their King, the son of David,
At the time in which thou seest O God,
    That he may reign over Israel Thy servant,

And gird him with strength that he may
    Shatter unrighteous rulers,
And that he may purge Jerusalem from
    Nations that trample her down to destruction."

The rhapsodists of the Vâlmîkian cycle sang verses like these to millions of men and women, teaching them the doctrine of *Avatâra* (human incarnation of Divinity) and reciting the story of the advent of the Messiah. During these very times the poets and monks of the Sâkyasimhan order were building up the materials for similar Messiah-legends about the great teacher of the sixth century B.C.. Sâkyaites and Râmaites represent the same Indian mentality from slightly different angles. The Hindu sculptures of the period, *e.g.*, those at Bharhut, tell the same tale; for in these we find scenes from the Sanskrit *Râmâyana* forming motives, decorative as well as didactic, together with the legends described in the Pali *Jâtakas*. We see both in literature and art how the historical Sâkya and the semi-historical Râma were simultaneously getting deified in people's imagination. The same emotionalism and romanticism were at work in both.

CHAPTER V.

The God-lore of China and India under the First Emperors

(B.C. 350-100)

SECTION 1.

Progress in Hagiology and Mythology.

(a) INVENTION OF NEW DEITIES

We have noticed the continuity and growth of the pre-Confucian Cult of World-Forces in Confucius' time. The development continues along the same lines after Confucius too. During the latter half of the Chou Period and the succeeding epoch of Imperialism we can observe the progress of this pluralistic godlore.

According to La Couperie, "there was a remarkable dualist worship established in Tcheng in B.C. 524 to *Hwei-luh*, god of light and fire, and *Hiuen Ming*, god of darkness and water, then known in Chinese Mythology for the first time. * * * It was the custom at Yeh in the state of Wei in Honan to give a wife to the river-god, Hopeh, annually by throwing a girl into the river. It was suppressed during the reign of Marquis Wen of Wei, B.C. 424-387. * * * It was the custom in the state of Lu, at the above date, in time of drought, to leave a person exposed to the sun, to die of thirst and hunger. * * *

The worship of the fire-goddess *Hwei-luh* was adopted by the Emperor in B.C. 133 and afterwards became that of the kitchen-god."

Mr. Werner quotes the *China Review* (XII. 417) from which it is apparent that the worship of the five emperors "was not completed till the Han Dynasty, the second century before Christ." "The worship of the five emperors was still more developed in the Tsin and Han Dynasties."

The God of Literature (Wen Ti) was, like the God of War, "called into being by an Imperial Mandate," as the writer in the North China Branch of Royal Asiatic Society's Journal (vi. 31-3) remarks.

The First Emperor perpetrated vandalism on the Confucian Classics and the *literati*, but he was himself a great patron of the orthodox religion which they represented. For he was the innovator of the worship of Mt. Tai in Shantung, which is now a part of the popular faith. Mt. Tai has since then been the most important of the five sacred mountains of China. As Giles observes, "it is, in fact, a divinity manifesting itself from time to time under human form. * * * The chief favours sought from the mountain were (1) rain and fine weather in due season, in order to produce abundant crops for the farmer, and food for the people at large; (2) protection from earthquakes, thunder-storms and such dangers as were supposed to be connected with the appearance of comets, eclipses and other natural phenomena."

The worship of Mother Earth as a deity is also described by Giles in this connexion: "The soil with its apparent powers of yielding or withholding its vegetable products, became a god—a fifth among the cluster of family-deities, the gods of the kitchen-stove, of the well, of the front door, and of the parlour."

In India, also, during this period, the people were inventing new deities exactly like the Chinese.

The following verses, in Waterfield's translation, describe how the new god Shiva compelled recognition from those who had been used to the earliest Vedic deities:

Daksha for devotion made a mighty feast;
Milk and curds and butter, flesh of bird and beast,
Rice and spice and honey, sweetmeat, ghee and gur,
Gifts for all the Brahmans, food for all the poor.
At the gates of Gangâ Daksha held his feast;
Called the gods unto it, greatest as the least.
All the gods were gathered round with one accord,
All the gods but Umâ, all but Umâ's lord.
Umâ sat with Shiva on Kailâsa hill;
Round them stood the Rudras watching for their will.

* * *

Wroth of heart was Umâ; to her lord she spake:—
"Why dost thou, the mighty, of no rite partake?
Straight I speed to Daksha such a sight to see:
If he be my father, he must welcome thee."

* * *

Spake the Muni Daksha, stern and cold his tone:—
"Welcome thou, too, daughter, since thou com'st alone.
But thy frenzied husband suits another shrine;
He is no partaker of this feast of mine."

* * *

Words like these from Daksha, Daksha's daughter heard;
Then a sudden passion all her bosom stirred:
Eyes with fury flashing, speechless in her ire,
Headlong did she hurl her 'mid the holy fire.

* * *

Hushed were hymns and chanting; priests were mocked
and spurned;
Food defiled and scattered; altars overturned.

* * *

Prostrate on the pavement Daksha fell dismayed:—
"Mightiest, thou hast conquered; thee we ask for aid."

* * *

Bright the broken altars shone with Shiva's form;
"Be it so!" His blessing soothed that frantic storm.

—Indian imagination thus brought to the forefront a new god who had been in the background in Vedic, post-Vedic and Sâkyasimhan times. The worship of Shiva in the form of *lingam* (phallus) is taken as a matter of course in the *Mahâbhârata*. Fundamentally the worshippers of world-forces, the Hindus like the Chinese can manufacture a god every ten years.

The Hindus of the Maurya and post-Maurya epoch had other things to do besides the creation of gods and goddesses. And when they did care for the creation of gods and goddesses they were not exclusively bent upon elaborating the traditions of the Sâkyasimhan cycle. We have noticed how in Sâkyasimha's time the old Nature-deities had been getting definite shapes and were being transformed into more or less new divinities. Some of these have been mentioned and described with illustration in Grunwedel's *Buddhist Art in India*. The process went on during the post-Sâkyan era also and gave rise to all the gods and goddesses known to us in the *Râmâyana*, *Mahâbhârata* and some of the *Purânas*. Râma-cult, Krishna-cult, Vishnu-cult and Shiva-cult, in fact, all the cults and all the mythologies which were to have powerful influence on Indian character in subsequent times may be said to have formed themselves during this period. It is difficult to trace the successive stages in the Hindu mythologies as it is difficult to fix a date for every Chinese god. But it may be asserted with tolerable certainty that the epoch of the Mauryas and their successors was the formative period of the later Buddhist, Brâhmanic and Jaina saint-lores and godlores. So that towards the end of the first century B.C. and the beginning of the first century A.D., we witness the emergence of Shaivaism, Buddhism, Vishnuism, Jainism, etc., as more or less full-fledged religious systems with all the paraphernalias of ritualism known to mediæval and modern Hindus.

(*b*) Simultaneous Development of diverse god-lores.

It is superfluous to observe that the folk-ideas about animals, trees, fetishes, etc., continue to develop along the usual lines as in previous centuries. Changes in myths and superstitions, whether they be regarded as animistic or taoistic or primitive, must not be ignored in any account of Chinese Religion during this period.

The "Calendrical mode of life" goes on as ever. "The propitious days are named on which to contract marriages or remove to another house or cut clothes: days on which one may begin works of repair of houses, temples, ships or commence house building by laying the upper beam of the roof in its place by means of a scaffolding, or putting up the first pillar; days on which one may safely undertake earth works, bathe, open shops, have meetings with relations, and friends, receive money; days on which one may sow or reap, send one's children to school for the first time, bury the dead, etc." (De Groot).

The following account of the first Emperor's Taoistic leanings from Gowen's *Outline History* is a good picture of the prevailing eclecticism in Chinese Society: "During the Tsin dynasty the Emperor was wont to expound Taoism to his courtiers and caused those who yawned to be executed. Tsin Shih Hwang Ti, the 'Burner of the Books' was an ardent Taoist and sent a famous expedition to Japan in search of the *Elixir Vitæ.*" And the facts that the first sovereign of the Han dynasty was also much devoted to Taoism and the hierarchy of Taoist Popes dates from about this time, point inevitably to the conclusion that the Chinese mind was as elastic as ever in socio-religious beliefs inasmuch as it never recognised the monopoly of any.

The following extract from De Groot's *Religion in China* is another illustration of the tendencies of the time:

"As early as the time of the Han Dynasty, Taoism had grown to be an actual religion with a pantheon with doctrines of sanctity, with ethics calculated to teach sanctity, with votaries, hermits and saints, teachers and pupils." About the Han Emperor Wuti (B.C. 140-87), whose long reign of fifty-four years was one of the most splendid in the whole history of China, Gowen remarks: "He did much to promote the study of the re-discovered Confucian classics, * * * displayed in his later life a great devotion to the superstitious and magical rites of Taoism and is said to have been the author of the so-called 'Dew-receiving vase' in the belief that the drinking of the dew thus collected would secure immortality."

Thus Confucius and Laotsze flourish side by side. It is impossible to make a bipartite or tripartite division of Chinese mentality and study each separately. Likewise it is misleading to represent Hindu religious consciousness as divided into water-tight compartments, *e.g.*, of Vaishnavism, Shaivaism, Jainism and Buddhism.

The following history of Jainism given by Stevenson is typical of every Indian *ism*: "As the Jaina laity had been drawn away from Hinduism by their adhesion to Mahâvira, they were left without any stated worship. Gradually, however, reverence for their master and for other teachers, historical and mythical, passed into the adoration and took the form of a regular cult. Finally, images of these adored personages were set up for worship, and idolatry became one of the chief institutions of orthodox Jainism. The process was precisely parallel to what happened in Buddhism. It is not known when idols were introduced, but it was probably in the second or first century B.C.."

The simultaneous growth of Taoism and so-called Confucianism during Tsin-Han period is paralleled by simultaneous growth of all the isms in contemporary India:

"The third and second centuries B.C., must have been a period of great activity amongst the Jaina. Under Asoka the religion is said to have been introduced into Kashmir. Under Suhastin, the great ecclesiastical head of the order in the second century, Jainism received many marks of approbation from Samprati, grandson of Asoka. Inscriptions show that it was already very powerful in Orissa in the second century and in Mathura in the northwest in the first century B.C..".

It is interesting to note that the Brahmanist Chandragupta, the first Emperor of India, is claimed by the Jainas as an adherent of their faith, exactly as the first Chinese Emperor was a patron of both the cults of his time. Again in the 3rd century B.C., there is reported to have been a Council of Jainas held to fix their Canon. Sâkyasimhans also are credited with having had a Council of their own about the same time.

The parallel development of Jainism, Buddhism and other Indian isms can be lost sight of only to misunderstand the working of the forces that made the actual life of the Hindus in the pre-Christian era. In their zeal to prove an ascendency of Buddhism during certain ages of Indian history, some scholars have minimised the actual position and importance of the Vedic and Brahmanic rites. They have also totally ignored the existence of other powerful cults, *e.g.*, Jainism, and the faith of the "folk" which has been the parent of all new-fangled ideas in every epoch. For the culture of Hindusthan has been the making, not of the princes and rulers alone, nor of the scholars, philosophers, moralists, priests, *bhikshus*, or monks alone, but of the people and the lower orders as well. The 'folk-element' in Hindu civilisation has yet to be studied. The more it is studied the more would it be clear that the origin and development of Indian religious systems owes a great deal to the imagination and inventiveness of the dumb millions. This can be said equally about the folk-element in Chinese culture as well as Japanese.

However, the following remarks of Mrs. Stevenson give an idea of the common fund of convention out of which all the founders of Indian religions have drawn, and explain why it is so important not to dogmatise about any age as being dominated by a certain *ism*: "The lack of knowledge on the part of early scholars which accredited all *Stupa* and all cave-temples to Buddhists, robbed Jainism for a time of its earliest surviving monuments. It is only recently, only in fact since students of the past have realised how many symbols, such as the wheel, the rail, the rosary, the *svastika*, etc., the Jaina had in common with the Buddhists and Brahmanas that its early sites and shrines have been handed back to Jainism. * * * Jaina and Buddhist art must have followed much the same course, and the former like the latter erected stupa with railings round them in which to place the bones of their saints. But such has been the avidity with which everything possible has been claimed as Buddhist that as yet only two *stupas* are positively admitted to be of Jaina origin."

Asoka had been harsh to the Brahmanical sacrificers as Shi Hwangti was to the Confucian literati but neither could and did extirpate them. So the old cult of the World-Forces was not dead during their rule. In fact a vehement pro-Brahmanic and anti-Asokan propaganda began about B.C. 184, when the last of the Mauryas was put to death by a popular general Pushyamitra. It was signalised by the *Aswamedha* or horse-sacrifice. The religion of sacrifices and Nature-deities thus ran smooth both in China and India.

(*c*) Deification of Men as *Avatâras*

Meanwhile Confucius and Laotsze the rivals in lifetime begin to wax prominent in the pious thoughts of their adherents and admirers. They become first saints or sages, then gods. It is difficult to trace the whole process of heroification and deification. But evidences of Chinese imagination gradually constructing out of these two historic personalities 'things that never were on sea or land' are not wanting.

Ssu-ma Chien the historian, who lived in the second and first centuries B.C., thus records his opinion about Confucius. "Countless are the princes and prophets that the world has seen in its time; glorious in life, forgotten in death. But Confucius * * * remains among us after many generations. He is the model for such as would be wise. By all, from the son of Heaven down to the meanest student, the supremacy of his principle is fully and freely admitted. He may indeed be pronounced the divinest of men." Even in this ecstatic eulogy Confucius is not yet a god, but only a 'hero,' to use Carlyle's language, or the more recent 'Super-man.' But he will soon have a shrine, then a temple, and be adopted into the pantheon of *Shângti*.

The same historian mentions the following about Laotsze's adherents: "Those who attach themselves to the doctrine of Lao-tsze condemn that of the *literati*, and the *literati* on their part condemn Lao-tsze." On this Dr. Legge remarks in *The Religions of China*: "The students of the Tao had * * become a school distinct from the adherents of the orthodox Confucianism, and opposed to and by them. But there is no account of Lao-tsze's deification, nothing of his pre-existence."

This is, however, the opinion of one who belonged to the opposite party. In any case we see here both Confucius and Lao-tsze in that stage at which their godhood is in what may be called the "period of gestation." They are already saints and surely gods-on-probation.

A picture of the thoughts that were moving in the Chinese mind of the later Chou, Tsin and Han periods would come up before our mind's eye if we only notice what is going on among the Hindus of to-day.

To mention only a few names from among the Indian celebrities who have worked in the field of religion, morals and social service during the last century. Râmamohana and Dayânanda are already *avatâras* or incarnations of God to their devotees. Devendranâth, the father of the 'knight-poet' Sir Rabindranâth Tâgore of *Gitânjali* fame is a *maharshi*, *i.e.* a Great Sage; Râm Tirath is, if not anything more, at least a saint. Vivekânanda, the Nietzschean Energist, is a demi-god; and his *guru* or spiritual preceptor, Râmkrishna *Paramahamsa* is nothing short of a god occupying almost the same rank as Râma, Buddha, Krishna, etc. And there are hundreds of others who have been receiving homage as saints, *avatâras*, gods in *esse* as well as in *posse*. They have temples consecrated to them and are worshipped if not yet in stone-images, at least in oil-paintings. These have their following not only among the women and the half-educated masses who in every age and every clime have contributed to the building up of the world's hagiology and mythology, but also among Justices of the High Courts, Barristers of the British Inns, botanists, engineers, chemists, medical men, journalists, social reformers, political agitators, educationists, theists, monotheists, and of course, atheists and positivists with their *New Calendars of Great Men*.

The doctrine of *Avatâra* (*i.e.* the idea of Divinity embodying itself in human beings to save mankind), which has been the bedrock of later Indian life and thought, must have been developed during the Maurya and post-Maurya epoch. It was utilised by the Vaishnavaites (Krishnaites), Râmaites and even Sâkyaites and Mahâvirites. The birth-stories, called the *Jâtakas* in Pali language, deal with the previous births of Sâkyasimha the Buddha; and the *Tirthankara*-legends of the Jainas in Prakrit language deal with their own Messiahs. Both have their future *avatâras* too.

All these are derived from the same stock of tales about the past and future saviours of mankind which had been floating in the atmosphere of India in those days. The orthodox Brahmanical version, in Sanskrit language, of these incarnation-myths is to be seen in that huge encyclopædia of Indian beliefs, practices, superstitions, arts, and sciences known as the *Mahâbhârata* and also in some of the Purânas. It has to be noted also that the great theory of *Yugântara* (or Cycles, at the end of which the Divinity incarnates itself to found a new *Zeitgeist*) is enunciated in the *Gîtâ*, which is only a chapter of the encyclopædic *Mahâbhârata*. The pre-eminence of Krishna in the *Gîtâ* is an aspect of the Vaishnavite environment noticeable in the multifarious contents of the huge work.

Neither Sâkyasimha nor Mahâvira has any place in the whole *Mahâbhârata* literature. But both of them have been receiving almost the some homage as these gods among their own adherents.

It need only be added that whatever be the date of the final form in which we have the *Mahâbhârata*, some of the stories related in it describe facts and phenomena of pre-Sâkyan ages, and a great portion of the verses must have been composed during the post-Sâkyan, Maurya, post-Maurya but pre-Christian centuries. The same remark can be made about the Râma-legends compiled by the *Vâlmîkian* bards.

The development of godlore was thus proceeding on the same lines among the Celestials and the Hindus. The two peoples were approaching an identical consummation.. The religious imagination of the Chinese is made of the same stuff as that of the Indians.

The types of Perfection or Highest Ideals which were being evolved both in China and India during the previous millennium at last began to crystallise themselves out of the spiritual solution and emerge as distinctly individualised entities. The Classical World-Forces supplied the basic foundation of these types or entities. Folk-imagination in brooding over the past and reconstructing ancient history had sanctified certain historic personalities, legendary heroes or eponymous culture-pioneers, and endowed their names with a halo of romance. Philosophical speculation had been groping in the dark about the mysteries of the universe and had stumbled upon the One, the Unknown, the Eternal, the Infinite. Last, but not least, are the contributions of the "lover, the lunatic, and the poet" who came to weld together all these elements into artistic shapes, 'fashioning forth' those "Sons of God"—concrete human personalities to embody at once the man-in-God and the God-in-man. In the *Avatârahood* of every superintendent of the *Zeitgeist*, *e.g.*, that of a Confucius or a Laotsze, a Râma, or a Krishna or a Buddha or a Mahâvira, the philosophical historian has to read at once the same ethnic, physical, legendary, mystical and imaginative factors of the Indo-Chinese world.

SECTION 2

Images as Symbols

(*a*) IN CHINA

According to De Groot, the Confucianists are idol-worshippers and Confucianism is "a system of idolatry." Of course it is too late in the day to repeat that the worship of idols in China, Japan and India, whether Buddhistic, Taoistic, Jaina, Vaishnava, Shaiva, or Shâkta is not worship of 'stocks and stones.' As Johnston says in *Buddhist*

China: "In the East as in the West there are many people who are, or believe themselves to be, incapable of dispensing with all sensuous aids to religious imagination, and who find in outward signs and emblems a means of preserving undimmed within their hearts and minds the light of a lofty spiritual ideal. * * * The image or sacred picture is merely a symbol of divinity. * * *

"No sanctity attaches to images and pictures as such, their sole use is to stimulate the religious imagination and to engender feelings of veneration for the spiritual reality of which they are an imperfect expression. * * * The image serves its purpose if it helps to bring the human spirit into communion with the divine. but it is rightly to be regarded as a means and not as an end."

The so-called Confucian idolatry is thus described by De Groot: "It represents the gods, even Heaven and Earth, by wooden tablets inscribed with their titles, and some of them by images in human form. These objects it holds to be inhabited by the gods themselves, especially when, as always occurs at sacrifices, the spirits or *shen* have been formally prayed to or summoned with or without music, to descend and take up their abode therein. * * *

Its ritual, based on the Classics, was codified during the Han dynasty. * * *

The images of gods exist by tens of thousands, the temples by thousands. Almost every temple has idol gods which are of co-ordinate or subordinate rank to the chief god. * * * For the mountains, rocks, stones, streams and brooks which the people worship, images in human form are fashioned, to be dedicated to their souls, that these may dwell therein."

This can stand as a correct picture of the religious systems of the folk in Japan and India also.

It would be interesting to know exactly when image-worship began to occupy a place in Chinese religious consciousness. There are reasons to believe that like every other item of socio-religious life, image-worship was autochthonous in China and not imported from abroad. The legend of the first image of Buddha being placed by the king in a temple which already had other images would indicate this. This was in 121 B.C.

Dr. Legge in his paper on Taoism in *The Religions of China* remarks: "Indeed it was not till after the image of Buddha was brought to the capital in A.D. 65 that images or statues of Confucius and other great men of the past began to be made."

This does not seem to be correct. For images and representations of deities have been prevalent in China since 4th century B.C.. Terrien de La Couperie observes that a name of the Fire-goddess about that time was "*Ki*, which is the tuft or coiffure of a Chinese lady, the deity was then represented as a beautiful woman dressed in red. Her worship was recognised * * * by Kao-tsu, the first emperor of the Han dynasty in B.C. 204." (*Western Origin* pp. 160-1 quoted by Werner).

Images have existed in China before the Celestials came into contact with the Hindus.

The personifying and concretising tendency of the Chinese mind would also be evident from the cosmogony of the Celestial people described in *Chinese Repository* (iii. 55): "The warm influence of the *Yang* being condensed produced fire; and the finest parts of fire formed the sun. The cold exhalations of the *Yin*, being likewise condensed, produced water; and the finest parts of the watery substance formed the moon. By the seminal influence of the sun and the moon, came the stars."

The following is taken from Davis' *Chinese* ii. 67-8:

"The above might, with no great impropriety, be styled, 'a sexual system of the universe.' They maintain that when from the union of the *Yang* and *Yin* all existences, both animate and inanimate, had been produced, the sexual principle was conveyed to, and became inherent in, all of them. Thus heaven, the sun, day, etc., are considered of the male gender; earth, the moon, night, etc., of the female. This notion pervades every department of knowledge in China."

It requires but a single step to come from this materialising tendency to the *iconising* of the Nature-Energies or World-Forces. In fact, the images that have been already formed through poetry, legends, ballads and folk-songs have only to be transferred to the sculptor and the painter. Images are images whether expressed through the medium of sounds as in literary and musical arts, or through that of sights as in the sister plastic and pictorial arts. The very moment that a hymn has been sung, and a piece of poetry composed, the idea has become embodied, the invisible visible, and "airy nothings have got a local habitation and a name." Idol-worshipper every man has been, every man is, and every man will be—so long as man is a speaking animal.

During the period under review, Confucius had been slowly extending an empire over the heart of the Celestials.

He was not yet formally deified but there were signs that he would soon have a place with the gods, as an assistant of Shâng Ti. The process of this heroification and deification does not seem to have been clearly described by any scholar. But by the end of the first century A.D., says Giles in his *Confucianism*, "the birthplace of Confucius had become a goal for the Confucian pilgrim; a shrine had been built there, and even Emperors found their way thither, to do honour to the great Teacher." Soon there would be images, and tablets and rituals for Confucius the god as for the gods described in the Classics by Confucius the historian. To quote Giles: "In 505 A.D., the first Confucian temple, as we now understand the term, was built and dedicated. Images of Confucius were then introduced into the temple, some say for the first time; others hold that in A.D. 178 a likeness of Confucius had been placed in his shrine, a substitute for the wooden tablet in use up to that date. * * * Gradually, the people came to look upon Confucius as a god to be propitiated for the sake of worldly advantages."

Confucianism ultimately becomes like the modern Hindu Shaivaism, Vaishnavism, etc., the cult of Confucius as a Deity, a Nature-Force or Energy. So that even without Buddhism the Celestials are like the Indians in religious conceptions.

In China as in India the course of cultural evolution had passed through almost the same stages. About 3rd century B.C., we see that landmark at which the Arts of Poetry and Music requisitioned the Arts of Sculpture and Painting to assist them in being handmaids to Religion. The mythology which had up till then been elaborated only by poets and singers began now to be enriched and receive a new character in bronze, clay, stones, and ink. The master-minds of the age thought not only in words but also in metals and *kakemonos*. Henceforth we have to decipher the signs of Chinese religious consciousness in the world of hieroglyphics and picture-writings as well as in the realm of bas-reliefs, statuettes, drawings, pencil-sketches, and fully-wrought images and portraits. In the history of every religion the thinkers in bronze and canvas demand as much attention as the intellectuals of letters. So the *literati* alone, whether Confucian, Taoist or Buddhist, must not be our sole guides as interpreters of Chinese Religion after the fourth century B.C..

(*b*) In India

In his *History of Fine Art in India and Ceylon* Mr. Vincent Smith quotes Prof. Percy Gardner to modify his own statement that the "history of Indian art begins with Asoka." Gardner's words are: "But there can be no doubt that Indian art had an earlier history. The art of Asoka is a mature art." No specimens of images, however, whether Hindu, Buddhist or Jain, have been yet discovered to illustrate the religious sculpture of the Asokan age.

It is probably in the post-Asokan Bharhut *stupa* (3rd.-2nd cent. B.C.?) that we come across the first Indian images. The following is quoted from Cunningham's *Stupa of Bharhut* by Vincent Smith: "Besides these scenes, which are so intimately connected with the history of Buddhism there are several bas-reliefs which seem to represent portions of the history of Râma during his exile. There are also a few scenes of broad humour in which monkeys are the chief actors.

Of large figures there are upwards of thirty alto-rilievo statues of Yakshas and Yakshinis, Devatâs, Nâga Râjas. * * * We thus see that the guardianship of the north was entrusted to Kuvera, King of the Yakshas, agreeably to the teaching of the Buddhist and Brahmanical cosmogonies. And similarly we find that the other gates are confided to the Devas and the Nâgas."

The image of Sirimã, the goddess of Luck, comes also from this age. In modern mythology *Sri* or *Siri* is the consort of Vishnu.

Rhys Davids remarks about this image: "It may be mentioned in passing that we have representations, of a very early date, of this *Siri*, the goddess of Luck, of plenty and success, who is not mentioned in the Veda. One of these is marked in plain letters *Sirimâ Devatâ;* and like Diana of the Ephesians, she bears on her breast the signs of her productivity. The other shows the goddess seated with two elephants pouring water over her. It is the oldest instance of the most common representation of this popular goddess."

Grünwedel in his *Buddhist art in India* also gives a similar story.

The following is taken from *The Heart of Jainism:* "It was during this time (*c.* 397 B.C.) that the two sects of Osavâla Jaina and Srimâla Jaina arose. It is also said it was now that the image of Mahâvira was enshrined at Upakesâ Pâttana. This is probably a reference to the first introduction of idol-worship into Jainism."

Smith begins his treatment of post-Asokan sculpture with the following remark:

"A detached pillar standing to the northeast of Besnagar has been invested with special interest by the recent discovery of a long concealed inscription on the base which records the erection of the monument in honour of Vishnu by Heliodoros, son of Dion, envoy from the great king Antalkidas of Taxila to a local prince. Antalkidas is supposed to have reigned about B.C. 170. The inscription states that the column was crowned by an image of Garuda, the monstrous bird sacred to the god."

The following is quoted by Smith from Cousens about the gateways at Sanchi which also represent post-Asokan but pre-Christian art: "The faces, back and front of the beams and pillars, are crowded with panels of sculpture in bas-relief representing scenes in the life of Buddha, domestic and silvan scenes, processions, sieges, adoration of trees and topes, etc."

Images of Buddha do not occur at this period, which is represented by Besnagar, Bodhgaya, Bharhut, and Sanchi. "The early artists did not dare to portray his bodily form * * * being content to attest his spiritual presence by silent symbols—the footprints, the empty chair and so forth."

In the Sanchi sculptures "we see the worship of a Nāga spirit represented by an image of the hooded cobra housed in a shrine with a domical roof. It is possible that the object of worship may be Buddha himself sheltered by the hoods of Muchalinda, the Snake King. The Real Presence of Buddha in these sculptures is always indicated symbolically."

"A relief of unknown origin depicts * * * the famous visit of Indra to Buddha seated in a cave." The specimen dates "probably from the first century B.C.."

Some Jaina bas-reliefs in Orissa, "the oldest of which date from the second century B.C.," describe a procession in honour of Pârswanâtha, the precursor of Mahavira as the founder of Jainism.

The oldest image of Buddha is a battered seated figure at Tantrimalai in Ceylon, wearing a conical cap, and is believed by Mr. Parker, author of *Ancient Ceylon*, to "date from about the beginning of the Christian era."

The following is quoted from the *Chinese Recorder* ii.1:

"In the reign of King Wu (B.C. 140-86) of the West Han Dynasty a (gigantic) gold image of Buddha was brought (in B.C. 121) to China (forming part of the spoils of these campaigns) and set up in the sweet spring temple. This served as the model according to which the images of Buddha were afterwards made. King Hi of the same dynasty (B.C. 6 to A.D. 1) sent learned men to search for images and books of the Buddhist religion but they returned without having reached their destination."

Giles also in his *Confucianism* refers to the tradition that in B.C. 121 an image of Buddha was secured for the first time. "This is further said to have been taken by a victorious Chinese general from a Hun chieftain who was in the habit of worshipping it. A later history says that when the Emperor received the image, he had it placed in the palace among some other images, all of which averaged about ten feet in height. He did not sacrifice to it; but merely burnt incense and worshipped it with prayer."

The history of Indian art would thus indicate that in Asoka's time Sâkyasimha was being deified and worshipped as the *Buddha*, the Buddha-cult was recognised as the other cults *e.g.*, *Vishnu-cult*, *Râma-cult*, *etc.*, but the paraphernalia of worship did not probably include an icon. In the post-Asokan age, *i.e.*, the second century B.C., there were images of gods and goddesses, saints and *avatâras*, Brahmanic as well as non-Brâhmanic. But the real age of Image-worship had not yet come. It can be safely stated, however, that the religious consciousness was fully ripe for it, and that this aid to religion was to be exploited by the follower of every cult.as soon as sculptors and painters were able to supply their handiworks in large number. The moment came towards the end of the pre-Christian and beginning of the Christian era, when the Graeko-Roman artists were firmly established in the north-western hinterland of India.

It has to be observed, finally, that image-worship has passed through the same stages both in India and China, and the process of deification of Confucius and Laotsze is exactly parallel to that of Sâkyasimha and Mahâvira. The recognition of Confucius as a god to be worshipped like other gods through an image is a few centuries later than that of his more favoured colleagues of India. But images as symbols of divinity have been synchronous among the two peoples.

CHAPTER VI.

The Birth of Buddhism

(B.C. 150—A.D. 100)

SECTION 1.

Introduction of Buddha-cult into China.

(*a*) CHINESE ROMANTICISM.

Historically speaking, Buddhism was introduced into China under Mingti, the Han Emperor, in A.D. 67. There are legendary traditions of the Celestials having had knowledge of the new faith in Chou times and at least since the time of the first Emperor, the contemporary of Asoka. The traditions do not seem to have been thoroughly unhistorical in view of the fact that the Maurya Emperor (*c* B.C. 250) was a great internationalist and was always ambitious to extend the Indian sphere of influence in every direction, and also because the Han Emperor Wuti (B.C. 140) was a great explorer of Central and Western Asia.

But even if the Asokan or later Indian Missions to China are unfounded and be regarded as impossible, the Chinese sympathy with, and knowledge of, Buddhism during that early period were, at any rate, philosophically very probable, in fact, almost a psychological necessity. That the Chinese intellect of the period was eminently adapted to a new mythology of Romanticism would be apparent from Fenollosa's remarks in his chapter on "Chinese Art of the Han Dynasty":

"The poetry of Han * * * remained largely Taoist or Individualistic, enforcing the prime fact which all later Chinese critics, and their European Sinologist pupils have ignored, that almost all the great imaginative art work of the Chinese mind has sprung from those elements in Chinese genius, which if not anti-, were at least non-Confucian. This poetry is almost always in the southern romantic style."

Professor Fenollosa also speaks of the "philosophical and romantic interest in the Taoist stories of the West" which inspired the great Han Emperor Wuti "to inaugurate the Turkestan campaigns. He summoned about him the individualistic genius of his day, professed to believe in and share the Taoist mystical powers, and determined to revisit the Queen of his Taoist paradise."

The romantic story of the actual introduction, also, points to the same inevitability of the Buddha-cult extending sway over the spiritual consciousness of the Celestials. The dream of the Emperor was not the "fine frenzy" of an individual but an index to the whole race-psychology. "Imagination bodies forth the forms of things unknown." So the Chinese imagination evolved the Buddha-cult in the guise of an Imperial dream as it had produced so many other cults in other guises.

The story is told by Hackmann thus: "The commonly accepted date of the real entrance of Buddhism into China is during the reign of Emperor Mingti (A.D. 58-76). This ruler is said to have had a dream in which a high, shining gold image of a god appeared to him, which entered his palace. The interpreter of the dream—a brother of the Emperor—attributed this apparition to the Buddha Sâkyamuni, who was revered in Central Asia and India, and who demanded worship in China also. * * * The Emperor sent an embassy through Central Asia to Khotan (the land of the Yueh-chi) to procure the things requisite for the practice of the new religion. The emissaries—eighteen in number—left the imperial court in the year A.D. 65 and returned in 67, accompanied by two monks, Kâsiapa Mâtanga and Gobharana (the latter arriving a little after the former), as well as in possession of Buddha images and scriptures. A temple was built for the new religion, in which the two representatives lived, and gave themselves to the work of translating the most important Buddhist instructions into Chinese. The imperial palace of residence at that time was Loyang, the present Honan-fu. It was here that Buddhism first took root in Northern China."

The admission of Buddha into the Chinese pantheon in the first century A.D. was not an extraordinary incident in the life of the Celestials. It belongs to the same category as the promulgation of the worship of Tai Mountain by the First Emperor in the 3rd century B.C., and of other cults in the pre-Christian era, and also as the recognition of Confucius as a god about A.D. 555 when, to quote Giles, it was enacted that a Confucian temple should be built in every prefectural city in the empire. Chinese mentality had ever been manufacturing myths and deities out of forces scattered here and there and everywhere. The only contributions of India were (1) a few new names, e.g., those of Buddha, Avalokiteswara, etc., and (2) a new form or mould in which the original myth-creating and iconising instinct of the Chinese was to express itself.

The traditional Chinese literature and philosophy represented, on the one hand, by Laotsze and Chuangtsze, and on the other, by Confucius and Mencius, had pre-disposed the people for the new cult and were quite adequate to assimilate it when it was introduced. For as yet the influence of

Indian thought was insignificant. The number of Sanskrit works translated into Chinese was very meagre, intercourse between Hindus and Chinese infrequent, and in the realm of sculpture and painting there are absolutely no evidences of any contact between the two peoples. The great epoch of the Hindu sphere of influence in China's world of letters and art was to come under the mighty Tângs about six hundred years later, after Hiuen Thsang's return from India (A.D. 645).

Hindu missionising activity, during this period, for the propagation of the Buddha-cult, since the pioneer work of the first two missionaries, is described in the following extract:

"In the reign of Changli (A.D. 76-89) the chief of the Chu Kingdom became a devoted follower of Buddhism and many more books were imported. Eighty years afterwards a Parthian monk arrived at Loyang (Honan) with a collection of *sutras* some of which he translated with great intelligence and perspicuity. More monks arrived in the reign of Lingli (168-170) from the country of the Getæ and from India, and translated the Nirvâna and other *sutras* with great spirit and fidelity."—Werner's *Chinese Sociology*.

(*b*) The Religion of Love

It need only be stated here (1) that what has generally been known to scholars as *Mahâyânism* (Greater or Higher Vehicle), as contrasted with the *Hinayânism* (Lesser or Lower Vehicle) of Sâkyasimha's apostles, has been called *Buddhism* in these pages;

(2) That the mythology, iconography and canon which were introduced into China from Central Asia were neither

what the *man* Sâkya had taught as *Nirvânism* nor what Asoka had propagated as his *Dhamma*, both probably coming under *Hînayânism*,—but formed the ingredients of Mahâyânism*, which alone I have ventured to call Buddhism as being the cult of Buddhas and Bodhisattvas;

And (3) that the language of Mahâyânic Bibles was not Pâli, like that of Hînayâna, but Sanskrit, the language of universal culture in India.

It is beyond the scope of the present work to prove the connection of Hînayânism with the *Chhândogya Upanishad* or with the *Sâmkhya Darsana* of India. Nor is it the object to catalogue the gods and goddesses of the *Mahâyânic* pantheon so carefully done by Mrs. Getty. The processes, also, by which *Mahâyânic* eschatology and metaphysics were disentangling themselves from the previous *Hînayânic*, *Upanishadic*, and *Darsanic* systems need not detain us.

I have already mentioned Avatârahood and image-worship. A few more characteristics of Mahâyânism are being given in the words of Dr. Richard in his *New Testament of Higher Buddhism*:

1. "Help from God to save oneself and others from suffering.

2. Communion with God, which gave the highest ecstatic rest to the soul.

3. Partaking of the nature of God by new birth so as to become Divine and Immortal oneself."

---

*The image and the Sanskrit language indicate that the faith was Mahâyânic. Evidently this form of Buddhism had been well established in Central Asia before A.D. 65. What, then, is the date of Kanishka, especially of his famous council associated with the name of Aswaghosha, where Mahâyânic Buddhism is alleged to have been formulated for the first time? Kushan chronology seems to require fresh revision in the light of facts from Chinese History. Vincent Smith considers A.D. 78 to be the date of Kanishka's accession, but adds: "The substantial controversy is between the scholars who place the accession of Kanishka in B.C. 58 and those who date it in or about A.D. 78." He dates the council somewhere about A.D. 100.

The following characteristics may be added from Hackmann's account:

1. The conception of an Eternal Deity.
2. The Bodhisattvas or Buddhas in *posse*.
3. The attainment of the Bodhisattvahood as the ideal of life—consisting in "sympathy with all beings, and a world-encompassing love."
4. The invocation of the Bodhisattva becomes the central point to the householders. Remarkable stress is laid on Faith.
5. The idea of a Paradise or a happy state of existence as opposed to Hell.

These are the marks of a Religion with Love, Faith and Hope as its basis and Romanticism as its inspiring force. Its Bible has, therefore, been rightly called the *Awakening of Faith*. It is a work in Sanskrit by Aswaghosha* (1st century A.D.?).

The same Emotionalism and Idealism could be noticed in the whole super-natural and anthropomorphic god-lore of contemporary India. One common ocean of Devotionalism was being fed by Mahâyâna, as by Shaiva, Saura, Vaishnava, Jaina, and other theologies.

For the first time in world's religious history men opened their hearts and began to love. It was not an age of passionless stoics, mere brain-labourers and cold book-lorists, but of lovers, *bhaktas*, devotees, Messiahs and apostles. The Jâtaka-stories, the Râmâyana-verses and Gîtâ-literature could flourish not in an atmosphere of "sophists, calculators and economists" but in the world of warm-blooded enthusiasts, men of faith and hope "believing

---

* The Doctrine of *Sunya, i.e.* Void, as an important feature of Mahâyânism is attributed to Nâgârjuna, one of its founders like Aswaghosha.

where we cannot prove." These were meant not for abstract academicians but for such as could inhibit their senses in order to focus their whole attention on the culture of the heart so that it might be the capital of the 'Kingdom of God.'

Each of these Religions of Love embodied—

"The devotion to something afar
From the sphere of our sorrow."

The apostles of *Bhakti* or Heart-culture asked the questions :

" Would you understand
The language with no word,
The speech of brook and bird
Of waves along the sand ?
Would you know how sweet
The falling of the rill,
The calling of the hill,
All tunes the days repeat?"

And the right romantic reply that was preached to the devotees was the following *sutra*:

"The secret of the ear
Is in the open heart."

It was the creed or message of the "open heart" that the Mahâyânists and others were propagating in India. A similar situation came to pass when centuries later Jesus was repudiating the "Legalism" of the scribes and the Book-religion of Judaism.

The human and mystic elements in these faiths which postulate the Infirmity of Man and the Mercy of God are as different from the primitive Nature-cult as from the practice of Dhamma or the study of Sâkyan and Confucian *Dialogues*, but have historically grown out of both.

The Buddhism that came into the land of Confucius was thus only one of the expressions of the comprehensive cult of Love and Romanticism which manifested itself at the same time in the promulgation of the worship of Vishnu, Krishna, Shiva, etc.. And the same religious emotionalism was being exploited by sculptors to enrich their Buddhist or Shaiva arts.

This common origin it is which makes it often so difficult to distinguish between the images of the gods and goddesses belonging to the Buddhistic and non-Buddhistic pantheons of Hinduism. This is why Chinese, Korean and Japanese forms of Buddhism look so similar to the many varieties of present-day Indian religion in spite of modifications under the trans-Himâlayan soil and race-characteristics. This is why in spite of the disappearance of Buddha as a god from Indian consciousness, Buddhism may be said to live in and through the other cults of modern Hinduism, *e.g.* Vaishnavism, Shaivaism, Jainism, etc..

SECTION 2.

Exit Sâkya, Enter Buddha and His Host.

(*a*) THE PSYCHOLOGY OF ROMANTIC RELIGION.

Psychologically speaking, therefore, as we have indicated above, Buddhism was born almost simultaneously in China and India. It need not be considered as a foreign commodity imported into China but the inevitable outcome of its age-long social evolution. The religious consciousness of the Chinese has ever had the some stuff as that of the Hindu, and each had paved the way quite independently for the recognition of an *Avatâra*, a deified man or a God incarnate in human form. Invention of deities out of historical, semi-historical or legendary characters or out of Nature-Forces had been going on among both peoples all through their history. Sooner or later the "Enlightened" One was to get a place in the pantheon, sooner or later the Great Sage was to be a colleague of the Elemental Forces. It was an accident that Buddha was the name of the god to be worshipped first in both countries. It was an accident also that this Buddha was supplied to China from an Indian theological laboratory.

The contrast between Sâkya the preacher and Buddha the god, or Confucius the moralist and Confucius the god, has its parallel in Christology also. Professor Bacon writes in his *Making of the New Testament:* "Modern criticism expresses the contrast in its distinction of the gospel *of* Jesus from the gospel *about* Jesus."

The Pauline "doctrine of Incarnation appealing to the eternal manifestation of God in man," *i.e.*, of Jesus as an *Avatâra*, is thus explained by Dr. Bacon: "Whether Paul himself so conceived it or not, the Gentile world had no other moulds of thought wherein to formulate such a Christology than the current myth of Redeemer-gods. The value of the individual *soul* had at last been discovered, and men resorted to the ancient personifications of the forces of nature as deliverers of this new-found soul from its weakness and mortality. The influential religions of the time were those of personal redemption by mystic union with a dying and resurrected saviour-god, an Osiris, an Adonis, an Attis, a Mithra. Religions of this type were everywhere displacing the old national faiths. The Gentile could not think of the Christ primarily as a son of David who restores the kingdom to Israel. * * * The whole conception was spiritualised. The enemies overcome were the spiritual foes of humanity, sin and death; redemption was not the deliverance of Israel out of the hand of all their enemies, * * * it was the rescue of the sons of Adam out of the bondage to evil powers.'' It is human instinct to manufacture a god out of a great Teacher.

We have traced in the preceding chapter the development of the *avatâra*-cult in China and India. It is always difficult to point historically to the exact date when an idea is started. But so far as India is concerned, the best 'external evidence' is that supplied by the sculptors of the post-Asokan age (2nd century B.C.?).

These bear at once the indelible impressions of the Vishnu-Sirimâ worship, the avatâra-myths of the Râmâyana, and similar legends of the Jâtakas.

"It stands there," says Lloyd in his *Creed of Half Japan*, "in the clear-cut stone monuments of India that pre-Christian India believed in Buddha as a being whose birth was supernatural, the result of a spiritual power overshadowing the mother; as one whose birth was rejoiced over by angels and testified to by an aged seer; as one who had been tempted by the evil one and had overcome; as one whose life had been one of good deed and holy teachings; as one who had passed into the unseen, leaving behind him a feeling of regret for him who had thus gone away."

(*b*) SPIRITUAL EXPERIENCE OF IRAN AND ISRAEL

It is a significant fact that the first epoch of Internationalism in world's history beginning with the Hellenistic period was the time of gestation for new emotional cults throughout the world. The spiritual experience of all mankind was passing through the same stages. Zoroastrianism was evolving Mithraism, Chinese Classics were evolving the worship of Confucius, Hinduism was evolving Buddha-cult, Shiva-cult, Râma-cult and so on, and Judaism was in the birth-throes of the Christ-cult.

With regard to the development in Iran we read in Moulton's *Early Religious Poetry of Persia:* "We still meet the old familiar names: Ahura Mazdah is still supreme, with the Amesha Spentas around him, and Zarathustra is still the Prophet of the Faith. But even while we shut our eyes to the new divine names which crowd upon us, we cannot help seeing that the familiar names carry new associations. The Prophet is no longer a man of like passions with ourselves, a fervid religious and moral Reformer, eagerly pressing his lofty doctrine of God and duty against much opposition, and exhibiting very human emotions of elation and discouragement as the fortunes of the campaign sway to and fro. He is a purely supernatural figure, holding converse with Ahura Mazdah on theological and ritual subjects, which rarely come near the practical and homely religion inculcated by the singer of the *Gâthâs*. * * * His own name had become semi-divine."

Rev. Charles, Canon of Westminster, writes in his *Religious Development between the Old and New Testaments:* "One of the strongest impressions experienced by the reader who studies in their historical order the Canonical and non-Canonical Books of the Old Testament is the consciousness of the continuous, and in most instances, the progressive, re-interpretation of traditional beliefs and symbols.

* * *

Down to the fourth century B.C., progress was slow and hesitating, but from the third century onwards the work went on apace, not through the efforts of the official religious leaders of the nation, but mainly through its unknown and unofficial teachers, who issued their writings under the names of ancient worthies in Israel. The anonymity or pseudonymity * * characterised all the progressive writings in Judaism from the third century B.C. onwards. * * * All real progress in this direction was confined to a school of mystics and seers. * * *

During this interval a new and more ruthless power had taken the place of the Greek empire in the East, *i.e.*, Rome. This new phenomenon called, therefore, for a fresh re-interpretation. * * * Every conception was undergoing development or re-interpretation. Whole histories centre round such conceptions as soul, spirit, sheol, Paradise, the Messianic Kingdom, the Messiah, the Resurrection."

(*c*) Buddha-cult and its Indian "Cognates."

We have noticed in the previous chapter how the whole Indian atmosphere was surcharged with the doctrines and ideas described in the above extract. The following lines of the Vâlmîkian bards—

"For Vishnu's self disdained not mortal birth,

And heaven came with him as he came to earth"—

were the stock-in-trade of every religious sect. So that centuries before the one "beneath the Syrian blue" declared "I am the Way, the Life, the Truth," his brother-Messiah, the Hindu Krishna, had asserted in the *Gîtâ*: "Forsake all *Dharmas* (*i.e.*, Ways, Taos, religions or creeds), make Me alone thy way."

The following declaration of the Lord is from Griffith's *Specimens of Indian Poetry*:

"I am the Father, and the fostering Nurse,
Grandsire, and Mother of the Universe,
I am the Vedas, and the Mystic word,
The way, support, the witness and the Lord.
The Seed am I, of deathless quickening power
The Home of all, and mighty Refuge-tower.

* * *

When error leads a worshipper astray
To other Gods to sacrifice and pray,
Faith makes his gift accepted in my sight—
'Tis offered still to Me, though not aright.
Faith makes the humblest offering dear to Me,
Leaves, fruit, sweet water, flowers from the tree;
His pious will in gracious part I take,
And love the gift for his devotion's sake."

The lengthy oration of Lord Krishna proceeds in this strain, which is nothing short of Romanticism carried to the *nth* power. Here is the Yankee idealist Whitman's individualism lifted up to the transcendental plane. One is reminded of his characteristic *Song of Myself:*

"Magnifying and applying come I,
Taking myself the exact dimensions of Jehovah,
Lithographing Kronos, Zeus his son, and Hercules his grandson,
Buying drafts of Osiris, Isis, Belus, Brahma, Buddha,
In my portfolio placing Manito loose, Allah on a leaf, the crucifix engraved,
With Odin and the hideous-faced Mexitili and every idol and image,
Taking them all for what they are worth and not a cent more," etc., etc.

Whitmanism spiritualised is the mysticism of *Gītā*.

These verses from the *Gîtâ* give a picture of the common spiritual *milieu* in the midst of which the various cults of Hinduism were born. The new mythologies are therefore "cognates" and all present a family-likeness.

Sâkyasimha had been one of a legion of "cognates." His *Nirvânism* was one of the numerous metaphysico-moral systems of the Hindus in the 6th century B.C.. Similarly during this period (B.C. 150-100 A.D.) Buddhism or Mahâyânism was one of the numerous "cognate" cults that had been developing among the people of Hindusthân. This Buddhism should be called Hinduism of the Buddha-cult, just as Vaishnavism of the period was Hinduism of Vishnu-cult, and Shaivaism was Hinduism of the Shiva-cult, and so on.

Buddha was only one of the gods of a vast pantheon. It consisted of the Supreme Being variously conceived and diversely named, as well as the full-fledged deities, *avatâras*, and the gods in *posse*. Among Buddha's host are to be included not only Âdi-Buddhas, Avalokiteswaras, the Bodhisattvas and the other " Gods of Northern Buddhism," but also Râma, Krishna, Vâsudeva, Pârsvanâtha, Tirthankaras, etc., to mention a few semi-historical names, and Brahmâ, Vishnu, Shiva, etc., descended from the Vedic deities.

That Mahâyânism and other forms of Hinduism were not mutually exclusive would be evident from the policy of Kanishka, the Indo-Scythian monarch, generally regarded as the Asoka of the "New" Buddhism. Says Mr. Vincent Smith: "Such a Buddha (a god with his ears open to the prayers of the faithful and served by a hierarchy of Bodhisattvas) rightly took a place among the gods of the nations comprised in Kanishka's wide-spread empire, and the monarch, even after his 'conversion,' probably continued to honour both the old and new gods, as, in a later age, Harsha did alternate reverence to Siva and Buddha."

Almost all the coins of Vasudeva I, the last powerful Kushan ruler (A.D. 140-73?), "exhibit on the reverse the figure of the Indian god Siva, attended by his bull Nandi, and accompanied by the noose, trident and other insignia of Hindu iconography." The thoroughly Indian name of this King, which is a synonym for the god Vishnu, is a proof, according to Smith, of the rapidity with which the foreign invaders had succumbed to the influence of their environment. The coins of Kadphises II, the predecessor of Kanishka, also tell the same tale.

It is clear that Buddha, Shiva and Vishnu existed side by side as deities in Hindu religious consciousness during the first and second centuries of the Christian era.

Section 3.

The " Balance of Accounts " in International Philosophy

(*a*) Rival Claims of the East and the West

The relations between Greek thought and the Asiatic religions during the Hellenistic period may be understood from the following account.

According to Emmet in Charles' *Apocrypha and Pseudepigrapha*, the third book of *Maccabees* written about B.C. 100 in Hebrew "expresses a bitter opposition to the attempts at hellenising, which so nearly overwhelmed Judaism in the second century B.C., and shows no sympathy with the developments of thought and doctrine, which at that time were growing up within the Jewish Church."

So also the Hebrew *Book of Jubilees* written between B.C. 135 and B.C. 105 defends, in Canon Charles' words, "Judaism against the Hellenistic spirit which had been in the ascendant early in this century, and to prove that the Law was of everlasting validity."

Dr. Moulton writes in his *Early Religious Poetry of Persia:* "Are we justified in claiming Zarathustra's right to be acknowledged as the founder of apocalyptic? It is too large a question to answer here in any adequate way, but we may briefly recognise the strong probability that contacts with a Zoroastrianised Persia did much to stimulate in Israel the growth of a form of literature which from the Maccabean era downwards dominated Jewish thought and created the *milieu* of the Gospel proclamation."

Mr. Hogarth writes in the *Ancient East:* "His (Alexander's) recorded attitude towards the Brahmans of the Punjab implies the earliest acknowledgment made publicly by a Greek that in religion the West must learn from the East."

Further, "the expansion of Mithraism and of half a dozen other Asiatic and Egyptian cults, which were drawn from the East to Greece and beyond before the first century of the Hellenistic Age closed, testified to the early existence of that spiritual void in the West which a greater and purer religion, about to be born in Galilee and nurtured in Antioch, was at last to fill.

A ring of principalities, Median, Parthian, Persian, Nabathœan, had emancipated the heart of the Orient from its short servitude to the West; and though Rome, and Byzantium after her, would push the frontier of effective European influence somewhat eastward again, their Hellenism could never capture again that heart which the Seleucids had failed to hold."

In his *Studies in Chinese Religion* Parker records the opinion that "it is impossible to deny that the ideas of a Messiah of Salvation, good works and so on, may reasonably have suggested themselves to the Nazarenes through the efforts of Buddhist monks."

The following is from Lloyd's *Creed of Half Japan:* "The existence of Buddhism in Alexandria has often been suspected. Scholars have seen Buddhists in the communities of the Essenes in Palestine, in the monastic congregations of the Therapentœ described by Philo, in the Hermetic books of Egypt. * * * It has also been often suspected that Gnosticism was derived from Buddhism."

On the other side have been opinions that Iranian, Hindu and Chinese religions of B.C. 200—A.D. 100 owe their origin to Biblical lore. According to Rev. Timothy Richard, "it is more and more believed that the Mahâyân Faith is not Buddhism, properly so-called, but an Asiatic form of the same gospel of our Lord and Saviour, Jesus Christ." And Lloyd believes that the religious mission to China during the reign of Mingti in A.D. 67 was "not a Buddhist mission at all" from India, but a Christian propaganda, and "that under Indian names of these two missionaries there may have lurked a Greek nationality."

Mr. Lloyd refers to the tradition of the visit of the *Magi* or the Iranian 'Sages' to the cradle of the Infant Saviour as an indication of the way in which the wind was blowing. But the tradition should be regarded as having the same value as that of pious Buddhists who have recorded the legend of Vedic deities dancing attendance on the infant Sâkyasimha on his nativity. It proves really, on the contrary, that the philosophy and metaphysics as well as theology of the Persian "wise men" were the most powerful factors in the socio-religious world of the time, and, therefore, it was a pardonable vanity on the part of the apostles of the Galilean to imagine the representatives of the established order as having paid homage to the newly risen Star.

Any reader of Lloyd's chapter on 'The New Testament in touch with the East' in his *Creed of Half Japan* would see how impossible and hopeless a task it is to prove the early influence of the Christ-cult on the lands of Zarathustra, Sâkyasimha and Confucius. In the first place, the chronology of Biblical literature itself is not yet beyond criticism. In the second place, according to Prof. Bacon, in the *Making of the New Testament*, it was not before the end of the second century A.D. that the New Testament was canonised. For, on the authority of the Tubingen school of Bible-criticism founded by Ferdinand Baur, "the period covered, from the earliest Pauline Epistle to the latest brief fulminations against Gnostic Doketism and denial of resurrection and judgment, is included in the century from A.D. 50 to 150."

The Sanskrit Râma-stories and Pali Jâtaka-stories which are related on the stupas of the 2nd century B.C. could not certainly be influenced by stories which became current several centuries afterwards. Buddha-cult, Râma-cult, Krishna-cult, Shiva-cult and Vishnu-cult had already been formed with icons and *sutras* before Christ-cult was definitely established in Asia Minor. Historically speaking, Christology and Mariolatry are later than similar '-logies' and '-latries' in Persia, India and China.

The following opinion of Giles may also be quoted: "It seems almost certain that the *Mahâyâna* School had already developed in western India before any knowledge of the Gospels could possibly have travelled so far. Nâgârjuna, its reputed founder, is generally assigned to the second century A.D., and it does not appear to have been earlier than the middle of that century, that the Christians at Antioch began to gather together the records of their Founder, nor indeed until the end of the second century that the Gospels became publicly known through the writings of Irenæus and Tertullian."

The conclusion of Mr. Vincent Smith regarding the "extent of the Hellenic influence upon India from the invasion of Alexander to the Kushân or Indo-Scythian conquest at the end of the first century of the Christian era" is thus given in his *History of India*:

"The Greek influence merely touched the fringe of Hindu civilisation and was powerless to modify the structure of Indian institutions in any essential respect."

The following statement of the same author, however, is unsupported by evidence and partially contradicts the above remark: "The newer Buddhism * * * must have been largely of foreign origin, and its development was the result of the complex interaction of Indian, Zoroastrian, Christian, Gnostic and Hellenic elements which had been made possible by the conquest of Alexander, the formation of the Maurya Empire in India, and above all by the unification of the Roman world under the sway of the earlier emperors."

(*b*) Parallelism and "Open Questions"

It is not justifiable to explain the problem of the nature of the relationship between Christianity and Buddhism except by the hypothesis of an original common fund of spiritual ideas. The following remark of Johnston can, therefore, be accepted:

"We may then admit the possibility that some of the characteristic doctrines shared by Christianity and the Mahâyâna—such as the efficacy of belief in divine or superhuman saviours incarnating themselves in man's form for the world's salvation—were partly drawn from sources to which the builders of both religions had equally ready access."

Dr. Timothy Richard remarks in *The New Testament of Higher Buddhism:* "It is getting clearer each year now that these common doctrines of New Buddhism and Christianity were not borrowed from one another, but that both came from a common source, Babylonia, where some Jewish prophets wrote their glorious visions of the Kingdom of God that was to come. Babylon then had much intercourse with Western India and Persia, as well as with Judæa, Egypt and Greece. From this centre these great life-giving, inspiring truths were carried like seeds into both the East and West, where they were somewhat modified under different conditions."

About Babylon and early Christianity, however, Mr. Johnston remarks: "It is in the discussions of these schools (Hînayâna) orthodox and unorthodox, not in Babylonian poetry or prophecy or in the missionary activity of a St. Thomas, that we must look for the ultimate sources of the principal streams that flow into the ocean of Mahâyânist belief."

In fact, as for the place of Babylonia in world's religious history and the general intellectual condition of the Hellenistic and Græco-Roman countries, the only statements that may be safely made seem to be the following :—

1. Hellenism was a composite product—neither thoroughly Greek nor thoroughly Asiatic. Therefore anything traced to Hellenistic influence must be considered as much oriental as occidental.

2. Hellenism was, after all, not very deep and wide. It may be *presumed* that the important landmarks in world's thought during this period bore the impress of the mutual influence of the East and the West, and that the Buddha-myth (as well as Râma-myth and Krishna-myth) of Eastern Asia and the Christ-myth of Western Asia were held in solution in the grand philosophic cauldron of post-Alexandrian eclecticism. But definite historic *evidences* to prove the impact in each case are not yet forthcoming.

Rather, as Vincent Smith observes, "the invasions of Alexander, Antiochos the Great, Demetrios, Eukratides and Menander were, in fact * * merely military incursions which left no appreciable mark upon the institutions of India; * * * the impression made by Greek authors upon Indian literature and science is hardly traceable until after the close of the period under discussion."

3. Each one of the systems of philosophy, metaphysics and eschatology which we notice full-fledged between B.C. 150 and A.D. 100 can be explained independently as the consummation of an evolutional process along traditional lines without any reference to the international *milieu* or the contact between the East and the West. Thus Platonism

might lead to Stoicism, "Cynicism" and Neo-Platonism without any so-called Oriental impact. So Judaism might lead to Gnosticism, Apocalypticism, and Christ-cult without the influence of Neo-Platonists or Zoroastrians. So also Zoroastrianism could be the basis of Mithraism without any Hellenistic or Hindu factors. Original Chinese mysticism might similarly give rise to later Taoism. The cult of *avatâras* in India and China also can be explained by totally ignoring the epoch of internationalism and *rapprochement* between East and West. The *Brâhmanas*, *Upanishads*, *Darsanas* and *Tripitakas* alone can explain Mahâyâna, Shaiva, Krishnaite and other faiths.

4. Under these circumstances it is desirable to recognise the parallelism in the trend of religious and philosophical growth in India, China, Persia and Syria, and not to dogmatise about the parenthood of any system with regard to the rest. The psychology and metaphysics of Hinduism with its Buddha-cult, Krishna-cult, etc., and those of Judaism with its Christ-cult were independent phenomena growing out of the same "conditions of temperature and pressure," to use a metaphor from physical science.

5. It may be stated that considerable research has to be bestowed on the Parthian, Bactrian, Persian, and Syrian languages and literatures, and the results of these investigations checked by comparison with the findings of Indo-Chinese scholarship, on the one hand, and Hellenic scholarship, on the other, before the problem of international debit and credit can be settled in that most fruitful period of world's religious history.

It is beyond the capacity of the present author to deal with that problem of the "Balance of Accounts" between Asia and Europe. It seems that for some time to come the following, among others, would still remain "open questions:"

1. How far Zeno, a Phœnician of Cyprus, the founder of Stoic Universalism, was a product of the wedlock between the East and the West.

2. What actual influence the missionaries sent out by Asoka to propagate his *Dhamma* had on the Magi of Iran (cf. Prof. Jackson's *Zoroaster*) or in the centres of Greek culture like Antioch, Tarsus and Alexandria. According to Vincent Smith, as would be apparent to every student of facts, "Asoka was much more anxious to communicate the blessings of Buddhist teaching to Antiochus and Ptolemy than to borrow Greek notions from them."

3. How far Saul, the Jew of Tarsus, an apostle of Christianity, was an "oriental who combined the religious instinct of Asia with the philosophic spirit of Greece."

4. (Coming somewhat later), to what extent Plotinus, the greatest of Neo-Platonists, who lived in the 3rd century of the Christian era, imbibed the mystical pantheism of Chuang-tsze's *Tao-te-ching* or the Indian *Gîtâ* and *Vedânta*. The following account from Webb's *History of Philosophy* would lead one to rank Plotinus with the Chinese *Taoists* and Hindu *Yogaists*. "The spiritual ambition of Plotinus was not to be satisfied by sympathy with the universal life, nor yet by contemplation of the eternal Intelligence. He sought, and was believed by his friends on several occasions to have attained, a union with the ultimate principle, the

highest God of all. * * * Union with the Highest can be attained only in a state in which all sense of distinction is lost, a state of ecstasy or rapture."

SECTION 4.

The "Middlemen" in Indo-Chinese Intercourse.

(*a*) THE TARTARS IN WORLD-HISTORY.

It was from Central Asia that the new mythology of India was introduced into China. It supplied two missionaries, several canonical manuscripts in Sanskrit language, and a golden image. Central Asia, as the connecting link between Chinese and Hindu culture, therefore, demands our attention during this period of the birth of Buddhism.

In the history of Indo-Chinese civilisation generally and of religious development in particular, the races of men inhabiting the region vaguely called Central Asia, have always played a prominent part. Their functions have never been creative but only those of carriers, distributors, intermediaries and middle-men. In the present instance, they are responsible (1) for the initiation in India of what is called the Græco-Roman art, and, (2) for the transportation of Buddhist religion, art and literature from India into China. A brief political anthropology would explain the inter-racial relations of the period.

The Maurya Empire of the Hindus (B.C. 320) was chronologically the first empire in world's history, if we leave out of consideration the ancient Assyrian, Egyptian and Persian Monarchies. Alexander's brilliant conquests did not lead to an empire because of his early death. The second Empire in world's history was that of the Chinese under Tsin (B.C. 220) and Han Dynasties. And the third Empire was that of the Romans (1st century A.D.). It is interesting to note that the first empire to be dismembered was the Hindu, the second, the Chinese, and the third, the Roman. It is still more interesting to note that the fall of all the three empires was due ultimately to the invasions of the same barbarian hordes.

These were the Central Asian races known under diverse names, e.g., Tartar, Scythian, Yuechi, Kushan, Saka, Hiung-nu, Hun, White Hun, and so forth. We need not enter into the question of their blood-connexions or linguistic affiliations nor tarry to inquire as to which of these names represents the genus and which the species, branch or family. The most important thing for us to know is that the homeland of peoples who could be successfully withstood neither by the Asiatic nor by the European civilised nations was the *terra incognita* named Central Asia. Readers of Gibbon's *Decline and Fall of the Roman Empire* are familiar with the story of "the barbarians of Scythia, * * * the rude ancestors of the most polished nations of the world."

Originally nomads, these Tartars had no culture of their own, but succeeded in swooping upon well-established civilisations through the vigour and virility characteristic of *pusne* races. And as always happened in history in such cases, "captive Greece captured Rome." The Tartars willingly allowed themselves to be captured by their slaves in India, China, as well as Europe, who were more enlightened than they. They took for their intellectual and spiritual masters those among whom they lived as conquerors, and thoroughly adapted themselves to the local conditions by matrimonial and other social connexions. In lieu of the refinements of culture they obtained they imparted the freshness of their blood and strength of their physique to the subject races. The "Barbarians" of Central Asia were thus vandals in no sense. Modern Hindus, modern Chinese, as well as modern Europeans, owe much of their ancient culture and present vitality to intercourse with these hardy races.

(*b*) The Indo-Scythian (Tartar) Kushans

By the middle of the second century B.C., a branch of the Tartar race, the Yuechi, was already on the move towards the hinterland of Northern and North-western India. There were no strong rulers either among Hindus or among the peoples of the neighbouring Hellenistic Kingdoms. The only powerful monarchy of the time was that of the Hans of China. The Yuechis, therefore, had smooth-sailing through the Indo-Bactrian and Indo-Parthian territories and also the regions now called the North-western Frontier Province of India.

By the first century A.D., *i.e.*, about the time of the founding of the Roman Empire, we hear of a first-class Hindu-Tartar (Kushan) Power under Kanishka (A.D. 78-123?)* with his capital at Purushapura (modern Peshawar). Kanishka was the patron of the celebrated Congress (A.D. 100?) of Hindu philosophers and metaphysicians under Vasumitra and Aswaghosha, to which tradition ascribes the first formulation of Mahâyânism. Just as the *Nirvânism* of Sâkyasimha had been brought into being and nurtured under more or less non-Aryan conditions of life in Eastern India, so *Mahâyânism* formally came into existence in Gândhâra in an atmosphere of newly Hinduised foreigners under the patronage of a monarch whose territory was situated within the westernmost confines of India and beyond. It must be

* Kushan Chronology is tentative.

remembered that a great part of the extra-Indian territory of the Kushans had been included within the Maurya Empire and hence had been the seat of Hindu culture since at least B.C. 320.

Kanishka's predecessors and compatriots had learnt sculpture from the Hellenistic schools of Bactria, and from there imported teachers into their territory called Gândhâra. On the Indian soil they devoted themselves whole-heartedly to Sanskrit language and literature as well as to the prevailing metaphysics and mythology, the first lessons of which they must have received in Bactria, Parthia, and Khotan. One would like to know how these Hellenistic art-traditions and Hindu culture-traditions were being transformed in the process of assimilation with the race-characteristics of these Yuechis (specifically, the Kushans). For the present it is clear that the Græco-Buddhist (also called Gândhâra) art and Hinduism of Buddha-cult were born in an environment of Indianised Scythian or Tartar Settlements. The place of Central Asia in the history of Buddhism is thus very large.

The Kushans were progressive monarchs. They maintained relations of international commerce and diplomacy with the Han Emperors on the East and the Roman Emperors on the West. They also succeeded in extending the Indian sphere of influence through their kith and kin who were rulers of the neighbouring Central Asian regions. External conditions for the propagation of Buddhism were thus thoroughly satisfactory, and we have seen that so far as the Chinese were concerned, their whole mental history had led them up to it.

The relations between the Chinese and those "middlemen" of Central Asia are being given in the words of Mr.

Vincent Smith, who describes the progress of Indian Buddhist art eastwards in his *History of Fine Art in India and Ceylon*:

"Communications between China and the Western countries were first opened up during the time of the early Han Dynasty (B.C. 226 to A.D. 25) by means of the mission of Chang-Kien, who was sent as envoy to the Oxus region and died about B.C. 114. That mission resulted in the establishment of regular intercourse between China and the Scythian powers, but did not involve contact with India. In the year A.D. 8 the official relations of the Chinese government with the western states came to an end, and when the first Han dynasty ceased to exist in A.D. 25, Chinese influence in those countries had vanished. But in A.D. 73 a great general named Pan-chao reduced the King of Khotan to subjection, and from that date continued his victorious career until his death in A.D. 102, when the power of China attained its greatest western extension. In the last decade of the first century Pan-chao inflicted a severe defeat on the Kushan King of Kabul somewhere beyond the Pamirs in the Yarkand or Kashgar country. Most probably that King was Kanishka. After Pan-chao's death the Kushan King retrieved his defeat and occupied Khotan at some time between A.D. 102 and 123. To that Indo-Scythian conquest of Khotan I would attribute the rapid spread of Indian languages, scripts, religion and art in Chinese Turkistan, as disclosed by the discoveries of recent years. I do not mean that Indian influence then first began to be felt, for there is reason to believe that it crossed the passes more than three hundred years earlier in the age of Asoka, but its great extension appears not to go back further than the first quarter of the second century of the Christian era, the very time when the art of Gândhâra was at its best."

(c) GRÆKO-BUDDHIST ICONOGRAPHY

A halfway house between Hindusthân and China was the kingdom of Kucha, situated in the heart of Chinese Turkestan. In the Royal Asiatic Society's Journal Dr. Sylvain Levi writes about this Central Asian region: "In the early centuries of the Christian era, Kucha received the Buddhistic creed and culture to such a large and overwhelming extent that the whole local situation became Buddhistic. Situated, on account of its connection with Khotan, well for commercial purposes, Kucha from this time onward became a very prosperous and flourishing place in which the activities of the merchants and the priests were equally vigorous and in which commerce and culture played an equally significant part. * * * Sanskrit became the sacred language and was assiduously taught and studied in the monasteries."

The following extract from Fenollosa's chapter on 'Græko-Buddhist art in China' would give the whole geography of the Kushan (Indo-Tartar) sphere of cultural influence in Asia: "This wave of civilisation from Gândhâra passed northward from the Indus valley into the great mountain passes of Balkh and Swat * * * and advancing over the roof of the world to the great Turkestan plain lying beyond the Pamirs, pushing up toward Kashgar and Samarkand, and downward again to skirt the southern borders of the great deserts which the Kunlung range * * separates from Tibet, and so on to kingdoms far towards the Chinese border, has been verified by the important recent explorations of Sven Hedin, Mr. Stein of the Indian Government, and others."

According to Vincent Smith the culmination of the Hellenistic sculpture of Gândhâra "may be dated from A.D. 50 to A.D. 150." "Thus the best productions of the Gândhâra Hellenistic school nearly synchronise with the art of the Flavian and Antonine periods in western Asia and Europe, and in India with the reliefs or the great rail at Amarâvatî in the Deccan, as well as with many sculptures at Mathurâ on the Jumna."

The Kushan-Hindus were great worshippers of images, as would appear from the thousands of icons which have come to light during the comparatively recent excavations. "All the sculptures come from the Buddhist sites and were executed in the service of Buddhist religion. * * * Buddha may appear in the guise of Apollo, the god Brahmâ, or in that of St. Peter. * * * However Greek may be the form, the personages and incidents are all Indian."

"The statues and small groups represent Buddhas, Bodhisattvas, or saints on the way to become Buddhas, besides minor deities of the populous Buddhist pantheon. * * * That system (Mahâyâna) practically deified Gautama Buddha, as well as other Buddhas, and surrounded them with a crowd of attendant deities, including Indra or Sakra, Brahmâ and other members of the Brahmanical heavenly host, besides a multitude of attendant sprites, male and female, of diverse kinds and varying rank, in addition to human worshippers."

It was this Indo-Tartar iconography that supplied models to the Chinese and Koreans and finally to the Japanese.

CHAPTER VII.

A Period of So-called Anarchy in China

(A.D. 220-618)

SECTION 1.

COMPARATIVE CHRONOLOGY AND COMPARATIVE HISTORY.

The powerful Han Dynasty of Celestial Emperors came to an end in A.D. 221 after a brilliant career of about four centuries and a quarter. The Empire fell to pieces before the inroads of the Tartar barbarians of the North. These foreigners occupied almost the whole northern half of the country and pushed the original Chinese dynasties down to the South which had received civilising influences only recently. It was a period of small contending states, native and foreign, till A.D. 589, when the whole country came under the Sui Dynasty, from whom the Tângs inherited a unified Empire in A.D. 618.

An epoch of consolidation has always been followed and preceded by an epoch of dismemberment. History has repeated itself on these lines not only on the Chinese and Indian continents and in other countries of Asia but also in Europe taken as a whole, and in the European states taken singly. Feudalistic disintegration is not due to the alleged political incompetency of the oriental peoples but has been a marked characteristic of the western races as well.

A parallel study of the dates and facts of political history of the Chinese and Hindu as well as the European races from earliest times down to 1815 (and even 1870) would bring out the facts:—

1. That there have been at least as many instances of strong and centralised rule in the Orient as in the Occident; and necessarily as many periods of anarchy also.

2. That the durations of unified administration have been equally long or short both in China and India as well as in Europe.

3. That Chinese and Hindu history as well as the history of other Asiatic peoples can present no fewer Alexanders and Napoleons than the history of European races.

4. That Asiatic aggressions upon Europe have been at least as frequent as the inroads of European races into the East.

5. That the defeat and expulsion of foreign invaders by Asiatic peoples are as solid facts of oriental history as the retreat of Persian, Saracen, Tartar and Turkish nationalities from the heart of Europe.

6. That the cases of successful resistance of enemies' military inroads in Asiatic or European history can not be conveniently explained away as instances of home-keeping conservatism, or desire for "splendid isolation," or absence of international spirit on the part of any people.

7. That the ability to bring within the pale of one culture three hundred or four hundred millions of people indicates as great "aggressiveness" on the part of the Hindus or the Chinese as the ability to spread a common civilisation among the heterogeneous races of Europe on the part of the Westerners.

8. That if twenty, thirty, or forty millions be the human basis of a 'nationality,' as has been the case in the

West during the last forty years, Asiatic peoples have always given rise to such nation-states.

9. That fratricidal and internecine wars between peoples of the same race and religion have been at least as frequent in the West as in the East.

10. That instances of one Asiatic people dominating another have not been greater than those of the exploitation or "government of one people by another" in Europe.

11. That in ancient and mediæval times the nations of Asia have had knowledge about one another as much as or as little as the nations of Europe about themselves.

12. That the ignorance of Europeans regarding the Asiatics in ancient and mediæval times has been, to say the least, as profound as that of the Asiatics regarding the Europeans.

13. That 'splendid isolation' was equally true of both Asiatics and Europeans.

14. Hatred of foreigners was as powerful in the West as in the East; such terms as "barbarians," "heathens," "infidels," "vile Turk," "nigger," etc., are found in non-oriental languages.

15. Besides, the morals and manners of the Court of Peking have been out-Pekinged in lands other than Cathay. Thus Macaulay speaks of court-life in England under the Stuarts with his characteristic eloquence in his *Essay on Milton*:

"Then came those days never to be recalled without a blush, the days of servitude without loyalty and sensuality without love, of dwarfish talents and gigantic vices, the paradise of cold hearts and narrow minds, the golden age of the coward, the bigot and the slave. The King cringed to his rival that he might trample on his people, sank into a viceroy of France, and pocketed, with complacent infamy, her degrading insult, and her more degrading gold. The caresses of harlots and the jests of buffoons regulated the policy of the state. The Government had just ability enough to deceive, and just religion enough to persecute. The principles of liberty were the scoff of every grinning courtier, and the Anathema Maranatha of every fawning dean. In every high place, worship was paid to Charles and James, Belial and Moloch, and England propitiated those obscene and cruel idols with the blood of her best and bravest children. Crime succeeded to crime, and disgrace to disgrace, till the race accursed of God and man was a second time driven forth, to wander on the face of the earth, and to be a by-word and a shaking of the head to the nations."

It is necessary to bear this skeleton of Comparative History in mind while noticing the anarchy and political chaos in China during the four hundred years between Han and Tâng dynasties. The strength and weakness exhibited by Chinese humanity during the several millenniums have been those of every other race of mankind. If the historical geography of China were studied on the lines of Freeman's *Historical Geography of Europe*, it would be quite clear that generation by generation, and area for area, the political fortunes of the Far Eastern nation as well as of the Western peoples have advanced in nearly the self-same way. There is nothing abnormal in the race-characteristics of the Chinese, and nothing exceptional need be assumed while studying their religion and culture.

This period of anarchy is, however, very important to students of Chinese religion. It was during those troublous times that Buddhism, Confucianism and Laotszeism (Taoism), as cults of *avatâras* or personal deities in which form we know them to-day, took their final shape.

SECTION 2.

CHINESE RELIGIOUS DEVELOPMENT.

For a long time after the formal introduction of Buddha-cult among the Chinese, "things Indian" remained mere curios to their "upper ten thousand." India was to them no more than what she was to Europe in the days of Goethe when *Sakuntalâ* was first translated into a western language, or what Japan was to the Occidental world prior to the event of 1905 or of 1895, or what China is to-day to all outsiders. A real Hindu movement was a long-delayed phenomenon in the Celestial Empire. "*Vini, Vidi, Vici*" is not the verdict about Indianism in China in spite of the Indian element in her character.

For the Chinese, like every other people, had begun to bring out their own *Jâtaka*-stories or incarnation-myths regarding their ancient sages. They were not in need of much foreign help in the direction to which their mentality led them independently. The account given of Laotsze in Taoist works is, according to Davis in *Chinese* (ii,115-16) "that he was an incarnation of some superior being, and that there is no age in which he does not come forth among men in human shape. They tell the various names under which he appeared from the highest period of fabulous antiquity down as late as the sixth century, making in all seven periods."

Mr. Werner gives an extract from the *Transactions* of the China Branch of the Royal Asiatic Society (Pt. V., pp. 83-98) in which we read of the Taoist "mode of self-training called *liau-yang*," the analogue of Hindu *Yoga*. "This method consisted of a hermit life, and sitting cross-legged in a mountain cave, and trying to hold the breath. * * * By continuing this process sufficiently long, the soul will at length become superior to the body, rise up out of it by its own power, ascend to heaven, and become one of the celestial genii."

The use of charms, amulets, etc., is mentioned by sinologues in connexion with Taoism of this period, as evidently there were other forms of folk-religion, also. The discovery of the "Elixir of Life," "philosopher's stone" and all other phenomena connected with alchemy is also traced to Taoism of this and previous ages. "Chin-Shi-Hwangti sent a party to look for the Elixir of Life in B.C. 219. Among mineral substances cinnabar was considered likely to yield it." "The Taoists call the process of manipulating substances to obtain the elixir *Liau-wai-tan*, 'the obtaining by purification of the external elixir.'" "Alchemy was studied in China for two centuries B.C. and therefore earlier than in the West." This would remind the Hindu of his *Tantras* and Nâgârjuna, the Mahâyânist Doctor of Tantric philosophy.

Laotsze was fast approaching deification. The following is taken from Watters' *Lao-Tzu*. "From the time of the Chin (A.D. 265-478) and Liang (A.D. 402-557) Dynasties down to the Great T'ang dynasty his doctrine and his name were glorified. He was promoted to be a God, and wonderful things were invented about him, and the Tao of which he spoke so much."

It seems that Taoist Papacy was instituted before Laotsze had received a place in the pantheon. Watters gives the following account: "The first of the Taoist patriarchs in China was Chang Tao-ling, who lived in the time of the Han dynasty. Lao-tsze appeared to him in the Stork-cry Hill and told him that in order to attain the state of immortality which he was seeking he must subdue a number of demons. Tao-ling in his eagerness slew too many, and Laotszu told him that Shangti required him to do penance for a time. Finally, however, he was allowed to become an immortal, and the spiritual chiefdom of the Taoists was given to his family for ever."

Giles gives the following stages in the process of deification through which Confucius passed. "In A.D. 178 a likeness of Confucius had been placed in his shrine as a substitute for the wooden tablet in use up to that date. * * * There is no doubt that the shrine played an important part in keeping alive the Confucian tradition. So far back as A.D. 267, an Emperor decreed that the sacrifice of a pig, sheep, and an ox should be offered to Confucius at each of the four seasons. Rules were drawn up about A.D. 430 for regulating the ceremonies to be performed. Gradually, the people came to look upon Confucius as a god to be propitiated for the sake of worldly advantages; and in A.D. 472 it became necessary to issue an edict forbidding women to frequent the shrine for the purpose of praying for children. About A.D. 555 it was enacted that a Confucian temple should be built in every prefectural city in the empire. * * * Some of the ancient sages who were admitted to share in the honors accorded to their master, appear in the shape of wooden figures; the portraits of others were painted on the walls. In the year 960 the wooden figures were abolished, and clay images were substituted."

It would appear that the idea of personal gods, *avatâras* or Messiahs, to be worshipped in their icons had been growing independently in Hindusthân, Iran, Israel and China. The following seems to be the chronological order in the history of world's modern deities :—

1. Shiva-cult, Râma-cult, Vishnu-cult (Krishna-cult).
2. Buddha-cult, Mahâvira-cult.
3. Mithraism, Christology, Mariolatry.
4. Laotsze-cult.
5. Confucius-cult.

The mentality expressed in each cult is the same, there are slight differences only in the technique and external paraphernalia.

SECTION 3.

"CONFUCIANISM," "BUDDHISM," "BUDDHIST INDIA," "BUDDHIST CHINA."

The term "Confucianism," as the name of a religion, like the names of other great religions, Hinduism, Christianity, etc., is ambiguous and very elastic.

(1) The Cult of the World-Forces that has been existing in China from time immemorial has been miscalled Confucianism, simply because Confucius the librarian at Loo happened to compile, or edit, or even lend his name to the collection of, the Ancient Classics in which that cult finds expression. In this sense Confucianism had existed in China before Confucius was born. As Hirth puts it, thus considered, the whole history of China becomes a tale of "retrospective Confucianism."

(2) Confucianism may mean a study of the Ancient Classics alleged to have been edited by Confucius, the *Vyâsa* or Pisistratus of China, and also the worship of the same Deities as have been adored by the Celestial people throughout the ages.

(3) Confucianism is sometimes wrongly taken to be equivalent to positivism. The sayings of Confucius as moralist which we get in the *Analects*, and the *Doctrine of the Mean*, have no reference to the supernatural, the unseen or the other world, and are supposed to convey the *whole* message of his life. But as we have indicated in a previous chapter, they are really *parts* of a system which embraces the entire classical literature, and is, therefore, as theistic as that of the pre-Confucian Chinese.

(4) Confucianism has become the worship of Confucius as a god since about the 5th century A. D.. This Confucius-cult is exactly like the Shângti-cult, Heaven-cult, Tai-cult, etc., of the Chinese, and the Varuna-cult, Indra-cult, Vishnu-cult, Buddha-cult, etc., of the Hindus, a cult of Nature-Force. This has, therefore, to be regarded as distinct from (3), the so-called Positivism of the Chinese supposed to have been taught by Confucius the moralist, (2), the study of the classics, etc., associated with the name of Confucius as editor, and (1), the Ancient Chinese Religion. Rather it should be regarded as a branch of (1), because Confucius is a god among gods.

It may be remarked, in passing, that the trend of the foregoing pages has been to indicate that Confucianism taken in any sense is easily comprehensible to the Hindu mind.

Likewise, the term 'Buddhism' also is ambiguous. It may mean at least two things: (1) the religion that was founded by a man named Buddha, (2) the religion which recognises Buddha as *a* or *the* god in its pantheon. This ambiguity is shared with it by the term 'Christianity' as we have seen in the preceding chapter.

Now in India no religion has been named after its founder. It is the custom to designate religions according to the cult. In that case, if the teachings of the historic person Sâkyasimha, surnamed the Buddha, may be considered as constituting a religion, it should be called *Nirvânism* or Cessation-of-Misery-ism after its most prominent metaphysical tenet. The current term *Hînayânism* is quite good.

Buddhism in its second meaning has practically no or very indirect connexion with this *Nirvânism*, though evolved out of it. It is a cult like *Shaivaism* with Shiva as the principal god, or *Vaishnavism* with Vishnu as the principal god, or *Shâktaism* with *Shakti* as the principal goddess, or *Sauraism* with Suryya, the Sun, as the principal god, etc.. Buddha here is on a par with the elemental forces of the universe, Fire, Air, Water, Sky, etc., named Agni, Indra, Varuna, Dyaus, etc., in Vedic literature, or Brahmâ, Vishnu, Shiva, etc., the descendants of Vedic deities.

It is necessary to bear this distinction always in mind because Sâkyasimha the founder of *Nirvânism* (the philosophy of twelve *Nidânas** and eight-fold path) did not and naturally could not claim the rank of a god or a son of God or even a prophet. Buddhism or the cult of Buddha-worship therefore should not be fathered upon Sâkyasimha. This Buddhism, called also *Mahâyânism*, is like every other ism in India not the making of a single brain or character, but

*Links between Ignorance and Birth.

is the outcome of communal religious consciousness, the embodiment of a collective race-ideal. It is the growth of generations and sums up the accumulated spiritual experience of ages.

What, then, does the term *Buddhist India* mean? It should mean (1) *Nirvânist* India, and (2) India in which Buddha-cult has been supreme. But either way it is a misnomer. There has been no period of Indian history in which Sâkyasimha's *Nirvânistic* teachings had exclusive sway over the mind of the people. There were other sources of inspiration to Indian humanity both in Sâkyasimha's time as well as before and after. There was the *Upanishad*-India, there was the *Darsana*-India, there was the *Folk*-India, there was the *Mahâvira*-India, there were probably the *Mahâbhârata*-India and *Râmâyana*-India too, and there were many other Indias at the same time. No chapter of Indian history can be called after Sâkyasimha, or *Nirvânism*, if that be his exclusive patent.

Secondly, if we take Buddhism in the second sense, here also we can never speak of a Buddhist India. Because when Buddha had a place in the pantheon, he was only a god among the gods worshipped by the people of Hindusthân. Besides, just as the metaphysics of *Nirvânism* was not Sâkya's original discovery, so also the metaphysics of Buddhism was not the patent of any sect. If any chapter of Indian history is to be named after the gods worshipped by the people or the metaphysical systems they embody, Brahmâ, Vishnu, Shiva; Târâ, Krishna, Râma, Pârswanâtha and a thousand others have equal claim with Buddha.

But Rhys Davids has used the term *Buddhist India* in such a way as leaves the wrong impression that for certain consecutive periods of Indian history the religion founded by Sâkyasimha as well as the religion of Buddha-cult monopolised the faith of the people and probably eclipsed all their secular and materialistic activities. If by *Buddhist India* he meant all those epochs of Indian history in which Buddhism in any sense has existed and all those peoples of India, past or present, who have professed Buddhism in any shape, there would have been no misunderstanding. Mr. Johnston, for example, in his *Buddhist China*, has done exactly what is being suggested here. Readers of Johnston's work get an idea of what Buddhism is and has been, as taught and professed by the Celestial People. They are never misled to believe that there is a Buddhist epoch of Chinese history. But readers of *Buddhist India* by a greatest student of Indian Buddhism have been thus misled for a long time.

In fact, the whole division of Indian history into the so-called epochs has up till now been thoroughly misleading. It has been the fashion to name the chapters after a race or a religion. If this were the fashion with students of European history, they would have to describe some of their epochs as those of *Mahometan Europe*, *Turkish Europe*, *Tartar Europe*, and so forth. Students of Indian history should have to proceed to their work with the object of elucidating the operation of forces, both national as well as international, and secular as well as non-secular, that have contributed to the building up of a varied and complex civilisation. Sometimes the most prominent culture-force is probably race-mixture, at other times it is probably an intellectual upheaval. And it may often be difficult to get a convenient word for defining all the activities throughout India. The work, therefore, has to be commenced in the spirit of a Guizot or a John Richard Green. Vincent Smith may be said to have given a thousand years' chronological scaffolding. Much spade-work yet remains to be done before India can be presented in an understandable form.

SECTION 4.

THE PIONEERS OF ASIATIC UNITY.

The fortunes of Buddhism during the period of so-called anarchy in China may be thus described in the words of Hackmann:

"The most striking fact, to which too little notice has so far been given, is that it was not till the beginning of the fourth century A.D. that the Chinese were allowed to become monks in the Buddhist religion. The authorised representatives, therefore, of the new religion were foreigners during the first two and a half centuries. A roll of names of foreigners has been handed down to us who came from India, from the Himalayan states, and from Central Asia, to take charge of Buddhism in China. For a long time their most important labours consisted in translations of the books of the Buddhist Canon. * * * Till about A.D. 300 the translators were all foreigners (with the exception of one Chinese layman)."

The following is taken from Giles: "It was not until A.D. 335 that the Chinese people were allowed to take Buddhist orders. This permission was due to the influence of a remarkable Indian priest, named Budhachinga, who reached the capital in A.D. 310. * * * Buddhism now began to take a firm hold; and under the year 381 we read of a special temple built for priests within the Imperial palace. A further great impetus to the spread of this religion was given by the arrival, about the year 385, of Kumârajîva. * * * He laboured for many years as a translator, dying in 417. * * * The work by which he is best known * * * is the translation of what is called *The Diamond Sutra* * * * which teaches that all objects, all phenomena are illusory, and have no real existence, * * * seems to show that faith in Buddha through the Buddhist scriptures can also make a man 'wise unto salvation.' * * * While Kumârajîva was spreading the faith in China, and dictating commentaries on the sacred books of Buddhism to some eight hundred priests, the famous traveller, Fa Hien, was engaged upon his adventurous journey."

The heroic idealism as well as lofty spirituality which inspired Fa Hien in his arduous journey (A.D. 399-413) were characteristics of the Chinese converts of the day. The following is taken from Legge's translation of Fa-Hien's *Travels:* "That I encountered danger and trod the most perilous places, without thinking of, or sparing myself, was because I had a definite aim, and thought of nothing but to do my best in my simplicity and straightforwardness. Thus it was that I exposed my life where death seemed inevitable, if I might accomplish but a ten thousandth part of what I hoped."

Fa Hien's noble personality can be understood also from the following account of Giles: "He brought with him a large number of books and sacred relics, all of which he nearly lost in the Bay of Bengal. There was a violent gale, and the ship sprang a leak. As he tells us in his own account of the journey, 'he took his pitcher and ewer, with whatever else he could spare, and threw them into the sea; but he was afraid that the merchants on board would throw over his books and images, and accordingly he fixed his whole thoughts upon Kuan-shih-yin or Kuan Yin, the Hearer of the Prayers of the World, and prayed to the sainted priests of his own country, saying, 'Oh that by your awful prayer you would turn back the flow of the leak and grant us to reach some resting place!' "

These are the words of a real *bhakta* or lover, be he a Shaiva, a Vaishnava, a Râmaite, a Jaina, or a Buddhist. The Religion of Love and Faith was established in China by genuine Romanticists and self-abnegating devotees of the Fa Hien-type.

With Kumârajîva and Fa Hien, *i.e.*, towards the beginning of the 5th century, we enter a new era of Indo-Chinese relationships. It marks the beginning of an intimate cultural and spiritual union between the two peoples, which, backed by equally deep commercial and political intercourse, has given rise to that composite crystal of human thought known as Asiatic Culture. The land of Sâkyasimha and the land of Confucius met at last in a real "Holy Alliance." For the next thousand years (*i.e.* down to about A.D. 1453, the year of the capture of Constantinople by the Turks), the life and activity of human beings from Kyoto to Cairo were governed by one Asiatic science, art and philosophy. This, carried to Europe by Arab intermediaries, became also the foster-mother of that Renaissance, the ultimate results of which we have been witnessing in the world since 1815. That chapter of world's mediæval history has yet to be written.

Hindu culture in general, and Buddha-cult in particular, may now be said to have come to stay in China. Indianism was no longer a mere "interest" of curio-hunters and faddists, but on the fair way to be a permanent factor in

Chinese civilisation. According to Hackmann, "perhaps the renown attained by the Chinese Buddhism of that period is best demonstrated by the striking event that in the year A.D. 526 the patriarch of Indian Buddhism, Bodhidharma, the twenty-eighth in the list of the Buddha's successors, left his native land and migrated to China, which thenceforward became the seat of the patriarchate."

It is now desirable to get a picture of Indian culture and religion, the fountain-head of the Asiatic life-stream, at the beginning of this momentous epoch in world's history. To this task I shall now address myself.

CHAPTER VIII.

The Beginning of Hindu Culture as World-Power

(A.D. 300-600)

SECTION 1.

INDIAN NAPOLEON'S ALEXANDRIAN MARCH.

We noticed in a previous chapter that, if we exclude the Assyrian, Egyptian and Persian Monarchies of ancient times, the Maurya Empire of the Hindus (B.C. 321-B.C. 185) was, chronologically speaking, the first Empire in world's history, and that, internationally speaking, it occupied the first rank in the contemporary state-system. We have now arrived at a stage in world's history when another Hindu Empire became similarly the very First Power of the world. This was the celebrated Empire of the Guptas (A.D. 320-606). There was now "anarchy" (?) in China. With the incursions of Barbarians into the Roman Empire, Europe was immersed in her "Dark Ages." The Saracenic Caliphate of the followers of Islam was not yet come. It was the people of Hindusthân who enjoyed the real "place in the sun."

While noticing the military and political achievements of Samudragupta (A.D. 335-375), one of the Emperors of this House, Mr. Vincent Smith—to whom Indologists owe the only "chronological narrative of the political vicissitudes of the land"—makes the following remarks:

"Whatever may have been the exact degree of skill attained by Samudragupta in the practice of the arts which graced his scanty leisure, it is clear that he was endowed with no ordinary powers; and that he was in fact a man of genius, who may fairly claim the title of the Indian Napoleon. * * *

By a strange irony of fate this great king—warrior, poet, and musician—who conquered nearly all India, and whose alliances extended from the Oxus to Celyon—was unknown even by name to the historians until the publication* of this work. His lost fame has been slowly recovered by the minute and laborious study of inscriptions and coins during the last eighty years."

It may be mentioned, in passing, that monarchs of the Samudragupta-type, who may be compared easily with a Charlemagne, a Frederick or a Peter the Great, have flourished in India almost every second generation. Hindu folk-lore has known them as Vikramâdityas (Sun of Power) and has invested their names with the halo of Arthurian romance.

It is unnecessary to wait long over the political achievements of the Gupta Emperors. The *Digvijaya* or 'Conquest of the Quarters' made by Samudragupta fired the imagination of a contemporary poet, Kâlidâsa, the Goethe or Shakespeare of Sanskrit literature. The following are some of the verses from Canto IV of his immortal epic, *Raghu-vamsam* ("The House of Raghu"), translated by Griffith for his *Idylls from the Sanskrit*, which describe the triumphal progress of his hero Raghu:

"Fortune herself, sweet Goddess, all unseen,
Held o'er his sacred head her lotus screen,
And Poesy in minstrels' form stood by,
Swept the wild string, and raised his triumph high.

* First Edition, Clarendon Press, Oxford, 1905.

What though the earth, since ancient Manu's reign,
Was wooed by every king, nor wooed in vain;
She came a bride, with fresh unrifled charms,
A pure young virgin, to her Raghu's arms.

* * *

Scarce was he ready for the sword and shield
When autumn called him to the battlefield,—
War's proper season, when the rains are o'er,
When roads are dry, and torrents foam no more.
Soon as the day to bless the chargers came,
The warrior's holy festival, the flame
Turned to the right, and with a ruddy hand
Gave him full triumph o'er each distant land.
Then when his Kingdom was secured, and all
His city fortified with tower and wall,
His hosts he marshalled, his broad flag outspread,
And to subdue the world his army led.
Forth as he rode, the city matrons poured
The sacred grain upon their mighty lord.

* * *

First to the East the hero takes his way,
His foemen trembling as his banners play.
Thick clouds of dust beneath his chariots rise,
Till dark as earth appear the changing skies;

* * *

He marked his progress with a mighty hand;
The fountain gushed amid the thirsty sand;
The tangled forest harboured beasts no more,
And foaming floods the freighted vessel bore.

* * *

Through all the East he passed, from land to land,
And reached triumphant, Ocean's palmy strand.
Like an unsparing torrent on he went,
And low, like reeds, the lords of Suhma bent.
Then fell the islets washed by Gangâ's wave,
Nor could their ships, the hosts of Banga save.

* * *

No wealth he sought, but warred in honour's name,
So spared his land but spoiled his warlike fame.

* * *

But louder, as the war-steeds paced along,
Rattled the harness of the mail-clad throng.

* * *

True to the Law thus Raghu marched by land
To Pârasîka with his conquering band.
He saw, indignant, to the lotus eyes
Of Yavana dames the wine-cup's frenzy rise.

* * *

Mad was the onset of the western horse,
And wild the fury of the conqueror's force;
No warrior saw—so thick the dust—his foe,
But marked him by the twanging of his bow.
Then Raghu's archers shot their keen shafts well;
The bearded head of many a soldier fell,
And covered closely all the battle-ground
Like heaps of honey that the bees surround.

* * *

Pale grew the cheek of every Huna dame,
Trembling in wild alarm at Raghu's name.

* * *

By him subdued, they forced their pride to bring
Coursers and gold as gifts to Kosal's King.
Borne by these steeds he climbed Himâlayas hill,
Whose crest now clothed with dust rose loftier still.

* * *

Fierce was the battle with the mountaineers
Armed with their bows and arrows, stones and spears,
The thick sparks flying as they met. Then ceased,
Slain by his arrows, from the mirth and feast
The mountain revellers, and minstrel bands,
That walked as demi-gods those lofty lands,
Were taught the hero's victories to sing,
And each hill tribe brought tribute to the King.

* * *

Thus when all princes owned the conqueror's sway,
He turned his chariot on his homeward way,
Letting the dust, beneath his wheels that rose,
Fall on the diadems of humbled foes."

It was the atmosphere of this poetry which nurtured the nation of Kumârajîvas. Fa-Hien and Kâlidâsa were contemporaries, and if the Chinese traveller had cared to know some of the prominent Hindus of his time, the first man to be introduced to him would have been Kâlidâsa. But it seems from Fa-Hien's diary that he had not much leisure to go beyond his special mission. However, it was the Indianism of Kâlidâsâ's age with which the Chinese Apostle came in contact. It was this Hindu Culture which was propagated in China and finally transmitted to Japan to build up her *Bushido* and *Yamato Damashii*. Buddha-cult was introduced into Korea from China in A.D. 372, and from Korea into the Land of the Rising Sun in A.D. 552.

SECTION 2.

"WORLD-SENSE" AND COLONISING ENTERPRISE.

The Hindus of the fourth, fifth and sixth centuries were not living in "splendid isolation," as it has been the fashion to suppose that the Asiatics have ever done. As in previous ages, so under the Guptas they kept up cultivating the "world-sense."

In the first place, it must be remembered that India alone is a world by herself—the whole of Europe minus Russia. Therefore, for the Hindus to be able to develop the "India-sense" in pre-Steam days must be regarded as an expression of internationalism of high order. Considered territorially, and also in terms of population, the world-sense of the Roman Emperors was not greater than that of the Hindu Imperialists.

The internationalism of the Hindus was extra-Indian too. It is well-known that the world of Kâlidâsa's poetry includes the whole of India and also the Indian borderland and Persia. The fact that with the fifth century is augmented the stream of traffic between India and China both by land and sea is itself an indication of the "Asia-sense" they had been developing. It may be said that the Mauryas had cultivated mainly the relations with West-Asia, the Kushans had opened up the Central-Asian regions, and the Guptas developed the Far Eastern intercourse. The Hindus could now think not only in terms of India but of entire Asia.

The larger world beyond Asia was also to a certain extent within the purview of the Hindus. Ever since Alexander's opening up of the West-Asian route, the Hindus had kept touch with the "barbarians." About the first century A.D. Hindu trade with the Roman Empire was not a negligible item of international commerce. The *Periplus of the Erythræan Sea* (*c* A.D. 100) is a document of that Indo-Roman Intercourse. Both the Kushans in the North and the Andhra Monarchs in the South were interested in Rome.

In the *Imperial Gazetteer of India* (*India*, Vol. II.) Sewell describes the foreign trade of the Hindus under the South Indian Andhras (B.C. 200—A.D. 250): "The Andhra period seems to have been one of considerable prosperity. There was trade both overland and by sea, with Western Asia, Greece, Rome, and Egypt, as well as with China and the East. Embassies are said to have been sent from South India to Rome. Indian elephants were used for Syrian warfare. Pliny mentions the vast quantities of specie that found its way every year from Rome to India and in this he is confirmed by the author of the *Periplus*. Roman coins have been found in profusion in the peninsula, and especially in the south. In A.D. 68 a number of Jews, fleeing from Roman persecution, seem to have taken refuge among the friendly coast people of South India and to have settled in Malabar."

The following picture of foreign settlements in Southern India is given by Vincent Smith: "There is good reason to believe that considerable colonies of Roman subjects engaged in trade were settled in Southern India during the first two centuries of our era, and that European soldiers, described as powerful Yavanas, dumb Mlechchas (barbarians), clad in complete armour, acted as body-guards to Tamil kings."

According to the same authority Chandragupta II. Vikramaditya (A.D. 375-413) of the Gupta dynasty was "in direct touch with the sea-borne commerce with Europe through Egypt."

Besides, intercourse with Further India and the colonisation of Java form parts of an adventure which in Gupta times was nearing completion. In fact, with the fourth century A.D. really commences the foundation of a "Greater India" of commerce and culture, extending ultimately from Japan on the East to Madagascar on the West. The romantic story of this Expansion of India has found its proper place in Mookerji's *History of Indian Shipping and Maritime Activity from the Earliest Times.* The heroic pioneers of that undertaking were all embodiments of the world-sense.

It would thus appear that the travels of Kumârajîva the Hindu Missionary (A.D. 405) and of Fa Hien the Celestial Apostle were facts of a nature to which the Indians had long been used. The Chinese monks came to a land through which the current of world-life regularly flowed. Hindusthân had never been shunted off from the main-track of universal culture. To come to India in the age of the Guptas was to imbibe the internationalism of the atmosphere.

Regarding the Indo-Chinese intercourse of this age the following extracts from *The Epochs of Chinese and Japanese Art* are interesting:

"Of what took place in the Tartar regions of the north we know little, since their dynasties have not been recognised by Chinese historians as legitimate. The true Celestial annals, indeed the lore of Chinese genius, belong at this time to the stimulus afforded by the new southern conditions. The new capital, near the present Nanking, was on the great Yangtse. * * * The Southern seats of the Chinese were in closer proximity to a new part of India, the south through Burma, or along the opening lines of coast trade. * * * It was here too, in the Southern Chinese nests, that Buddhism could drop her most fertile germs."

It may be mentioned that the patriarch Bodhidharma, originally a South Indian Prince, reached Canton by sea and was then invited to Nanking (A. D. 520).

The above is a picture of the sea-traffic. References to this are to be found in the *Kwai-Yuen Catalogue* (A.D. 730) of the Chinese *Tripitaka* which has been drawn upon by Prof. Anesaki for his paper in the J.R.A.S. (April, 1903).

It must not be forgotten, besides, that Kucha and Khotan, the halfway house between India and China, remained all this while the great emporium of Hindu culture and Graeko-Buddhist art. Manuscripts, unearthed by Stein and others, both in Kharoshthi and Chinese Scripts, prove that Central Asian Indianism flourished during the period from 3rd century A.D. to 8th or 9th. And it was the Central Asian land-route which was traversed by Fa Hien in A.D. 399 and later by Hiuen Thsang in A.D. 629 on their way to India, from which both returned home by sea.

SECTION 3.

A Melting-pot of Races.

(*a*) THE CAPACITY FOR ASSIMILATION.

The New Worlders of the United States take a great delight in describing their country as the 'melting-pot of races.' Similarly the statesmen and scholars in the Land of the Rising Sun have been giving out to the world during the last decade or so, that an extraordinary 'capacity for assimilation' is the characteristic of the Yamato race. Anthropologically speaking, the two claims are one and the same; and historically considered, the Japanese or American characteristic is not the exclusive feature of any race, but has been exhibited in the life of every race of human beings, and may be traced ultimately to the elemental instinct of self-preservation.

The ancient Chaldæans and Mycaneans could claim the same characteristic, as well as the Aztecs of Mexico and the Maories of New Zealand. Every inch of soil on the Old World from Korea to Ulster has been as great a melting-pot of races as any of the States in the New World. And the race-psychology of the Tartar, the Jew, the Briton, the Pole, the Hindu, the Pathan, the Chinese, the Bulgar, and the Slav displays the same assimilative capacity for utilising new conditions and thus growing by adaptation as that of the Far Eastern people.

In the following picture of "England under foreign rule" (1013-1204) given by Green in his *Short History of the English People* we see at once the American melting-pot and the Japanese assimilation:

"Britain had become England in the five hundred years that followed the landing of Hengest, and its conquest had ended in the settlement of its conquerors. * * * But whatever titles kings might assume, or however imposing their rule might appear, Northumbrian remained apart from West Saxon, Dane from Englishman. * * *

Through the two hundred years that lie between the flight of Æthelred from England to Normandy and that of John from Normandy to England our story is a story of foreign rule. Kings from Denmark were succeeded by kings from Normandy, and these by kings from Anjou. Under Dane, Norman, or Angevin, Englishmen were a subject race, conquered and ruled by foreign masters; and yet it was in these years of subjection that England first became really England. * * * The English lords themselves sank into a middle class as they were pushed from their place by the foreign baronage who settled on English soil; and this change was accompanied by a gradual elevation of the class of servile and semi-servile cultivators who gradually lifted themselves into almost complete freedom. The middle class which was thus created was reinforced by the up-growth of a corresponding class in our towns. * * *

At the same time the close connexion with the continent which foreign conquest brought about secured for England a new communion with the artistic and intellectual life of the world without her. The old mental stagnation was broken up, and art and literature covered England with great buildings and busy schools. * * *

Dane and Norwegian were traders over a yet wider field than the northern seas; their barks entered the Mediterranean, while the overland route through Russia brought the wares of Constantinople and the East. * * * Men from Rhineland and Normandy, too, moored their vessels along the Thames. * * *"

Further, "At the accession of Henry's grandson it was impossible to distinguish between the descendants of the conquerors and those of the conquered at Senlac. We can dimly trace the progress of this blending of the two races in the case of the burgher population in the towns."

Also, "It is in William (of Malmesbury) above all others that we see the new tendency of English literature.

In himself as in his work, he marks the fusion of the conquerors and the conquered, for he was of both English and Norman parentage, and his sympathies were as divided as his blood. The form and style of his writings show the influence of those classical studies which were now reviving throughout Christendom."

Every country presents the story of this fusion of races and blood-intermixture, and India is no exception. The purity of blood or race-type claimed by the Hindus is, in fact, a myth. It was certainly out of the question during the period of the Guptas which was preceded as well as followed by the military, political and economic settlements of Central Asian hordes in various parts of India.

(*b*) Tartarisation of Aryanised Dravidians.

Taking a vertical view of history, the following important race-elements must have contributed to the web of Hindu physico-social life of the Vikramâdityan era:

1. The Aborigines (pre-Aryans or so-called Dravidians) should be regarded as the basic factor in Indian humanity both in the North and in the South. The Mârâthâ race is Scytho-Dravidian ethnologically, and Mârâthâ scholars point out the non-Aryan or pre-Aryan strain in the Hindu characteristics of Western India. President Sâstri of Bangîya Sâhitya Parishat of Calcutta in his recent essays has been testifying to the predominance of primitive non-Aryan influences on Bengal's life and thought. As for South India, the following remarks of Prof. Pillai quoted in the *Tamilian Antiquary* (No 2, 1908) are eminently suggestive:

"The attempt to find the basic element of Hindu civilisation by a study of Sanskrit and the history of Sanskrit in Upper India is to begin the problem at its worst and most complicated point. India South of the Vindhyas—still continues to be India proper. Here the bulk of the people continue distinctly to retain their pre-Aryan features, their pre-Aryan languages, their pre-Aryan social institutions. Even here the process of Aryanisation has gone too far to leave it easy for the historian to distinguish the native warp from the foreign woof."

The blending of aboriginal races with newcomers has to be recognised through all the ages of Indian history. It was not finished in the prehistoric epoch of Aryan Settlements, but is going on even now. The Himalayan tribes and the races inhabiting the forests and hills of the whole peninsula have always contributed their quota to the making of the Hindu population. Thus among the so-called Rajput clans some are descended from the foreign Sakas and Hūns, while others have risen from the native pre-Aryan races. According to Vincent Smith, "various indigenous or aboriginal tribes and clans underwent the same process of Hinduised social promotion, in virtue of which Gonds, Bhars, Kharwârs, and so forth, emerged as Chandels, Râthors, Gaharwârs, and other well-known Rajput clans, duly equipped with pedigrees reaching back to the sun and the moon."

2. Aryanisation must be regarded as the second factor in this composite structure. It is this by which the Hindus become one with the Iranians of Persia and Græko-Romans and Teutons of Europe. Aryanisation has promoted in India a "fundamental unity" of cultural ideals, but must not be assumed to have effected any thoroughgoing transformation of race. The blending of the Aryan and non-Aryan has

proceeded in varying degrees in different places; and the civilisation bears marks of the different degrees of fusion. Scientifically speaking, the term 'Aryan' implies a certain culture of peoples speaking a certain language, it cannot refer to certain blood-strains or physical characteristics involved in the use of the word 'race.' The Aryanisation of India, as of other countries of the world, should, therefore, indicate the super-imposition of a new language, new religious conceptions, new domestic and social institutions, and a new polity upon those of the pre-Aryan settlers.

3. Persianisation or Iranisation, and, along with it, older Assyrian or Mesopotamian traces, need be noticed in the early civilisation of Aryanised India. Prof. Rapson in his primer, *Ancient India*, has dealt with the political relations between Persians and Indians in the sixth and fifth centuries B.C.. Here, again, the influence may be more cultural than racial. Prof. Fenollosa suggests Mesopotamian influence upon Chinese Art of the Han dynasty (B.C. 202-221 A.D.), especially in the animal-motives. This may be suggested about India too, as has been done by Grünwedel in his *Buddhist Art.* Vincent Smith also remarks: "The little touches of foreign manners in the court and institutions of Chandragupta * * * are Persian; * * * and the Persian title of Satrap continued to be used by Indian provincial governors for ages down to the close of the fourth century."

The Persian influence on Maurya India has been described in the *Indian Antiquary* (1905). Mr. Smith thinks that some features of Maurya administration "may have been borrowed from Persia;" and hazards the conjecture that the Persianising of the Kushan coinage of Northern India should be explained by the occurrence of an unrecorded Persian invasion in the 3rd century A.D..

4. Yavanisation or Hellenisation was effected both in blood and culture. Chandragupta himself had set the example of Indo-Greek matrimonial relations. The Hellenistic Legation-quarter, at Pâtaliputra (modern Patna), under Megasthenes, Asoka's propagandism in the Hellenistic Kingdoms of Western Asia and Egypt, Kushan patronage of Græko-Roman artists, the establishment of Roman colonies in parts of Southern India as well as the contact of the Hindus with Græko-Bactrians and Græko-Parthians as enemies on various occasions, suggest more or less inter-racial as well as inter-cultural fusion. It is difficult to prove, however, as has been stated in a previous chapter, what the extent or character of the fusion could amount to. Vincent Smith does not think it was much.

5. Tartarisation of India seems to have been as deep and wide in blood as Aryanisation was in culture. It is this by which the Hindus of mediæval India became one with the people of contemporary China. The Aryans had brought civilising influences into the land of the Dravidians; but the nomad hordes of Central Asia brought only vigorous and fresh blood, and accepted the civilisation of the new land in *toto*. Possibly some primitive folk-characteristics, traditions of pastoral and agricultural life in Mongolia, Turkestan and Bactria, the rude nature-deities and superstitions prevailing in the steppes and deserts of the wild homeland, were necessarily introduced as new factors into Indian social life. It is to this common ethnic element that the commonness of some of the folk-beliefs in different parts of Asia may have to be attributed. Howorth's *History*

of the Mongols is a monumental work on the Central Asian tribes in English.

Roughly speaking, Tartarisation or Scythianisation of the Aryanised Dravidians of India, was effected in three different, but not necessarily successive, waves. The first wave was that of the Sakas, that of the Kushans the second, and the third that of the Huns. The waves overwhelmed not only the Northwest, the Punjab, Sindh and Gujrat, but the whole of Northern India, and crossed the Vindhyas also to fertilise the Deccan plateau and Konkan plains. As has been noted in a previous chapter, the Central Asian migrations into the Indian sphere of influence can be traced to about the second century B.C.. Since then for about half a millennium the stream of immigration seems to have been continuous. The Central Asians poured in either as peaceful settlers or as invaders, so that layer upon layer of Tartar humanity began to be deposited on the Indian soil.

The Saka settlements at Taxila in the Punjab and at Mathurâ on the Jumna probably as 'satrapies' of a Parthian (Persian) power, the independent Saka Kingdom in Saurâshtra or Kâthiâwâr which was destroyed by the Gupta Emperor in A.D. 390, the Kushan Empire which under Kanishka extended in India probably as far South as the Vindhyas, the Saka Satrapy at Ujjain probably tributary to Kanishka, the Kshaharâta Satrapy of Mahârâshtra at Nasik which was annexed to the Andhra monarchy about A.D. 126, "the Abhiras, Gardabhilas, Sakas, Yavanas, Bâhlikas, and other outlandish dynasties named as the successors of the Andhras" in the Purânas,—all these are instances of Hinduisation of Tartar conquerors down to the time of the Gupta Emperors.

The Hun-element in the Tartarisation of India began towards the close of the Gupta era. It was the Huns who destroyed the brilliant Empire and occupied north-western Punjab. They invaded the heart of India also and left settlements in Râjputânâ, during the fifth and sixth centuries, but were finally defeated by the Vardhanas in A.D. 604.

Recent researches of archæologists have thrown a flood of light on the fusion of the Hunnic and the Indian races. The present tendency among scholars is to believe that almost all the important ruling dynasties in Northern India between Emperor Harshavardhana (*c* A.D. 647), the host of Hiuen Thsâng, and Mohammedan invasions, were descendants of the mixed races, and may be regarded as more or less Tartarised or Scythianised.

Thus (1) most of the Râjput clans, some of which continue as Feudatories of the British Empire, should trace their pedigrees back to the Se (Sakas), Kushan (Yue-chi), and Hun (Hiung-nu) barbarians of Central Asia, rather than to the Sun, or the Moon, or the Fire-god.

(2) The Gurjara-Pratihâras of Kanauj, whose dominions under Mihira Bhoja (A.D. 840-90), and Mahendrapâla (890-905?), according to Vincent Smith, "may be called an empire without exaggeration", "were the descendants of barbarian foreign immigrants into Râjputânâ in the fifth or sixth century;" "closely associated with, and possibly allied in blood to, the White Huns."

(3) Professor Jadunâth Sarkar, in reviewing Banerji's *History of Bengal* written in Bengali language, suggests that the ancestors of the Pâla Emperors (A.D. 730-1130), who, according to Smith, "succeeded in making Bengal one of the great powers of India," and established "one of the

most remarkable of Indian dynasties," were the Râjbhats of Gorakhpur in U.P.; and that these were, like the Gurjaras, Guhilots, Râshtrakutas, Solankis, etc., descendants of the Tartar settlers.

It may be remarked, therefore, that the democratic blood of the modern Bengal bourgeoisie and the blue blood of the Râjput aristocracy are both derived from the common spring of the uncouth blood of the savage Central Asian Huns.

6. Lastly, must be mentioned the race-fusion within the limits of India herself. The constant shifting of the political centre of gravity from place to place, and military occupations of the territories of neighbouring princes by ambitious monarchs—both afforded ample scope for social amalgamation and necessarily brought about inter-provincial blood-mixture. The effects of dynastic revolutions and territorial readjustments on the social status of tribes and castes should require a separate treatment.

It is not known what the Gupta Emperors were ethnologically; but that the people over whom they ruled were a composite product there is no doubt.

To bring the story of race-mixture and culture-fusion in India to a close, I need only mention the following three important stages:—

7. Islamite Invasions under the Pâthâns (A.D. 1300-1550). These commencing with the tenth century were of the nature of previous Tartar settlements or still earlier Aryan colonisings. The conflict of the Hindus with the new-comers was certainly very bitter like that described in the Vedic literature as having taken place between the Indo-Aryans and the aboriginal *Dasyus*. But

the Indian capacity for assimilation led to happy compromises as soon as it was found that the Pâthâns meant to adopt Hindusthân as their motherland, and not exploit it in the interests of a far-off Transoxiana.

8. Saracenisation of the Indian population was the result of these new conditions. It may be conveniently described as having taken place under the powerful Moghul Monarchy (A.D. 1550-1700). This was the period of Mahometans Hinduising and Hindus Islamising in every department of life. The glorious civilisation of the age was neither exclusively Hindu, nor exclusively Mahometan, but an off-spring of the holy wedlock between the two. It was Indo-Saracenic or Hindu-Islamic. The scars and wounds of the invasion-period had long been healed when the Imperial Head at Delhi was found to inherit the blood both of the Râjput and of the Mongol, when the *Tàj Mahal*, that dream-verse in marble, raised its stately domes and minarets on the fair Jumna,—a visible symbol of the marriage between indigenous and foreign art-traditions, when language,* literature, painting, music, religious preachings and philosophical teachings, folk-lore, fairs, processions, and even the commonplace superstitions testified to the eclectic spirit of the age.

Not only Chaitanya (1485-1533) and Nânak (1469-1538), Kabîr (1440?-1518?) and Tukârâma (1608-49), the Martin Luthers and Calvins of India, but the musician Tân Sen, the emperor Jahangir, the viceroy Man Singh, the statistician Abul Fazl, and the financier Todar Mall are all embodiments of that Indo-Saracenic life-fusion. The Renaissance that characterised the 16th and 17th centuries was

* See Naren Law's *Promotion of Learning in India by Mohammedan Rulers* (Longmans, 1915.)

as brilliant as the Vikramâdityan Renaissance of a thousand years ago, and must be evaluated as the result of naturalisation of Saracenic culture in India.

9. Deccanisation (or South-Indianisation) of Hindusthân under the Hindu Empire of the Mârâthâs. This may be said to have been a powerful factor in Indian civilisation during the period from the rise of Sivâji the Great (*c* A.D. 1650) to the overthrow of the last Peshwa by the British (1818). During all previous ages, generally speaking, it was the North that had influenced the South* both culturally and politically. Since the middle of the 17th century it was the turn of the South to influence the North. It was not only the reaction of the Hindu against the Mahometan power, but also that of *Dâkshinâtya* against *Âryâvarta*. To understand the race, religion, customs, and culture of Northern India from Orissa to Gujrat or from Assam frontier on the East to the territory of the Amir of Kabul on the West during the 18th century it is absolutely necessary to analyse the social influences of the splendid Mârâthâ conquests.

(*c*) CASTE-SYSTEM AND MILITARY HISTORY.

In this connexion it may not be inappropriate to enter into a digression concerning the blood-intermixture within the limits of the Indian continent, and thus throw a sidelight on the history of castes.

It has been the custom up till now to study the caste system of the Hindus from the socio-economic and socio-

* It need be noted, however, that of the greatest thinkers of Mediæval India, Sankarâchâryya (788-850), Râmânuja (12th century), Madhva (13th century), and Râmânanda (14th century) were all Southerners; and the Northerners, *e.g.*, Chaitanya, Nânak and Kabîr, were the disciples of their systems. Besides, the influence of the Tamil Napoleons on Orissa, the buffer between Bengalee and Chola Empires, (and ultimately on Bengal), during the 11th century, has to be recorded.

religious points of view. The fundamental fact about it, however, is physical. For all practical purposes the castes are groups of human beings designed for the regulation of marriages, *i.e.*, selection of mates. The Caste-system should thus form the subject matter not merely of Economics and Theology, but also, and primarily, of Eugenics. In fact, the eugenic aspect of the castes is the basis of the socio-economic and socio-religious problems as treated by such classical Hindu law-givers as Manu.

A scientific treatment of the Caste System, therefore, is tantamount to the history of marriages or blood-relationships among the Hindus, and of the changes in their eugenic ideas. It thus becomes a part of the larger subject of Race-Intermixture, *i.e.*, Ethnology, or Physical Anthropology.

It has been shown above that the Physical Anthropology of Indian population has been powerfully influenced by the political and military history. The study of castes, therefore, has to be undertaken from a thoroughly new angle, viz., that of dynastic changes, military expeditions, subjugation of races, empire-building and political disruption. It ultimately resolves itself into a study of the influence of warfare on social and economic transformation. When the caste system is thus studied as a branch of the military history of the people of India, it would be found—

1. That the facts of the present day socio-economic and socio-religious system cannot be carried back beyond a certain age.

2. That the attempt to understand Vedic, post-Vedic, Sâkyasimhan, Maurya, post-Maurya, Andhra-Kushan, Gupta, and even Vardhana, Pâla, Gurjara-Pratihâra and Chola societies according to the conventions of the Caste-system known to-day is thoroughly misleading.

3. That probably down to the 13th century, *i.e.*, the beginning of Islamite aggressions on India, the history of social classes supplies more data for the study of *races* than for *caste*-history.

4. That such terms as Brâhman, Kshatriya, etc., have not meant the same thing in all the ages down to that period—the same term may have covered various races and tribes.

5. That it is an open question how far the four-fold division of society in authoritative works down to that time was, like Plato's classification, a "legal fiction," and to what extent and in what sense it was an actual institution.

6. Since the 13th century there may have been formed eugenic groups like those we see to-day—but not necessarily four—in fact, innumerable.

7. These groups could never have been stereotyped but must have remained very elastic—because of the changes in the fortunes of the rulers, generals, viceroys, etc., and the corresponding changes in importance of localities, tribes and families. [The kaleidoscopic boundary-changes in Europe during the last five hundred years have repeated themselves on a somewhat smaller scale in the Indian world].

8. Under conditions which must be regarded as more or less feudal, the customs were always local and were never codified into fixed cakes as in the 19th century; and hence silent intrusions of new influences through economic pressure, or violent modifications through political revolution, were matters of course. It need be recognised, therefore, that the vertical as well as horizontal mobility of the population was greater under feudal than modern conditions.

9. The rise into prominence of a certain caste through military prowess or political aggrandisement led to a certain system of social values, which was sure to have been transvalued with its overthrow by another. In this way the political and military history of *races* down to the 13th century must have repeated itself in that of *castes* since then.

10. The consequence of changes in political and military history has been what may be described as a regular "convection-current" throughout the socio-economic system, making the elevation and depression of castes exactly parallel to that of races—the leading classes of one age being the depressed classes of another, and so on. The race-history and class-history have been affected in the same way all the world over by the history of warfare.

11. In each case of socio-economic transformation brought about by military-political revolutions the new orders have tried to preserve the old "legal fiction" by affiliating themselves to the traditional orders. The dynamic principle of 'progress' has thus been in operation in each synthesis, though the statical principle of 'order' has never been lost sight of. The student of Caste-history should recognise these successive syntheses as the milestones of Hindu social evolution.

12. The economic aspect of the castes as occupational grades, and the auxiliary religious aspect which ultimately implies only the guardianship of the Brahman caste in theological matters, must be regarded as an appendix, rather than as a prelude, to the political-cum-military treatment of the subject.

13. To understand the caste-system historically it has to be clearly realised that there was no *Pax Britannica* in

ancient and mediæval times, and that warfare was a normal phenomenon with the Hindus as it has been with every race of human beings from the earliest times down to the present day. In India as in Europe there has been no generation without war.

14. Under these circumstances both the orthodox metaphysical Doctrine of *Adhikâra* (*i.e.*, intellectual and moral 'fitness' as the regulative principle of caste-distinction), as well as the *doctrinaire* Social-Reform-theory of Equality of Rights (which is supposed to be infringed by the caste system) are equally irrelevant and unhistorical. They seem to have been started by those who were led to consider the social order under peace-conditions to be the same as that under conditions of normal progress through struggle for existence.

15. (*a*) That, after all, the classes in Hindu Social life have evolved on almost the same lines as those of other peoples, (*b*) that blood-intermixture has been no less potent in Indian society than in others, (*c*) that the abnormalities supposed to inhere in the system of social groups called castes have not really existed in history, but are the myths invented by the ignorant Portuguese settlers in the 16th century, who were struck by the superficial distinctions between their own life and that of the Hindus, and subsequently perpetuated by Orientalists who have not cared to compare the actual conditions and history of matrimonial relations among the Hindus with those among their own races, (*d*) that even at the present day the scope for intrusion of new blood into the Hindu castes is *actually* not less than that in the groups of other communities; and (*e*) that a historical study for the state of things obtaining in the past,

and a statistical-comparative study for that in the present, would be the solvents for the erroneous theories regarding the origin as well as nature of the institution.

SECTION 4.

A WELL OF DEVOTIONAL ECLECTICISM—THE RELIGION OF THE PURÂNAS.

With the establishment of the Guptas at Pâtaliputra we enter modern India. The beginning of Vikramâdityan Imperialism is the beginning of modern Hindu religions. It was the age of Purânas, of Sanskrit revival, of well-peopled pantheons of deities, of spiritual inspiration as the nurse of sculpture, and of religion as the handmaid of Art. The modern Hindu of any denomination, Jaina, Mahâyânist, Shaiva or Vaishnava, can easily understand the Vikramâdityan Kâlidâsa, and parley with him without a special preparation. But the preceding Andhra-Kushans and the still older Mauryas are to him considerably antique and archaic. The currency of thought, the conventions and technique of life obtaining in the age of the *Raghu-vamsam* are almost the same as to-day, but the Hindus of the age of *Arthasâstra* or even of Aswaghosha's *Awakening of the Faith in the Mahâyâna* thought in other terms and lived in other spheres. To take a simple analogy. As Chaucer is to Shakespeare, so is Kautilya to Kâlidâsa; and as Shakespeare-cum-Bacon is to Bernard Shaw, the socialist, so is Kâlidâsa-cum-Varâhamihira to Rabindranâth Tâgore, the modern nationalist. And this as much in religion and morals as in literature and art.

(*a*) PAURÂNIC SYNTHESIS.

It has been well said that the appreciation of Milton's poetry is the last test of consummate Classical scholarship.

It may be said with the same force that the appreciation of Kâlidâsan literature is the last test of consummate Paurânic scholarship. To enjoy the merits of this art one must be well grounded in the Purânas. The religious life of the Purânas is the atmosphere of Kâlidâsa's poetry; and the Purânas (including the *Râmâyana* and the *Mahâbhârata*) are repositories of whatever had been taught in the *Vedas*, *Upanishads*, *Nirvânistic suttas*, *Arthasâstra*, *Gîtâ* and *Vedânta*. In reading Kâlidâsa we seem to be turning from the *Sântiparva* of *Mahâbhârata* to a chapter of Paurânic mythology; at one place we seem to be listening to the lectures of Manu the law-giver, at another the sublime rhapsody of the Vâlmîkian bards. Kâlidâsa wrote of Râma-incarnation, sang hymns to Vishnu, the Lord of the Universe, dipped his pen deep in the Shaiva lore, and had thorough mastery over the Renunciation-cult, the doctrine of self-sacrifice, etc., preached by Sâkyasimha. The literature of Kâlidâsa is thus the art-form of that religious eclecticism which has characterised Hindu life in every age. The sculpture of the Gupta era also bears eloquent testimony to the same toleration and goodwill between sects and denominations.

The Purânas had been growing since at least Maurya times, as Smith notes in reviewing Pargiter's *Dynasties of the Kali Age;* in the time of the Guptas they were fully recast, re-interpreted and brought up to date, as Sir Bhândârkâr suggests. The days of the Prâkrit languages had long been over. Sanskrit was now the language of culture and religious literature with all sects of Hinduism. No longer the uncouth *Vedas*, no longer the Pâli *Tripitaka* or the Prakrit Jaina Canon, but works like the *Purânas* in simple, chaste and elegant Sanskrit were the Bibles of the

Gupta age. The eclectic religion of these Sanskrit Purânas was but a representative expression of that Religion of Love which had by this time established a secure empire over the Hindu heart,—Jaina, and Mahâyâna, Shaiva and Vaishnava. We noticed the beginnings of *Bhakti*, modern mythology, *avatâra*-cult, etc., in Maurya times, and traced their well-formed limbs in Andhra-Kushan era. By the time of the Guptas they had become the A.B.C. of Hindu thought.

(*b*) Jainism

The spiritual trend of the times that can be known from the scriptures of the Jainas, Shaivas, Vaishnavas and Buddhists indicates a common belief in human infirmity, and the efficacy of prayers to a loving personal god. Sanskrit literature became one vast ocean of love and devotion. The note of *Bhakti*, *i.e.*, devotion or love, is obvious in the following extract from Barnett's *Heart of India:*

"To thee, whose footstool buds with serried beams
From gems of all god-emperors' stooping crown,
Disperser of the banded powers of sin,
Friend of threefold world, great Victor, hail.

* * *

The sins that cling from birth to bodied souls,
Fade all, and are no more, through praise of thee;
Before the fiery sunlight's serried rays
How long can dreary darkness hold its place?

* * *

Fain for salvation, I am come to Thee,
The guide to cross the forest-wilds of Life;
Wilt thou not heed when Passion's robber band
Would snatch from me thy Treasure's trinity?"

This is part of a favourite Jaina hymn, called the *Bhûpâla-stotra.* "This is addressed to one of the twenty-four Redeemers, who, according to Jaina doctrine, have appeared in successive ages on earth, teaching mankind to spare all life, even of the lowest creatures, and to hasten the salvation of their souls by mortification of the body."

That this Jainism was, like Shaivism and Vaishnavism, only one of the sects of Hinduism, would be apparent from the following account in Stevenson's *Heart of Jainism.* "It had always employed Brahmans as its domestic chaplains, who presided at its birth rites and often acted as officiants at its death and marriage ceremonies and temple worship. Then, too, among its chief heroes it had found niches for some of the favourites of the Hindu pantheon, Râma, Krishna and the like."

It is thus difficult, as has been indicated in a previous chapter, to distinguish the images of Jaina gods from those of the Buddhist, Shaiva and Vaishnava pantheons. The *bhakta* could not do without the *form* of his love, and converted religion into a handmaid of art. The lover and the artist have ever been convertible terms, because self-expression is the common characteristic of both. In the present instance, the bhaktas or artists of all denominations *expressed* the same self. The same religious imagination was drawn upon by sculptors whether for the Jaina devotee or for the Shaiva. Images originating from the same heart could not but come out with the same marks. Art could not improvise or manufacture differences where the inspiration was the same. The differences have to be made out only in a few externals.

Jainism in the form in which it is difficult to distinguish from other isms of India had a prosperous career since the beginning of the Christian era. Mrs. Stevenson says: "The faith spread over the whole of the west and rose to great prominence and power in Gujrat. We have also evidence of its activity in most parts of Southern India during the first millennium of the Christian era."

"In South India earliest literary movement was predominantly Jaina. In Tamil literature from the earliest times for many centuries Jaina poets hold a great place. The *Jivaka Chintâmani*, perhaps the finest of all Tamil poems, is a Jaina work. Eight thousand Jaina, it is said, each wrote a couplet, and the whole when joined together formed the famous *Nâlâdiyâr*. * * * More famous still is the *Kurrul* of Tiruvalluvar, the masterpiece of Tamil literature."

The whole Jaina canon was reduced to writing in A.D. 454 at the Council of Vallabhi in Gujrât. "The zenith of Jaina prosperity lasted from the Council of Vallabhi to the 13th century." Consequently when in the middle of the 7th century Hiuen Thsang visited India he saw numbers of Jaina monks in prosperous temples, especially in the south.

(c) Shaivaism

The worship of Shiva also has been handed down from earlier times and counted many votaries in the Gupta age. Specimens of Shaiva faith are being given from South Indian Tamil literature of a later date. Barnett writes:

"No cult in the world has produced a richer devotional literature, or one more instinct with brilliance of imagination, fervour of feeling, and grace of expression. Of its many great poets the greatest is Mânikka-Vâchakar (11th century A.D.)"

The following is a quotation from the Tamil Shaivite's *Tiru-Vâchakam :*

O barrer of ways of beguiling sense, who wellest forth in my heart,
Pure fount of nectar, O Light supreme, shew Thyself unto me as thou art.
Of thy grace appear, Thou clearest of clear whose home is the Mighty Shiva Shrine,
Thou Bliss transcending all states unending, O perfect Love that is mine !

"Manikka-vâchakar is the favourite poet of the orthodox Sivaite Church. Its rites inspired many of his hymns, and he has found his reward in being sung in numberless temples."

The ecstasy of a Shaiva devotee finds vent in the following verses translated by Dr. Pope from Tâmil *Tiruvâsagam*:

"Sire, as in union strict, thou mad'st me thine; on me didst look, didst draw me near ;
And when it seemed I ne'er could be with thee made one—when nought of thine was mine—
And nought of mine was thine—me to thy feet thy love
In mystic union joined, Lord of the heavenly land,—
'Tis height of blessedness."

It may be mentioned that Kâlidâsa's epic *Kumâra-Sambhavam* or "The Birth of Kumâra (War-Lord)" is a study in the Shaiva mythology of his age, and that he begins his *Raghu-vamsam* with invocation to the Shaiva deities.

(*d*) VAISHNAVISM

The Gupta Emperors themselves were the worshippers of Vishnu. Prof. Barnett in his *Heart of India* gives the following verse as characteristic of the Vaishnavite "god-ward love in utter self-surrender:"

Oh, give me a love firm-set on Thee
Janârdana, and blind to gain;
I will joyfully turn from heavenward hopes,
And on earth in the body remain.

Also,

"Dear Lord, no peer in misery have I,
No peer hast thou in grace.
This binds us twain; and canst Thou then deny
To turn to me thy face?"

In the words of the Vaishnava follower of the 'religion of love,' "what avail offerings, holy places, penances, or sacrifices to him in whose heart is the shrine of Hari's presence?"

The Imperial faith in Vishnu and the Paurânic legends of Krishna is well illustrated by an interesting incident in connection with Skandagupta's defeat of the Huns between A.D. 455 and 458. Vincent Smith narrates the story thus: "His mother still lived, and to her the hero hastened with the news of his victory, just as Krishna, when he had slain his enemies, betook himself to his mother Devaki. Having thus paid his duty to his living parent, the king sought to enhance the religious merit of his deceased father by the erection of a pillar of victory, surmounted by the statue of the god Vishnu, and inscribed with an account of the delivery of his country from barbarian tyranny through the protection of the gods."

The above interpretation of the Purânic Krishna-story has a parallel in the annals of Europe also. In the 17th century William of Orange was regarded as an *avatâra* of the Old Testament gods who had come down among the Dutch to deliver the people from the fetters of Louis XIV and thus effect an *Yugântara* or revolution in *Zeitgeist.* Thus Macaulay writes of the mission of William in his *History of England*, vol. I:

"The French monarchy was to him what the Roman republic was to Hannibal, what the Ottoman power was to Scanderbeg, what the southern domination was to Wallace. Religion gave her sanction to that intense and unquenchable animosity. Hundreds of Calvinistic preachers proclaimed that the same power which had set apart Samson from the womb to be the scourge of the Philistine, and which had called Gideon from the threshing floor to smite the Midianite, had raised up William of Orange to be the champion of all free nations and of all pure churches."

In Canto X of *Raghuvamsam* we have the following hymn to Vishnu addressed by the gods praying for His intervention in order to overthrow their enemy Râvana:

"Glory to Thee in triple form adored,
Creator, Saviour, and destroying Lord!
Each of these forms, unchanging God! is thine,
Even as the mystic triad may assign.

* * *

Omniscient Lord, but known to none art thou;
Subject to none, to thee all creatures bow.
Maker of all things, Self-existent still;
One, yet the wearer of all forms at will.

* * *

None e'er may know Thee, God without a birth
Yet born in many a mortal form on earth.

* * *

What though in scripture many a way we see
That leads to Bliss, they all unite in thee:
* * *
To those who fix on Thee, their heart and mind,
And trust in thee, with every wish resigned.
Thou art the way that leads to endless joy,
Which none can lose again, nor time destroy."

It is essential to remember that instances of a Vaishnava Shaivaising and a Shaiva Vaishnavising were as common as those of a Jaina Vaishnavising and a Vaishnava Jainaising, and so forth. Thus, declarations of the Lord like "I am Vishnu, I am Brahmâ, I am Shiva" abound in *Mahâbhârata* and *Purâna* literature.

(*e*) Buddhism Mixed up with other isms

This was the fountain at which the great *bhakta* of China, Fa-Hien, came to quench his spiritual thirst. The Celestial missionary found *bhaktas* everywhere in India. It was the era of romanticism and spiritual ecstasy—known under diverse names, Jaina or Vaishnava, Buddhist or Shaiva. If the devotees differed from one another at all, it was only in the *name* of their Love and Lord, not even in the method of approach, because the approach to Love must ever be the same. They differed probably in some externals of life, *e.g.*, as to the method of using the toothpick, or shaving the head, or as to the proper times for religious worship, ablutions, etc..

It was impossible for Fa-Hien to get a "well" of Buddhism "undefiled," as it was impossible for others to get a "well" of Vaishnavism "undefiled" or a 'well" of Shaivism "undefiled." All these isms were gushing forth mixed up with one another from the same whirlpool of devotion. It was out of the question for those who lived at the time to mark out the individual characteristics of each faith, as it is hopeless to-day for scholars in the library to dissect the special strands. The anatomist of those Religions of *Bhakti* or Heart-Culture would only succeed by sacrificing the unifying physiology of Love.

The Mahâyânist follower of the *Awakening of Faith* joined the other votaries of Love to sing one common chorus of devotion:

"We have but faith: we cannot know;
For knowledge is of things we see;
And yet we trust it comes from thee,
A beam in darkness: let it grow.
Let knowledge grow from more to more
But more of reverence in us dwell;
That mind and soul according well,
May make one music as before,
But vaster."

So the Vaishnava and the Jaina, the Shaiva and the Buddhist of the Gupta era sat at the same well of devotional eclecticism and raised "one music as before but vaster," thereby developing the Bhakti-cult and Romanticism of the Purânas.

SECTION 5.

The Age of Kâlidâsa.

(a) RENAISSANCE AND THE *Navaratna*.

It was a New India, this India of the Guptas—a new stage, new actors, and what is more, a new outlook. Extensive diplomatic relations with foreign powers, military renown of *digvijaya* at home, overthrow of the 'barbarians' on the western borderland, international trade, maritime activity, expansion of the motherland, missionising abroad, the blending of races by which the flesh and blood of the population was almost renewed, and social transformation as epochmaking as the first Aryanisation itself—all these ushered in in the fourth and fifth centuries of the Christian era a thorough rejuvenation and a complete overhauling of the old order of things in Hindusthân. The Indians of the Vikramâdityan era started their life afresh—with young eyes and renovated mentality.

Edmund Spenser dedicating his *Faerie Queene* to the "most mighty sovereign" referred to the wonders of his age as the inspiration of "merrie England:"

"Who ever heard of the Indian Peru?

Or fruitfullest Virginia who did ever view?"

To the Indians of the Gupta age also it was a veritable age of wonders. That was the time

"When meadow, grove and stream,

The earth, and every common sight"

To them did seem

"Apparell'd in celestial light,

The glory and the freshness of a dream."

Hindu tradition has ever known this era to be the age of *Navaratna* (or Nine Gems, *i.e.*, celebrities). In modern times since the publication of *A Peep into the early history of India from the foundation of the Maurya Dynasty to the downfall of the Imperial Gupta Dynasty (B.C. 322—A.D. 500)* by Sir Bhândârkâr of Bombay, it has become a commonplace with indologists to call it the age of Hindu Renaissance.

The colours, the sunshine, the bursting vitality of the spring, and the joy of life, which characterised this age would appear from the following verses: *

See, no more languid with the heat of day,
A hundred fair ones, all mine own, at play
In Sarju's waves, which, tinted with the dyes
That graced their bosoms, mock the evening skies,
When dark clouds roll along, and, rolling, show,
Upon their skirts, the lines of sunset's glow.
Stirred by their play, the gently rippling wave
Steals from their eyes the dye the pencil gave;
But quick the light of love and joy returns,
And each moist eye with brighter lustre burns.
See, as they revel in their merry sport,
Their bracelets' weight the girls can scarce support,
Well nigh o'erladen with their wealth of charms,—
Their broad full bosom, their voluptuous arms.
Look, how the flower that decked that lady's ear
Slips from her loosened hair, and floating near
The river's bank, deceives the fish that feeds
On the sweet buds of trailing water-weeds.
To meet the wave, their heads the bathers bend,
And the large drops adown their cheeks descend:
You scarce can tell them from the pearls that deck—
So pure and bright are they—each lady's neck.
Now at one view I see the beauties there,
The poet-lovers in their lays compare:
The curling ripples of the waves, that show
Her eye-brow's arching beauty, as they flow;
The two fond love-birds, on the wave that rest,
And the twin beauties of a lady's breast.

* Griffith's *Idylls from the Sanskrit.*

I hear the sound of plashing waves, that comes
Mixed with sweet singing like the roll of drums.
The peacocks, listening on the shore, rejoice,
Spread their broad tails, and raise the answering voice.
Still the girls' jewelled zones are gleaming bright,
Like stars, when moonbeams shed their pearly light.
But now no more the melody can ring
Upon those waists, to which the garments cling,
Showing their graceful forms; the water fills
The bells that tinkled, and their music stills.
Look! there a band of ladies, bolder grown,
O'er a friend's head a watery stream have thrown;
And the drenched girl, her long black hair untied,
Wrings out the water with the sandal dyed.
Still is their dress most lovely, though their play
Has loosed their locks, and washed the dye away,
And though the pearls, that wont their neck to grace
Have slipped, disordered, from their resting place.

This is a description of the Ladies' Bath fifteen hundred years before the age of Vaudevilles, Dancing Parlours and Swimming Pools. It would remind at once of the carnalism and realistic coarseness of the mediæval *Le Roman de la Rose* and of the romantic Provencal literature that grew up round the 'Courts of Love,' or of the Renaissance sonneteers of England who showed "the tender eye-dawn of aurorean love" and disdained the joys of paradise since they excluded the joys of loving.

We have no time to see specimens of the Hindu delight in " a thing of beauty," which "is a joy for ever;" but may quote the following words of Smith: "The Gupta period, taken in a wide sense as extending from about A.D. 300 to 650, and meaning more particularly the fourth and fifth centuries, was a time of exceptional intellectual activity in many fields—a time not unworthy of comparison with the Elizabethan and Stuart period in England. In India all the lesser lights are outshone by the brilliancy of Kâlidâsa, as in England all the smaller authors are overshadowed by Shakespeare. But, as the Elizabethan literature would still be rich even if Shakespeare had not written, so in India, if Kâlidasâ's works had not survived, enough of other men's writings would remain to distinguish his age as extraordinarily fertile in literary achievement.''

It has to be added that this quickening of intellectual life was not confined to Northern India. The Renaissance had begun in the south earlier than in the north. Mr. S. Krishnaswâmy Âiyangâr in his *Ancient India* places the golden age of Tamil literature in the first century A.D.. But Mr. Gover in his *Folksongs of Southern India* would place it in the third.

Nor need we linger over the sculptures* of the age, the merits of which have been attracting notice in recent years, or of the Ajanta paintings renowned in world's art-history.

The nine celebrated luminaries of Hindu folk-lore associated with the patronage of Vikramâditya were :—

1. Dhanvantari—the physician.
2. Kshapanaka—the philologist.
3. Amarasimha—the lexicographer.
4. Sanku—the elocutionist.
5. Vetâlabhatta—the necromancer.
6. Ghatakarpara—the politician.
7. Kâlidâsa—the poet.

* See Smith's "Indian Scupture of the Gupta Period" in *Ostasiatische Zeitschrift* (April-June, 1914).

8. Varâhamihira—the astronomer and mathematician.
9. Vararuchi—the grammarian of Prakrit languages.

It is an open question if these celebrities were contemporaries, like Kâlidâsa, of the great Guptas. It has been now established that Kâlidâsa flourished during the reigns of Chandragupta II. and Kumâragupta I. when the Gupta power was at its height (A.D. 390-450). His literary activity, therefore, extended during the period while the Chinese Missionary Fa-Hien was a state-guest at Pâtaliputra.

Varâhamihira belonged to the sixth century. He lived between A.D. 505 and 587. Amarasimha also might have been a Guptan. But how far they were contemporaries of the great poet cannot be known for certain. As for others in this sweet company of "strange bed-fellows," the mists of folklore are as yet too deep to allow any light upon their historic personality.

The tradition, therefore, has to be taken as an indication of the wonderful influence the Gupta age had upon the imagination of the people. We see in it the all-round intellectual activity of the period from physical science to oratory. It may also be mentioned that among these Kshapanaka and Amarasimha have been claimed as Jainas, Kâlidâsa is alleged to have been a peasant or agriculturist by family profession, and Ghatakarpara a potter. The futility of trying to understand India through the spectacles of a particular caste or creed would thus be apparent. The Indian *Vidyâs*, or sciences, and *Kalâs*, or arts, were never Brâhmana, or Buddhist, or Jaina, or Kshatriya or Vaisya or Sudra.

Another name which historically belongs to this age but has not been included in the *Navaratna* is that of *Âryabhata* (*c* 490) the mathematician.

In Varâhamihira's *Brihat Samhitâ* we have an interesting passage which indicates that the Hindus were willing to learn from anybody who could teach them: "Even the Mlechchhas and Yavanas who have studied the sciences well are respected as Rishis." Here is a confession of Varâhamihira's indebtedness to Greek Astronomy. He was not an advocate of 'splendid isolation,' but wanted to keep abreast of the times.

The *Opus Majus* of Roger Bacon, the intellectual precursor of the Elizabethan Francis Bacon, has been described by Dr. Whewell as "at once the Encyclopædia and the Novum Organum of the 13th century." So the works of Varâhamihira are not merely astronomical but sum up the whole Positive Science of the Hindus of the Vikramâdityan age. They constitute a very important landmark in the thought of Mediæval Asia.

When we speak of Hindu* and Oriental physical sciences it is again necessary to refer to Comparative Chronology. It has to be remembered—

1. That the Western discoveries—mechanical, chemical and biological—which have revolutionised world's movements and have given birth to modern life, cannot, strictly speaking, be traced further back than 1815.

2. That the Western achievements of the 18th century down to 1815 had been of a very tentative character, and that during that period both the East and the West were what may be called mediæval.

3. That the Renaissance in Europe which produced a Leibnitz, a Descartes, a Bacon and a Newton in the

* See Prof. Brajendranâth Seal's *Positive Sciences of the Ancient Hindus* (Longmans Green and Co., 1915.)

middle of the 17th century did not, after all, effect that transformation which we are accustomed to associate with the Industrial Revolution of the 19th century.

4. That the modern world should therefore be considered as only 100 years old.

5. That during this period of 100 years the people of Asia have not contributed a single truth to the culture of mankind. Asia may be said to have been expunged from the map of the world throughout the 19th century, the era of modernism. This has been the only dark age for Asia.

But the achievements of the Orientals in physical science and industry down to the age of Descartes and Newton, and even so late as 1815, have as good a place in the history of human progress as those of their Occidental colleagues. It would be quite irrelevant here to elaborate the original contribution of the Hindus to each department of mediæval science, but it may be mentioned, in passing, that among others the decimal system of notation, circulation of blood, use of Zinc in pharmacopœia, evaluation of π, and an exact anatomical system were known in India earlier than in Europe.

(*b*) Kâlidâsa, the Spirit of Asia

If it is at all necessary to single out one name as synonym for India and Hindu culture, it is not that of Manu, Yâjnavạlkya, Sâkyasimha, Asoka, Samudragupta, Ṣankarâchâryya, Tulṣidâsa, Sivâji or Chaitanya, but of Kâlidâsa the poet of the 4th-5th cent. A.D.. If it is at all possible to regard any one work as the embodiment of Indianism, it is not the *Rig Veda*, the *Arthasâṣtra*, the *Tripitaka*,

Gîtâ, *Vedânta*, *Kurâl* (Tâmil work—3rd century A.D.), *Sakuntalâ*, *Dâsa-bodha* (Mârâthi work—17th century), or *Kavi-kankana Chandi* (Bengali work—17th century), but the *Raghu-vamsam* of Kâlidâsa. And if it is required to point to single passages in this epic which may be regarded as the most convenient *Sutra* or mnemonic formula for *Indono Damashii* (the spirit of Hindusthân), these are:—

Â-samudra-kshitîshânâm
*Â-nâka-ratha-vartmanâm**
Vârdhakay muni-vrittînâm
Yogenântay tanutyajâm.

i.e., Lords of the lithosphere from sea to sea,
Commanding the atmosphere by chariots of air;
Adopters of the life of the silent sage when old,
And passing away at last through *Yoga's* aid.

These four phrases occur in the very prelude to *Raghu-vamsam* where the poet invokes the deities to help him in describing the achievements of the House of Raghu. The following English translation is by Griffith:

"Yes, I will sing, although the hope be vain
To tell their glories in a worthy strain,
Whose holy flame in earliest life was won,
Who toiled unresting till the task was done.
Far as the distant seas allowed their sway;
High as the heaven none checked their lofty way,
Constant in worship, prompt in duty's call,
Swift to reward the good, the bad appall,
They gathered wealth, but gathered to bestow,
And ruled their words that all their truth might know.

* Literally, whose chariot-tracks went up to the skies. Pseudo-scientists may read in this and similar other passages in Sanskrit an anticipation of aeroplanes.

In glory's quest they risked their noble lives;
For love and children, married gentle wives,
On holy lore in childhood's days intent,
In love and joy their youthful prime they spent,
As hermits, mused, in life's declining day,
Then in Devotion dreamed their souls away."

Here is a Hegelian synthesis of opposites—the Machiavellian Kautilya shaking hands with the *Nirvânist* Sâkyasimha. Here are secularism and other-worldlyism welded together into one artistic whole, a full harmony of comprehensive life. This is Indianism; and if 'the East is East,' this is that East.

European travellers in ancient and mediæval times were impressed by the "wealth of Ormus and of Ind" and the "barbaric pearls and gold" of "the gorgeous East." They had no philosopher like Matthew Arnold going out of his way to poetise about 'the legion,' or stylist like Kipling to write pseudo-anthropological stories about foreign races and to start fascinating theories of race-psychology. They, therefore, did not notice any abnormal mentalities in the Orient, but found activity and the joy of life scattered everywhere. The globe-trotters of the steam-age, however, begin their first lessons in Oriental lore with the dictum that "the East is East, and the West is West." They therefore make it a point to find evidences of 'Oriental Sun,' 'Oriental atmosphere,' 'Oriental lethargy,' 'Oriental intrigue,' 'Oriental superstition,' 'Oriental corruption,' and 'Oriental immorality.' To make "confusion worse confounded," historians and philosophers who ought to be able to dive beneath the surface have been misled by the theory of Schopenhauer about Hindu pessimism. Though Schopenhauer's ideas do not count for much in the present day life and philosophy of the western world, the cue supplied by him regarding the Orient bids fair to be a permanent superstition with those who should understand better.

That Hindu culture could have expressed itself in an objective philosophy of energism and positivism would, therefore, appear paradoxical to those who have been taught to know India only in her subjective metaphysics of Nirvânism and mysticism. Strictly speaking, each represents 'the truth, and nothing but the truth,' but not 'the whole truth;' for as the poet has said, "we are but parts and can see only but parts." As for the travellers of ancient and mediæval times, or the tourists and scholars of the modern world, they have certainly seen only parts, because they came to see only parts. They were *specialists* commissioned to study definite interests. Thus there have been political ambassadors like Megasthenes, commercial agents like Marco Polo and Tavernier, sightseers, curio-hunters, and sensation-mongers, newspaper-reporters who are deputed to get the 'inside view' of things, Christian missionaries who must force their gospel, archæologists whose interests, if really honest, must only be the unearthing of 'fossils' from the dead past, and others, who like all these have been born into the faith that the Oriental human beings belong to a fundamentally inferior race.

The whole India is an organic synthesis of the two philosophies. That synthesis cannot be interpreted fully by bringing about a mechanical adjustment of the conflicting reports of tourists and scholars. To unbiassed students of the philosophy of history, however, that is the only framework through which the signs of life have to be read. Besides, the synthetic race-ideal can be studied in the representative creations of constructive national imagination. Hindu Culture found its best expression in the mind and art of Kâlidâsa. For the complete view of Indian life and thought, therefore, one should turn to Kâlidâsan literature. And to do justice to it one must apply the same Method of Literary Criticism as is used in the interpretation of Dante, Shakespeare, Vondel and Goethe as exponents of their times. A part of my remarks on the *Raghu-vamsam* of Kâlidâsa made elsewhere* may be reproduced in this connexion :

"It is impossible to study it from cover to cover without noticing how profoundly the greatest poet of Hindusthân has sought to depict this Hindu ideal of synthesis and harmony between the positive and the transcendental, the *bhoga* (enjoyment) and *tyâga* (renunciation). *Raghu-vamsam* is the embodiment of Hindu India in the same sense that *Paradise Lost* is the embodiment of Puritan England. The grand ambitions of the Vikramâdityan era, its colossal energies, its thorough mastery over the things of this world, its all-round economic prosperity and brilliant political position, its Alexandrian sweep, its proud and stately outlook, its vigorous and robust taste are all graphically painted in this national epic, together with the "devotion to something afar from the sphere of our sorrow," the "light that never was on sea or land," the *sanyâsa*, *vairâgya*, *ahimsâ*, *yoga*, preparation for the other world, the idea of nothingness of this world, and the desire for *mukti* or the perpetual freedom from bondage.

This antithesis, polarity or duality has not, however, been revealed to us as a hotchpotch of hurly-burly and

* Foreword to *The Positive Background of Hindu Sociology* (Panini Office, Allahabad, India).

pellmell conflicts and struggles, but presented in a serene, sober and well-adjusted system of harmony and synthesis—which gives 'the World, the Flesh, and the Devil' their due, which recognises the importance and dignity of the secular, the worldly, and the positive, and which establishes the transcendental, *not to the exclusion* of, but only *above*, as well as *in* and *through*, the civic, social and economic achievements."

It was when this synthetic ideal of the One in the Many, the Infinite in the Finite, and the Transcendental in the Positive, was uttering itself in literature, sculpture, mythology and philosophy that Hindusthân first became what may truly be called the school of Asia. Kâlidâsa as the embodiment of Hindu nationalism is thus the spirit of Asia. Nobody understands Asia who does not understand Kâlidâsa. He is the "God-gifted organ-voice" of the Orient.

CHAPTER IX.

The Augustan Age of Chinese Culture

(A.D. 600 — 1250)

SECTION 1.

THE GLORIOUS "MIDDLE AGES" OF ASIA.

The darkest period of European History known as the Middle Ages is the brightest period in Asiatic. For over a thousand years from the accession of Gupta Vikramâditya to the throne of Pâtaliputra down to the capture of Constantinople by the Turks the history of Asia is the history of a continuous growth and progress. It is a record of the political and commercial as well as cultural expansion—and the highest water-mark attained by oriental humanity.

(*a*) ENTER JAPAN AND SARACEN.

Kâlidâsa was the harbinger of spring all through Asia. The Chinese Renaissance followed hard upon the Hindu Renaissance of the fifth century A.D.; and immediately afterwards from two wings two new actors appeared on the scene to participate in the general awakening and to add to the splendour of the Asiatic Middle Ages. These were the Japanese on the East and the Saracens on the West.

The beginning of this great epoch of Chinese history is thus characterised by Fenollosa:

"We have described the extraordinary invigoration of Chinese genius due to the sudden fusion into the Dzin and Tâng empires, apparently for the moment complete, of all hitherto separate movements and scattered elements,—Buddhist, Taoist, Confucian, Northern, Southern, Tartar and

Miaotsze. The Tâng Dynasty had come in as a military colossus in 618; but the great soldier and leader of Tâng who consolidated Chinese strength and expanded it again far towards the west, was the second Tâng Emperor Taiso (Tai Tsung), one of the greatest and wisest of Chinese rulers, who reigned from 627 to 650. It was in this great westward expansion that the introduction of Græko-Buddhist art was effected. Chinese armies and peaceful missions now marched again westward into Turkestan; and the pious pilgrim Hiuen Thsâng stopped at all the famous Græko-Buddhist sites in Khotan, Turkestan, Gândhâra and Central India, collecting manuscripts, drawings and models of every description, which were all safely brought back to China in the year 645.

Meanwhile communications by sea had been opened up with Sassanian Persia; princes and scholars of the western kingdom had been received as guests in Taiso's capital and wrote in Persian the world's first careful notes of the Middle Empire. * * * There is reason to believe, too, that the Byzantine Emperors, or their governors in Syria, had held communication with China and even implored the assistance of her powerful ruler to make common cause against Mohammed, who was just starting a conflagration on the borders of both. Taiso apparently agreed to the alliance, and his armies were preparing to advance from Turkestan to the relief of Persia, when the Saracens with Napoleonic haste, frustrated the junction by driving a wedge eastward across the Chinese path."

While reading this account one is led to think that all the conditions of the preceding Hindu Renaissance were repeating themselves on the land of Celestials. In the Land of the Rising Sun it was the brilliant Nârâ period (A.D. 710-94). And in the land of the Tigris

"By Bagdat's shrines of fretted gold,
High-walled gardens green and old,
* * *
In sooth it was a goodly time,
For it was in the golden prime
. . Of good Haroun Alraschid*."

Hindusthân had really crossed the Himâlayas. The Sanskrit *Panchatantra* was translated into Persian in the sixth century in order to be palmed down into Europe as Æsop's *Fables*, Hiuen Thsâng was propagating Hindu Culture in Far Cathay, and Japanese scholars were imbuing themselves with Hindu ideals at the feet of the Chinese Masters of Law. For a time, Hindu and Asian became almost synonymous terms. The intellectual and spiritual currency of the Eastern world was strück off in the Indian mints of thought. India became the heart and brain of the Orient.

It was the message of this Orient that was carried to Europe by the Islamites and led to the establishment of her mediæval universities. In describing the origin of Oxford, Green remarks in his *History of the English People:* "The establishment * * * was everywhere throughout Europe a special work of the new impulse that Christendom had gained from the Crusades. A new fervour of study sprang up in the West from its contact with the more cultured East. Travellers like Abelard of Bath brought back the first rudiments of physical and mathematical science from the schools of Cordova or Baghdad."

* *c.* A.D. 800.

(*b*) THE EXPANSION OF ASIA.

The chief feature in the history of Asiatic peoples in the Middle Ages is their phenomenal expansion.

A glance at the historical atlas of the world from the time of Attila the Central Asian Hun's havoc on Europe (A.D. 442-47) down to the establishment of the Ottoman Islam Empire in the place of the Greek (Eastern or Byzantine) Empire would show that, during all this period, not an inch of Asiatic soil was under foreign rule or even 'sphere of influence,' except certain parts of Asia Minor.

Rather, on the one hand, the amazingly rapid conquests of the followers of Mahomet carried the frontier of Asia to the Pyrenees mountains and converted the Mediterranean Sea almost into an Asiatic lake. The story of that Expansion of Asia is to be read best in the history of the Christian *jihâds* or Holy Wars against Islam. These Crusades undertaken by Pan-European or Pan-Christian Alliances were but attempts at self-defence on the part of the Westerners against a wholesale Orientalisation.

And, on the other hand, the avalanche of the Barbarians of Scythia kept the whole territory of the Slavs to the east of the Carpathian Mountains as a mere appendix of Asia. Princes of Moscow were feudatories and tax-"farmers" to the Mongol masters. The blood of the modern Russian reveals the story of that Asianisation.

The freedom of the rest of Christian Europe against the aggressions of Islamite Arab and the Buddhist Tartar remained precarious for several centuries. As Yule observes in his edition of *Travels of Marco Polo:* "In Asia and

Eastern Europe scarcely a dog might bark without Mongol leave from the borders of Poland and the Gulf of Scanderoon to the Amur and the Yellow Sea." This is a picture of the 13th century (A.D. 1260).

Wordsworth eulogises Venice, "the Queen of the Adriatic," as the bulwark of Europe:

"Once did she hold the gorgeous East in fee,
And was the safeguard of the West."

These lines indicate incidentally how far into the heart of Europe Asiatic sphere of influence penetrated.

The fierce contests between the Turk and the army of the Holy Roman Empire at the very gates of Vienna in later times (1529 and 1682) also point to the same fact. That account is given in *The Two Sieges of Vienna*, a work translated into English from Schimmer's German.

The contributions of Islam to European civilisation have a place in the pages of Gibbon's *Decline and Fall* and of the works of more modern specialists in Saracenic culture. I may mention also the Indian scholar Ameer Ali's luminous *History of the Saracens*.

The Expansion of Asia from the Tartar (Scythian or Mongol) side also was not a mere barbaric raid. Howorth writes in his monumental *History of the Mongols:*

"From China, Persia, Europe, from all sides, where the hoofs of Mongol horses had tramped, there was furnished a quota of ideas to the common hive, whence it was distributed. Europe which had sunk into lethargy under the influence of feudal institutions and of intestine wars, gradually awoke. An afflatus of architectural energy, as Colonel Yule has remarked, spread over the world almost directly after the Mongol conquests. Poetry and the arts began rapidly to revive. The same thing occurred in Persia under the Ilkhans, the heirs and successors of Khulagu, and in Southern Russia at Serai, under the successors of Batu-Khan. * * * The art of printing, the mariner's compass, fire-arms and a great many details of social life, were not discovered in Europe but imported by means of Mongol influence from the furthest East."

In the volume, entitled *The So-called-Tartars*, of the same work on Mongols, Howorth describes the Asiatic expeditions into Central Europe and the permanent conquests effected thereby. "This comprised the country from the Yaik to the Carpathian mountains, and included a suzerainty over Russia. * * * These various tribes * * owing more or less supreme allegiance to the ruler whose metropolis was Serai on the Volga, and the whole were comprised in the phrase the Golden Horde."

The following is taken from the Preface: "In these four chapters I have endeavoured to trace out the story of the original conquest of Russia during the Tartar domination * * * and have tried to point out how far the conquest has affected the history and the social economy of that great and interesting empire. I have also tried to show how during the Tartar supremacy the south of Russia, under the influence of a strong rule, was the focus of a vast trade and culture, and the means by which Cairo, Baghdad and Peking were brought into very close contact with Venice, Genoa and the Hanseatic towns."

The story of the Middle Ages is really the story of a Greater Asia.

Asiatic genius has ever been aggressive. The achievements of that Aggressive Asia are to be noticed not only in the victories of war but also in the "more glorious" victories of peace. It is not the purpose of this work to indicate even in brief outline the landmarks in the story of those victories; or exhibit the various threads of Hindu-Islamic intercourse, on the one hand, and of Indo-Mongol, on the other, which brought about the simple but composite web of Asiatic life. Nor would the more important contributions of the Chinese to world's culture during the most brilliant epoch of their history detain us. I shall only give a picture of the common Asiatic fountain of religious ideas and conventions which was set up under the Tâng and Sung Emperors and has since then been quenching the spiritual thirst of eight hundred million souls in *San-goku*, *i.e.*, the *three* countries, China, Japan and India. It would, however, be necessary to have before us a chronology of events for the period from A.D. 600 to A.D. 1250.

SECTION 2.

San-goku, *i.e.*, "CONCERT OF ASIA."

It may be mentioned at the outset that an idea of Asiatic unity is evident from the Japanese word *San-goku* which is a common term embracing the three peoples. Such a phrase as "So and so is *San-goku ichi*, *i.e.*, the first in the *three* regions" is very common in Japan. It indicates the Yamato consciousness of a common standard of merit and efficiency as governing the Japanese, Chinese and Hindus. *San-goku* may be thus taken to be the Asiatic equivalent of what in modern times is known as the "Concert of Europe."

(*a*) THE WORLD-TOURISTS OF MEDIÆVAL ASIA

The idea of a "Concert of Asia" may be regarded as having been well established during the epoch we have been considering. We may look upon Hiuen Thsâng as the great embodiment of that idea. The six hundred years that had elapsed between Mingti's dream and this Chinese scholar-saint's pilgrimage to India had led up to this conception which on Japanese soil became crystallised as *San-goku*.

We have already remarked that the period of so-called anarchy in China was a great period in her religious history, both Taoist and Confucian as well as Buddhist. It was marked also by the travels of Kumârajîva the Indian and Fa-Hien the Chinese. The consciousness of a common world of life and thought was greatly promoted by the journeyings to and fro of men like these. The number of such travellers during the four centuries was not insignificant. The following list is being given from Beal's account in his *Buddhist Literature in China* compiled from Chinese sources.

Wei Dynasty (A.D. 220-60)

(1) Dharmakala, an Indian. (2) Kong-Sang-Kai, a man of India. (3) Tan-ti, a Parthian. (4) Pih-yen, a man of the western* countries. (5) An-fa-hien.

Wu Dynasty (A.D. 222-64)

(1) Chi-hien, a Hun. (2) Wei-chi-lan, an Indian. (3) Chu-liu-yen, a fellow-traveller of the last. (4) Kong-sang-ui, a man of Samarcand. (5) Chi-Kiang, a man of the west.

Western Tsin Dynasty (A.D. 265-313)

(1) Dharmaraksha, a Hun. (2) Kiang-liang-lu-chi, a man of the west. (3) An-fa-Kin, a Parthian. (4) Won-lo-yan-che, a man of Khoten. (5) Chu-shuh-lan, a man of the west. (6) Pih-fa-tsu of Kong-niu (Within the River). (7) Chi-fa-to. (8) Shih-tao-chi. (9) Fâ-lih.

* India.

Eastern Tsin (Capital Kien Kang)

(1) Pi-si-li-mih-to-lo (Srimitra), a man of the western countries. (2) Chi-to-lin. (3) Chu-tan-won-lan (Dharmânanda), a man of the western world. (4) Kiu-tan-sâng-kia-ti-po (Gotamasangha Deva) a man of Cophene (Kabul). (5) Kia-lan-to-kia (Kaludaka) a man of the west. (6) Kang-tao. (7) Fo-to-po-to-lo (Buddhabhadra), a man of Kapilavastu and a descendant of Amritodana Râja (the uncle of Sâkyamuni). (8) Tan-ma-pi. (9) Pi-mo-lo-cha (Vimalâksha), a man of Cophene. (10) Fa-hien. (11) Chi-ma-to, a western man. (12) Nanda, a man of the west. (13) Chu-fâ-lih, a man of the west. (14) Kao-Kung. (15) Shih-lang kung. (16) Shih-fâ-yung. (17) Tan-mo-chi. (18) Shii-hwei-shang. (19) Kiu-mo-lo-fo-te (Kumârabodhi), a western man. (20) Sang-kia-po-ching, a Cophene (Kabul) man. (21) Tan-mo-ping, an Indian. (22) Dharmânanda a Turk (?)

Yaou Thsin Period (Capital Changan)

(1) Chu-fo-nien. (2) Tan-mo-ye-she (Dharmayasas), a Cophene man. (3) Kumârajîva, originally a man of India but afterwards of Karashar. (4) Fo-to-ye-she, a Cophene man. (5) Fo-ye-to-lo (Punyatara), a Cophene man. (6) Fá-kin. (7) Shih-tan-hioh. (8) Kih-kia-ye (Kakaya), a man of the west.

Northern Liang (Capital Ku-tsang)

(1) Shih-tao-kung. (2) Fâ-Chung, a man of Turfan. (3) Sang-kia-to, a man of the west. (4) Tan-mo-tsien (Dharmakshya), a man of mid-India. (5) Buddhavarma, a man of the west (A.D. 450). (6) Shi-chi-mang.

Sung Dynasty (Capital Kien Kang)

(1) Buddhajiva, a man of Cophene. (2) Tan-mo-mi-to (Dharmamitra), a Cophene man. (3) Kalayasas, a western. (4) I-ych-po-to (Iswara), a man of the west. (5) Sheh-chi-yan. (6) Gunavarma, a man of Cophene (A.D. 440). (7) Gunabhadra, a man of mid-India (A.D. 436). (8) Dharmavira (A.D. 420-53). (9) Chu-fa-chuen, an Indian (A.D. 465).

Tsi Dynasty (Capital Kien Kang)

(1) Tan-mo-kia-to-ye-she (Dharmajâtayasas), a man of India. (2) Mo-ho-shing (Mahayâna), from the west (A.D. 490). (3) Sanghabhadra, from the west (A.D. 489). (4) Dharmamati, a man of the west (A.D. 491). (5) Gunavati, a man of India (A.D. 493).

Southern Wei Dynasty.

(Capital Loyaug)

(1) Dharmaruchi of South India (A.D. 504), (2) Bodhiruchi of North India (A.D. 508), (3) Le-na-mo-ti (Ratnamati) of mid-India (A.D. 508), (4) Buddhasanda, of North India (A.D. 525).

Liang Dynasty.

(Capital, Kieng Kang)

(1) Mandala of Cambodia (A.D. 504), (2) Sanghavarma (of Cambodia 502), (3) Paramita (of Ujjein, A.D. 549).

Eastern Wei Dynasty.

(Capital Keng Nieh)

Gotamaprajnâruchi (of South India, born in Benares; A.D. 542)

Tsi Dynasty.
(Capital Nieh)

Nâlandayasas (of North India, 569)

Chen Dynasty.
(Capital, Nieh)

The son of the King of the country of Ujjein named Upasena.

Chow Dynasty.
(Capital Changan)

(1) Jnânabhadra (A.D. 560), (2) Jnânayasas from Magadha (A.D. 572), (3) Yasakuta, a man from Udyâna (A.D. 578), (4) Jnânakuta from Gândhâra (A.D. 588), (5) Dharmaprâjna (583), (6) Vinataruchi (of Udyâna, 583), (7) Dharmagupta (S. India, 591).

The list is not exhaustive, Bunyiu Nanjio's *Catalogue of the Chinese Translation of the Buddhist Tripitaka, the Sacred Canon of the Buddhists in China and Japan* may be referred to.

These are the names of scholars, lay as well as clerical, and Chinese as well as foreign, who settled in various parts of China to translate and propagate Indian thought during the four hundred years between Han and Tâng Dynasties. It is, therefore, natural that when the great Renaissance commenced under the unified rule of the mighty Tângs all this literature should have become the food of the master-minds of China. They got used to thinking not in terms of China alone but of the great western land of the Hindus as well. And when the great Hiuen Thsâng, "the Max Muller of his day," came back to his people, the conception of the Indo-Chinese world as a single unit became, as it were, a first postulate with them.

Hiuen Thsâng came back in A.D. 645, and It-sing, another equally famous pilgrim, went out on a tour in 671 which lasted for 24 years. His diary has been translated by Dr. Takakusu: *A Record of the Buddhist Religion as practised in India and the Malay Archipelago.* In it we get an account of no less than sixty Chinese Buddhist pilgrims who visited India in the latter half of the 7th century. It is thus not difficult to see why the Tâng epoch of Chinese history was a great age for the unity of Asia.

(*b*) Sino-Indic, Sino-Islamic and Sino-Japanese Sea-borne Trade

It was not only an age of foreign travel but an epoch of brisk foreign commerce as well with every people in Asia. In fact, the journeyings of those Asia-'trotters' were made possible through the establishment of well-laid-out routes between country and country. The routes were both overland and maritime.

It is needless to observe that the "Asia-sense" was promoted not only through the culture-missionaries, truth-seekers and religious pilgrims, but also through the commercial agents, brokers, sailors and speculative adventurers.

The sea-trade of the Asiatic peoples was, of course, facilitated by their shipping and navigation. Mookerji's *History of Indian Maritime Activity from the earliest times* throws a flood of light on this aspect of the question during the period under survey. During the Tâng age the command of the Indian Ocean was maintained by the powerful fleet of the Chola Emperors in Southern India.

The shipping was international. Both the Arabs on the West and the Chinese on the East were equally adept in using the highway of the seas. The following is taken from Hirth and Rockhill's *Chau Ju-kua:* "The pilgrim Fa Hien, the first Chinese who has left a record of a voyage from India to China (A.D. 413), came from Tamlook at the mouth of the Ganges to Ceylon to sail for Sumatra, and when in Ceylon he noted the signs of wealth of the 'Sa-po traders' on the island, and it does not seem unlikely that these foreigners were Arabs from Hadramant and Oman coasts." It is to be noted that Fa-Hien's fellow-passengers from Java to Canton were *Po-lo-mon* or Brahmans.

Further, Cosmas in the sixth century says of Ceylon: "The Island being, as it is, in a central position is much frequented by ships from all parts of India and from Persia and Ethiopia, and it likewise sends out many of its own. And from the remotest countries, I mean Tzinista (China) and other trading places, * * * while at the same time exporting its own produce in both directions."

The present position of Ceylon as the great port of call for world's shipping has thus been a historic one, coming down from the age when the Asiatic waters were navigated by their natural masters.

A history of Chinese maritime activity would show that the Celestial enterprise in navigation probably manifested itself a little later than that of the Arabs and Hindus. According to Hirth and Rockhill—"Notwithstanding the lack of enterprise on the part of the Chinese in the first centuries of the Christian era, * * * commerce by sea with south-eastern Asia and the countries lying to the west was steadily increasing through the continued energy and enterprise of the Arabs and the Indians."

But the sea voyages of the Chinese became considerable under the Tângs. It-sing mentions 60 Chinese pilgrims who in the latter part of the seventh century made the journey to India. Of these 22 travelled overland and 37 took the sea-route. The following itinerary is described in the Introduction to *Chau-Ju-kua:* " * * The port of embarkation being Canton, whence the travellers made western Java or more usually Palembang in Sumatra. Here they changed ships and taking a course along the northern coast of Sumatra and by the Nicobar Islands, came to Ceylon, where they usually took ship for Tamlook at the mouth of the Ganges and thence reached the holy places of India by land. The voyage took about three months, one month from Canton to Palembang, one to the northwest point of Sumatra and one to Ceylon; it was always made with the northeast monsoon in winter, and the return voyage to China in summer,—from April to October—with the southwest monsoon."

The "Asia-sense" of the Chinese, so far as it was developed through international commerce, was steadily on the increase during the 8th and 9th centuries, may have been a little retarded owing to the disorder following the fall of the Tângs, but revived in the 10th century "when they carried on direct trade with the Arabs, the Malay peninsula, Tongking, Siam, Java, western Sumatra, western Borneo and certain of the Philippine Islands." The more important ports like Canton and Tsuan-chou near Amoy began to have prosperous settlements of permanent Hindu and especially Moslem residents. The importance of Islam* in Chinese life during the 9th and

* It need be remarked incidentally that the Capital Singanfu received during this age Christian and Zoroastrian exiles who fled from their West Asian homes to escape the persecution of the Islamites.

subsequent centuries would be evident from the following statement: "From Chinese sources we learn that * * at Tsuan-chou, Hang-chou and elsewhere, the Moslems had their *kadi* and their *sheikhs*, their mosques and their bazaars." The institution of the Inspectorate of Maritime Trade at Canton, Kangshi (the capital), Tsuan-chou, Hang-chou and Minchou, also indicates the larger social life of the Celestials.

Chau Ju Kua was the Inspector of Foreign Trade at Tsuan-chou in Fukien in the latter part of the 12th century. His *Chu-fan-chi* or 'Description of the Barbarous Peoples' tells of what the Chinese at the beginning of the 12th century knew of the foreign countries, peoples and products of Eastern and Southern Asia, Africa and Europe. It precedes by about a century the account given by Marco Polo of Venice (1260) and "fills a gap in our knowledge of China's relations with the outside world extending from the Arab writers of the ninth and tenth centuries to the days of the great Venetian traveller." The English translation of this work by Hirth and Rockhill published by the Imperial Academy of Sciences, Petrograd, is of inestimable value to students of international commerce in Mediæval Asia.

When Japan entered upon the scene the Indo-Chinese world was expanded by the addition of a third member. The triple alliance of culture thus effected was the *San-goku*. Every Japanese thought in terms of the three regions, not of his native land alone. It was not enough, according to their conception, for any person to attain the highest position only in Japan. The most ambitious among them must have his worth recognised by China and India too. An international or Asiatic standard of science or *Vidyâs* governed the aspiration of all Japan. *San-goku* is thus a suggestive technical term contributed by the Japanese to the literature of world's international science.

It has to be observed that, culturally speaking, the heart of this Concert of Asia was Hindusthân, *Tienchu* or *Tenjiku* *i.e.* Heaven; but geographically, the heart was China. This "middle kingdom" may or may not be the middle of the whole world as the Chinese have believed it to be; but it was surely the middle or centre of *San-goku.* The Chinese received Hindusthân into their midst and then passed it forward to the Land of the Rising Sun. The first process was Indo-Chinese, and the second Sino-Japanese. It is doubtful if there was much direct Indo-Japanese intercourse. The Japanese depended for their Hinduism principally on their neighbours.

We know definitely that cotton was introduced into Japan from India. Prof. Takakusu in his paper on '*What Japan owes to India*' in the Journal of Indo-Japanese Association (1910), states that cotton was introduced into Japan through the Indians who were unfortunately carried over to that country by the "black current." The following is taken from Mookerji's *Indian Shipping:* "The eighth volume of the *Nihon-ko-ki* records how in July 799 a foreigner was washed ashore in a little boat somewhere on the southern coast of Mikwa province in Japan. He confessed himself to be a man from Tenjiku, as India was then called in Japan. Among the effects was found something like grass seeds, which proved to be no other than some seeds of the cotton-plant. Again, it is written in the 199th chapter of *Ruiju-kokushi* (another official record) that a man from Kuen-lum was cast upon Japanese shores in April 800, and that the cotton seeds he had brought with him were sown in the provinces of Kii, Awoji, Sanuki, Iyo, Tosa and Kyushu."

We hear also of Brâhman Bishops coming to Japan from countries other than China. But probably there are few evidences to connect them with India. They may have been Hindus from Annam, Cambodia or Indo-China. The principal reservoir of Indianism for Japan always remained China.

It is for this reason that we find innumerable materials for the history of India in China and Chinese literature; and materials for Chinese history in the Japanese and Chinese literature of Japan. The Island Empire thus happens to be the repository or museum of the Indo-Chinese world. It is perfectly natural, therefore, that *San-goku*, the technical term comprehending the three countries, should exist in the Japanese currency of thought.

SECTION 3.

THE "GREAT POWERS" OF *San-goku*.

The political history of China during this period falls into two divisions.

1. The Tâng Dynasty ruled from A.D. 618 to 905. Tai Tsung (627-50) is the most illustrious Emperor of this dynasty and is one of the Chinese Napoleons. He was the patron of Hiuen Thsâng.

2. The Sung Dynasty ruled over the whole Empire from A.D. 960 to 1127. In 1128 the northern half down to the Yangtse was conquered by the Tartars, who established their capital near the site of modern Peking. The Sung Dynasty continued to rule the southern half of China down to 1279 with capital first at Nanking, then at Hangchow.

The political strength and military achievements of the Tângs could not be maintained by the Sungs. But the people of China carried forward the intellectual and spiritual development of the 7th and 8th centuries down to the end of the period. So that the whole age was one of continuous cultural growth and expansion. In fact, the most brilliant era of Chinese literature, art and philosophy coincided with the last days of the Sungs.

The important landmarks in the political history of Japan are being indicated below:

1. From A.D. 552 to 710 the centre of government and culture was in the province of Asuka. This is, practically speaking, chronologically the first period of Japanese history. The most illustrious name is that of Prince Shōtoku Taishi (A.D. 573-621), who was regent for the reigning Queen Suiko. During this period the scholar Dosho is said to have come to China in 653 to study Hinduism with Hiuen Thsâng after his return from India in 645. Thus the conception of *San-goku* was forced upon Japan in her very infancy.

2. The Nârâ Period (from 710 to 794) was synchronous with the period of Tâng strength in China. The capital was removed to Nârâ near Osâkâ.

3. The Kyoto Period (782-1192) came down to the dismemberment of Chinese Empire under the weaker Sungs. The capital was transferred from Nârâ to Kyoto, which remained the Imperial seat till the beginning of the new era in the middle of the 19th century. Kyoto is thus the Delhi of the Japanese. During this period the famous scholar-saint Kōbō Daishi visited China (804-806) and came back to his native land to establish the Indo-Chinese culture on à thoroughly national basis.

The Nârâ and Kyoto periods are sometimes called the Fujiwara period because at both these centres the Fujiwara aristocracy lorded it over the whole administration. This period is of extraordinary interest to students of *San-goku*-culture, because specimens of Chinese life during its most brilliant epoch (and therefore of the Hindu also) are still preserved in the Japanese art of the age, but are lost elsewhere. Japan, thanks to her insular position like that of England, has been saved from the ravages of foreign conquests which have come upon her continental neighbours; and thus has been able to maintain intact the mediæval civilisation of Asia represented by the Kâlidâsas and Fa-Hiens of Vikramâdityan Renaissance.

5. Kâmâkurâ Period began with the establishment of the *Shogunate* or military Viceroyalty at Kâmâkurâ in 1192. The Emperor became a political cipher and remained virtually a prisoner at Kyoto until the glorious Restoration of 1868.

In India the political life of the period has to be studied in the following more important Empires:

1. The Empire of Harshavardhana who reigned in Upper India from 606 to 647. He was thus the contemporary of Tai Tsung and also of Prince Shōtoku. Hiuen Thsâng was the state-guest (629-45) of the Hindus under this monarch.

2. The Empire of the Châlukyas (550-753) in the Deccan. The most illustrious monarch of this dynasty was Pulakesin II (608-55) who inflicted a defeat on the northern Emperor Harshavardhana and thus maintained the sovereignty of the Southern Empire. Hiuen-Thsâng visited his court in 641. Pulakesin II is important to students of

art-history because some of the world-renowned paintings in the cave-temples of Ajantâ were executed during his reign, *e.g.*, those relating to Indo-Persian embassies.

3. The Empire of the Gurjara-Pratihâras at Kanauj in Upper India (A.D. 816-1194). Vincent Smith remarks: "Mihira, usually known by his title Bhoja, enjoyed a long reign of about half a century (*c* 840-90) and beyond question was a very powerful monarch, whose dominions may be called an 'empire' without exaggeration."

4. The Empire of the Bengalees under the Pâla Dynasty (A.D. 730-1175) in Eastern India. Vincent Smith remarks: "The Pâla dynasty deserves remembrance as one of the most remarkable of Indian dynasties. No other royal line, save that of the Andhras, endured so long for four and a half centuries. Dharmapâla and Devapâla succeeded in making Bengal one of the great powers of India."

A complete history of this 'great power' by Prof. Râkhâldâs Banerji written in Bengali language has been recently published at Calcutta. The Pâla age is important in the history of Tibet as having supplied her with Bengali art and Tantric* literature. Dharmapâla and Devapâla, whose reign extended from 780 to 892, were the Tai Tsungs of Bengal.

5. The Empire of the Cholas in Southern India (900-1300). The most illustrious monarchs of this dynasty were Râjarâja the Great (985-1018) and Râjendrachola

*See *Principles of Tantra* by Avalon (Luzac & Co., London); *Râmkrishna: His Life and Teachings* by Max Muller; *Kâli, the Mother* by Nivedita Longmans), and also the account of Tantric alchemy in Ray's *History of Hindu Chemistry*.

(1018-1035). The Cholas possessed a powerful navy, which led to the annexation of a large number of islands and the kingdom of Pegu in Further India across the Bay of Bengal. Mr. S. Krishnaswâmy Aiyangar's *Ancient India* is the most authoritative and complete work on Chola Dynasty and South Indian history available in English.

Section 4.

Indianisation of Confucianism.

The intercourse between India and China during this period is thus described by Okakura:

"Communication with India becomes more facilitated by the extension of the empire on the Pâmirs, and the number of pilgrims to the land of Buddha as well as the influx of Indians into China, grows greater every day. * * * The newly opened route through Tibet, which had been conquered by Taiso,* added a fourth line of communication to the former routes by Tensan and the sea. There were at one time in Loyang (Honanfu) itself, to impress their national religion and art on Chinese soil, more than three thousand Indian monks and ten thousand Indian families; their great influence may be judged from their having given phonetic values to the Chinese ideographs, a movement which, in the eighth century, resulted in the creation of the present Japanese alphabet."

Hiuen Thsâng had witnessed the processions, mystery-plays, and other folk-festivals patronised by Emperor Harshavardhana at Kanauj and Allahabad. The educative influence of these institutions worked upon his imagination; and it is likely that on his return to China he may have

---

* Japanese name of Emperor Tai Tsung.

played some part in the organisation of the popular dances, ballets and other amusements* which began to be important features of Chinese life under the Tângs.

Mr. Werner quotes from the *Contemporary Review*, (XXXVII. 123): "It was not until the sixth century A.D. that some travelling gymnasts from India initiated the people into the delights of the rude pantomimic dances and acrobatic performances of their native land." The French scholar Bazin's *Theatre Chinoise* throws interesting light on the history of games, festivals, ballets and pantomimes of China. Hindu influence is also suggested by scholars as having given the final shape to the drama which has been played in China since the time of the Tângs.

The following are the names of some of the Hindu scholars in China who helped It-sing in the propaganda work among his people early in the 8th century:

(1) Anijana, a priest from Northern India
(2) Dharmamatma, priest from Tukhara
(3) Dharmânanda, ,, ,, Cophene
(4) Sringisha, layman from Eastern India
(5) Gotamavajra ,, ,, ,, ,,
(6) Hrimati
(7) Arjun, Prince of Cashmere.

The list is taken from Beal's *Buddhist Literature in China*.

It is thus easy to understand why the whole world of Chinese letters and art should become Hinduised during their great age of Renaissance. Giles' *History of Chinese Literature* may be referred to for specimens of Tâng and Sung thought in prose and verse. The following is from

* The "No"-plays which became popular in Japan in the 14th century may have to be traced ultimately to Hindusthân.

Cranmer-Byng's *Lute of Jade:* "Po Chü-i (A.D. 772-846) is above all the poet of human love and sorrow, and beyond all the consoler. Those who profess to find pessimism in the Chinese character must leave him alone. At the end of the great tragedy of *The Never-ending Wrong*, a whispered message of hope is borne to the lonely soul beating against the confines of the visible world :

> 'Tell my lord,'
> She murmured, 'to be firm of heart as this
> Gold and enamel; then in heaven or earth
> Below, we twain may meet once more.'

It is the doctrine of eternal constancy, so dimly understood in the Western world, which bids the young wife immolate herself on her husband's tomb rather than marry again, and makes the whole world seem too small for the stricken Emperor with all the youth and beauty of China to command."

The Hindu, with his idealism of the *Satî*-institution which expresses itself in the determination of the widow not to re-marry, would easily understand this. Niveditâ's *Web of Indian Life* and *An Indian story of Love and Death* give excellent English studies in Hindu womanhood.

The result of the influx of Hindu ideas, institutions and practices was not confined solely to the popularisation of the Buddha-cult. The original Chinese ideas on every subject began also to be transformed, re-interpreted and Hinduised. The Augustan age of Chinese Culture was thus the age of a thorough-going Indianisation of China.

It must be understood that this Indianising affected not the religious sphere exclusively, but led also to the introduction of the secular *vidyâs* or sciences, and *kalâs* or arts. We have seen in the previous chapter that the Hindu Renaissance beginning with the Vikramâdityans of the 4th century and continuing through the succeeding centuries was as great in matters spiritual as in secular, economic, political and international. Influences emanating from India during this great age of China were, therefore, not likely to be one-sided. Smith's paper on Indian sculpture of the Gupta Period (300-650) may be referred to in the *Ostasiatische Zeitschrift.*

The *Journal of the Peking Oriental Society* (ii 228) is quoted by Werner:

"It remained for the authors of the Tâng dynasty to combine Taoism and Confucianism with a mixture of Buddhism, in a newly created poetry which was destined to raise literary art to a higher elevation that it had ever attained in China."

An instance of Hinduised Taoism is being given from the *Transactions* of the China Branch of Royal Asiatic Society, V. 83-98.

A Sung Emperor of the tenth century addressed the following rhapsody to Lao-tsze:

"Great and most excellent *Tau*
Not created, self-existent;
From eternity to eternities
Antecedent to the earth and heaven,
Like all-pervading light,
Continuing through eternity:
Who gave instruction to Confucius in the East
And called into existence Buddha in the West.
Director of all kings;
Parent of all sages;
Originator of all religions;
Mystery of Mysteries."

Indianism touched not only Taoism but also had a profound influence on traditional Confucianism. The Confucianism that has been prevalent in China for the last eight or nine hundred years is markedly different from the older one, and was born in the atmosphere of the Hindu Culture which prevailed under the Tângs and Sungs. Edkins has described the effect of Buddhism on the philosophy of the Sung Dynasty in chapter xx of his *Chinese Buddhism.*

About this neo-Confucianism a Japanese scholar writes in *An Official Guide to Eastern Asia, Vol. IV, China*, prepared by the Imperial Japanese Government Railways: "With the establishment of the Sung Dynasty * * * appeared philosophers who in expounding the classics brought to their aid certain cosmic and metaphysical ideas of India. * * *

Chu Hsi (1130-1200) is regarded as the founder of the Sung school of Confucianism. And whatever influence Confucianism exercised—and it has been great—in the training of a nation like Japan, must be largely ascribed to the works of this great philosopher and commentator."

Hindu *Dhyâna* or meditation is the chief characteristic of this re-interpreted Confucianism.

The art of painting as well as the criticism of that art were also being influenced by the new philosophy which finally received an authoritative stamp from Chu Hsi. The following is quoted from the section on "Art in the times of the Five Dynasties and of the Sung Dynasty (907-1279)" in the Japanese Official Guide: "Criticism, under the influence of the new subjective philosophy of the Sung period, took a fresh turn. Kuo To-hsü (in the Northern Sung Period) interpreted *Chi-yün* (life of the painting) in a subjective way, and pointed out that in the case of all kinds of painting, whether of animate or inanimate objects, the *Chi-yün* apparent in them was the personality of the painter. He said that an artist of noble character was sure to impress his personality on his production and that no skill in the technique could ever confer the refinement and grace which *Chi-yün* implied. He finally came to a bold conclusion that in true art there was no need of technique. * * * Su Shih (1036-1101) and Huang Shan-ku (1045-1105) * * * both held the opinion that the object of painting was not to make a sketch of the external appearance of things, but to give intimation of the life and power immanent in nature."

The *dhyâna*-element in art is thus emphasised in the Hindu work, *Sukranîti* (IV. iv. 147-9): "The characteristic of an image is its power of helping forward contemplation and *Yoga*. The human maker of images should, therefore, be meditative. Besides meditation there is no other way of knowing the character of an image—even direct observation (is of no use)." Here, then, is the fountain-head* of the neo-Confucianist art.

The Japanese term for *Dhyâna* is *Zen*. That this subjective philosophy of Meditation did not promote imbecility in secular life would be evident from the importance that the Buddhist scholars of Japan attach to the *Zen*-factor in the interpretation of their *Bushidō* or *Kshatriya*ism. It may be equally argued that Hindu *Samurai*-morality or Militarism was also strengthened by the element of *Samyama*, *i.e.*, temperance or self-restraint, involved in *Dhyâna* or *Yoga* discipline.

There is one fact about this Hinduisation of Asia which the most superficial student of mediæval history must notice. Indian missionising in foreign countries—

*See Laufer's *Das Citralakshana* in the *Ost-Zeit.* (January—March, 1914.)

(1) was not backed up or preceded by military, political or punitive demonstrations of any sort on behalf of the Indian States;

(2) was not carried on at the point of the bayonet or of the machine-gun or with the offer of inducements to a better socio-economic life;

(3) did not imply the direct or indirect domination of a "superior" race over semi-savage tribes or the so-called "arrested" sections of mankind.

It was, in fact, not a visible expression of Hindu Secular Power or the Might of the Indian State. Rather, the apostles of Hindu Culture consecrated their lives to the service of humanity. They

(1) adapted themselves to the manners, customs, sentiments and prejudices of the communities which they adopted as their own, thereby obliterating the distinction between alien and native;

(2) were absolutely non-political and non-commercial representatives of their mother-land, casting their lot with the "flock" which they came to tend;

(3) were deliberately accepted as *gurus* or preceptors by the first-class civilised Powers and the greatest intellectuals among their peoples, who wanted fresh light upon their problems.

Hinduising was thus the transmission of a new life and a new love from an equal to an equal. An "age of chivalry" was that.

SECTION 5.

"RINGING GROOVES OF CHANGE" IN ASIA

Prof. Takakusu makes the following remarks on Japanese Buddhism in *The Fifty Years of New Japan* issued by Count

Ōkuma as a manifesto for Japanese Culture after the event of 1905:

"It was not, therefore, a mere transplanting of the Buddhism of India, China, Annam, or of Korea, but a new and distinct form of religion. * * *

Thus Buddhism in Japan has never remained inactive or become effete, but reaction has followed reaction, and reformation reformation—a constant refining and remodelling going on to meet the needs of the people. * * * The old religion cannot satisfy thirsty souls, and this generation requires of the Buddhists not only new activities in their religion, but constantly renewed activity. * * * And if this ancient religion is to come forth into the arena of the twentieth century with fresh vigour and activity, and preach new glad-tidings to the world, it will be the Buddhism * * * of Japan."

To say that the Buddhism of Japan differs from that of China and of India, or that the Japanese Buddhism of the twentieth century will differ from that of the nineteenth as that again has differed from all previous, is to take a perfectly scientific attitude with regard to human civilisation.

A similar philosophic view about Christianity has been put into the mouth of Mr. "Little Boston" by the American humorist Oliver Wendell Holmes in his *Professor at the Breakfast-Table:*

"The divinity-student remarked, that it was rather late in the world's history for men to be looking out for a new faith.

I didn't say a new faith,—said the Little Gentleman; —old or new, it can't help being different here in this American mind of ours from anything that ever was before;

the *people* are new, Sir, and that makes the difference. * * *

* * * There was a great raft built about two thousand years ago,—call it an ark, rather,—the world's great ark! * * *

It's a slow business, this of getting the ark launched. The Jordan was not deep enough, and the Tiber was not deep enough, and the Rhone was not deep enough, and the Thames was not deep enough." * * *

"It must be done, Sir!—he was saying,—it must be done! Our religion has been Judaized, it has been Romanized, it has been Orientalized, it has been Anglicized, and the time is at hand when it must be Americanized!"

One might be inclined to smile over these outbursts of local patriotism, but it is impossible to deny the influence of Place and Race on Ideas.

Asiatic Culture is one, but is richly varied. It has grown from epoch to epoch and has changed in its transplantation from the banks of the Indus and the Ganges to the shores of the Hwang-ho and the Yang-tse, and thence again to those of the Yodo-gāwā and the Sumidā-gāwā. Unfortunately, however, scholars of the last century have been pleased to explain the whole history of Asia by such poetic and sonorous expressions as "unchanging East" or "Better fifty years of Europe than a cycle of Cathay." They have yet to learn that Asiatic history is as dynamic and as good a record of changes as the history of Europe.

Compared with the revolutionary changes that the world has witnessed since the Industrial Revolution of the second and third decades of the nineteenth century, the changes in previous five millenniums must be regarded as insignificant. It may be said that the world had not changed so much from the age of the Pharaohs down to 1815 as it has changed during the last hundred years. Thus considered, Ancient and Mediæval Europe down to 1815 must be treated as statical and unchanging, without any fundamental difference from Cathay, the proverbial land of sloth and conservatism. "Fifty years of Europe" in the 19th century are "better" than any cycle of Europe in the 17th, 16th, 15th and previous centuries.

Orientalists, sociologists and philosophers should, therefore, remember that it is not safe to take a Tennyson or a Whitman as the guide for historico-comparative investigations.

It was an altogether extraordinary state of things that Tennyson lived to see. The following remarks about his age—

"When more and more the people throng
The chairs and thrones of civil power,
    When science reaches forth her arms
    To feel from world to world, and charms
Her secret from the latest moon,"

could not be made with regard to any previous age in European history.

Tennyson's optimism was a product of the age which everywhere "rang out the old" "to ring in the new." He was writing of the "forward range" and "the ringing grooves of change," while the whole "old order" was crumbling down before his eyes, and the new order was apparently carrying everybody headlong to "that far-off divine event to which the whole creation moves."

The impulse of the age was equally potent in stimulating the imagination of Whitman when he wrote:

"The immortal poets of Asia and Europe have done
their work and pass'd to other spheres.
A work remains, the work of surpassing all they have
done."

It was an age when the New Englanders of the East coast were expanding towards the "middle West," "farther West" and "farthest West." In that colonising period every Yankee could talk glibly:

"For we cannot tarry here.
We must march, my darlings, we must bear the brunt
of danger.
We the youthful sinewy races, all the rest on us
depend.

Pioneers! O pioneers!

* * *

Have the elder races halted?
Do they droop and end their lesson, wearied over there
beyond the seas?
We take up the task eternal, and the burden and the
lesson,

Pioneers! O pioneers!

All the past we leave behind,
We debouch upon a newer, mightier world, varied
world,
Fresh and strong the world we seize, world of labour
and the march,

Pioneers! O pioneers!"

Any one in his cooler moments would see that these lines describe extraordinary conditions. The lofty flights of idealism and progressivism in the English poet-laureate of the Darwinian age and the American poet of the colonising period do not supply the norm by which to express the character of Eur-american civilisation previóus to the epoch-making changes. They cannot be *sutras* for the West down to 1815. The poet's *dicta*, therefore, should not be the formulæ with which to begin the study of Asiatic Culture. Unbiassed students of facts would find in the history of both Asia and Europe almost the same statical or dynamical pictures. Similarly the last "fifty years of new Japan" do not represent the previous fifteen hundred years.

Remarkable achievements and extraordinary successes of one's own generation may lead rhapsodists to poetise over one's race-history and race-destiny; but scientists must not forget to place them in their historical setting and read them in the light of the perspective. As it is, all the social sciences have been vitiated by poetry and race-pride during the last fifty years.

When Tennyson wrote "Cathay" he knew as much of China as we know of the moon. If anybody had suggested to him the name of "Mackay" or of "Pankhay," it would have suited the rhythm of his verse quite well; and as for readers, they would have to consult a *Dictionary of Unfamiliar Names* for 'Cathay' as well as for the others.

But a poet never errs. Therefore the verse is now the basis of sober history and the starting-point of race-theories. Thus an author begins his *Introduction to the History of England* with the following syllogism: "History is a record of changes. The Asiatic peoples have no history, because they have had no changes."

CHAPTER X.

Japanese Religious Consciousness

SECTION 1.

TOLERATION AND LIBERTY OF CONSCIENCE.

We have noticed that neither the Hindus nor the Chinese have ever been intolerant bigots. "Live and let live" has been generally their motto in matters of faith. The "individuality" which John Stuart Mill advocates in his *Liberty* may be regarded as the keynote of religious life among the Far Eastern races. Japan also has exhibited in her history the same spirit of freedom and toleration. Eclecticism and Syntheticism are the common characteristics of the peoples in India, China and Nippon. Not only geographically and historically, but also philosophically, Japan has ever been an appendix to Indo-Chinese Culture.

It is impossible to divide Hindu or Chinese religious consciousness into clean-cut, well-defined compartments, because the mentality is one organised whole. It is similarly impossible to label the different aspects of Japanese mentality according to certain stereotyped notions of Theological Doctors.

The most accurate statement about Japanese religious consciousness is the following short sentence of President Harada of Doshisha University (Kyoto) in his "Lamson Lectures" in America: "The Faith of Japan, to my mind, cannot be classified with satisfaction under any one religious system."

The relations obtaining between Shaivas and Buddhists and Vaishnavas and Jainas in India, or between Confucianists, Taoists and Buddhists in China are those that every observer notices between the various sects of the Japanese. Prof. Kumê writes for *The Fifty Years of New Japan*:

"In the present state of things the Japanese revere the *Kâmi* side by side with the Buddha, and are not very particular as to which is which."

In the same volume Prof. Takakusu has described how a new foreign and an old native faith live side by side in Japan, thereby promoting each other's growth: "These six sects (of the Nara period A.D. 710-94) having been founded soon after the introduction of Buddhism, were simply transplanted forms of the religion as it then existed in China, and were not well adapted to the condition of the Japanese nation. * * *

* * * It is true both sects (of the Kyoto period) were brought from China, but their doctrines were greatly modified to suit the Japanese, and, in order to adapt Buddhism to the new country, Saichō* and Kukai (Kōbō Daishi) freely admitted all the existing gods of Japan as incarnate forms of one or other of the Buddhas and treated them as such.

Almost all the principal Shintō shrines had some Buddhist priests attached to them, to whom the performance of half of the religious rites was entrusted."

Japanese religious consciousness would thus appear to be made of the same stuff as the Hindu and the Chinese.

* Both went to China in A.D. 804, Saichō came back in 805, Kōbō Daishi in 806.

In spite of differences in language and probably in race, the unity of mind is quite obvious. Freedom of conscience is the common watchword evolved in the religious history of the three peoples.

Writing about Michizane Sugawara, the most distinguished Japanese Confucianist of the Kyoto period (A.D. 704-1182), Prof. Inouye remarks in *The Fifty Years of New Japan*:

"A follower of Confucius, on the one hand, he was a worshipper of Buddhism on the other, and, as a result, the moral principles of loyalty and filial piety, and the religious doctrines of renunciation and *Nirvâna*, occupied their places in his mind without the least conflict or unity—thus evidencing that in those days even a man of his scholarship, not to speak of other men of lesser learning, did not venture to found views of life and of the world exclusively upon the basis of Confucianism."

Dealing with the Japanese Confucianism of the next, *i.e.*, Kâmâkurâ period, the same scholar refers to the influence of the Sung school of Chinese learning at Kyōtō and other centres in Japan. The Sung Confucianism differs from the original Confucianism, as has been indicated in the preceding chapter. "During the Sui and Tâng dynasties, Buddhism predominated throughout the Chinese Empire, and eventually almost stifled Confucianism. * * * Among a great many Confucianists of the Sung dynasty, Chutsze (A.D. 1130-1200), above all, grasped the spirit of Buddhism, and using it as framework, clothed it with the flesh and blood of Confucianism."

The Sung school of learning introduced into Japan was thus "a new form of the exposition of Confucianism with some admixture of Buddhist elements."

Even Shōtoku, the first great man of Japan, was a profound eclecticist. He was at once Chinese and Hindu—Confucian and Buddhist. A spirit of synthetic assimilation marks the Japanese race in the very first Act of its history.

It would thus appear that the "Doctrine of Infallibility" has seldom been the curse of the Far Eastern nations. Theirs has been the Doctrine of Love. They have kept their head and heart always open to new impressions and new emotions. The spiritual history of the *San-goku* is not therefore the record of dogmas or formulas, or creeds or so-called 'articles of faith.' It is an account of evolution from life-experience to life-experience. It presents a series of landmarks, each of which is a synthesis between Culture and Faith. These syntheses have been born organically out of the compromise between the brute-in-man and the god-in-man in the different stages of culture-history. Asiatic mentality, therefore, has a place for thousand and one heterogeneous elements in its scheme of attitudes to nature, man, and God. It is not at all perturbed by the apparent inconsistencies which are inevitable to human beings, but reconciles and harmonises them all in the grand crucible of Life.

The following is the confession of a modern Japanese *Kâmi* Professor in the *Fifty Years:*

"In what religion, then, do I believe? I cannot answer that question directly. I turn to the Shintō priest in case of public festivals, while the Buddhist priest is my ministrant for funeral services. I regulate my conduct according to Confucian maxims and Christian morals. I care little for external forms, and doubt whether there are any essential differences, in the *Kâmi's* eyes, between any of the religions of the civilised world."

This is the spirit of Asia. Johnston in his *Buddhist China* gives the following quaint little story of a certain sixth century Chinese scholar named Fu Hsi: "This learned man was in the habit of going about dressed in a whimsical garb which included a Taoist cap, a Buddhist scarf, and Confucian shoes. His strange attire aroused the curiosity of the Chinese emperor of those days, who asked him if he were a Buddhist. Fu Hsi replied by pointing to his Taoist cap. 'Then are you a Taoist?' said the Emperor. Fu Hsi again made no verbal answer, but pointed to his Confucian shoes. 'Then are you Confucian?' said the emperor. But the sage merely pointed to his Buddhist scarf."

And as for the polytheistic Hindu, he knows that Krishna the Vaishnava male-deity is none other than Kâlî the terrible war-goddess of the Shâktas, and that Brahmâ, Vishnu and Shiva are one and the same. The attitude of reconciliation could no farther go.

SECTION 2.

SHINTŌ, THE SO-CALLED *Swadeshi* RELIGION.

Like Minerva born *cap-a-pie* from the brain of Zeus, Japan was born in panoply out of Indo-Chinese life. We do not see the dawn or rising sun of civilisation in this 'Land of the Rising Sun.' Our almost very first acquaintance with the Yamato race is in what may be called a midday condition. The very first protagonist in the drama of Japanese history is the noble personality of Prince Shōtoku Taishi. This regent (A.D. 593-621) for Empress Suiko does not seem to be the representative of a young civilisation or an infant race. He embodies in his life and conception the maturest products of several millenniums of culture-history. On the one hand, in his celebrated *Constitution* he summarises for the land of the *Kâmi* whatever has come down in the land of Confucius from the earliest times down to the sixth century A.D.. On the other, he propagates among his countrymen the philosophy of the land of Sâkyasimha from *Rigveda* to *Raghu-vamsa*. The infancy of Japan is thus to be studied not in Dai Nippon itself, but, far away from Asukâ and Nârâ, on the banks of the Hoangho and the Yangtse and the Indus and the Ganges. All the preparatory work had been done for this insular people in the "green rooms" of the Continent as that for the Americans in Europe. The whole history of Asia down to the sixth century A.D. may be taken as the preface or fore-word to the study of Japanese civilisation.

In Japan, however, there has been a tendency among extreme nationalists to boycott the *continental* faiths, Confucianism and Buddhism, and adumbrate instead a pure Yamato religion. Shintō is this *swadeshî* (to use an Indian term) or "country-made" religion of the Japanese. With regard to this faith two important theories have been started:

(1) That Shintōism is nothing but ancestor-worship.

(2) That Shintōism is the original faith of the Yamato race—not derived from, or connected with, the religions of other peoples.

Both these theories are unhistorical, and neither can stand the criticism of the Comparative Method.

For any account of the archaic or prehistoric life in primitive Japan we must have recourse to the earliest documents of Japanese literature. Indigenous tradition has known the following three works to be the oldest:

1. *Kojiki* or "Records of Ancient matters" down to A.D. 500. This work was completed in A.D. 712.

2. *Nihongi* or "Chronicles of Japan from the earliest times down to A.D. 697." The alleged date for its completion is A.D. 720.

3. *Yengishiki* or "Institutes of the period Yengi" (A.D. 901-23). In this work we get the *Norito*, etc., prayers and rituals of Shintō cult. These were written down for the first time about this time but must have existed in previous ages.

A mere glance at the dates would lead to the presumption that the originality claimed for the matter chronicled for the first time about that period is out of the question. Korean Buddhism had invaded Japan at least two centuries before the completion of *Kojiki;* since then the great Shōtoku Taishi had introduced continental culture with remarkable avidity among his compatriots. Besides, it was now the heyday of the Nârâ period—an epoch of constant intercourse between Japan and the China of the mighty Tângs.

As for the unrecorded Chinese influence on primitive Japan, Kakasu Okakura writes in *The Ideals of the East:*

"We received Hang art from China, and were even perhaps acquainted with Chinese literature, long before Wani the Hakushi, the Korean scholar, came to expound Confucian texts. That there was a prior stream of influence is attested by the numerous inscriptions in Chinese. * * * Thus in Japan, as in China, Confucianism provided the soil on which the seed of Buddhism afterwards fell."

Internal evidences also betray foreign influences on the earliest Japanese literature. Chamberlain remarks in the preface to his translation of the *Kojiki:*

"It is of course not pretended that even those 'Records' are untouched by Chinese influence; that influence is patent in the very characters with which the text is written. * * * In the traditions preserved and in the customs alluded to, we detect the early Japanese in the act of borrowing from China and perhaps even from India."

About the *Nihongi* Chamberlain says :

"Not only is the style completely Chinese, * * * but the subject matter is touched up, re-arranged and polished, to make the work resemble a Chinese history. * * Chinese philosophical speculations and moral precepts are intermingled with the cruder traditions that had descended from Japanese antiquity."

Aston speaks about the *Nihongi :*

"Chinese ideas and traits of Chinese manners and customs are frequently brought in where they have no business. In the very first paragraph we have an essay spiced with Chinese philosophical terms which read strangely incongruous as a preface to the native cosmogonic myth. * * * We hear continually of the Temples of the Earth and of Grain, a purely Chinese metaphor for the State. * * * In one case the author has gone so far as to attribute to the Emperor Yûriaku a dying speech of several pages, which is taken with hardly any alteration from a history of the Chinese Sui dynasty, where it is assigned to an Emperor who died 125 years later."

Under these circumstances it is difficult to assert categorically how much of the original literature of Japan is pure *swadeshî* and how much foreign. Consequently it is not safe to regard the religious beliefs and practices embodied in it, viz., the *Kâmi*-myths or Shintō, as exclusively

Yamato. Continental influence on *Kâmi*-cult is probably very considerable.

The other theory of the Shintō Revivalists is that their faith recognises only one cult, viz., that of ancestors. It is alleged that ancestor-worship is the sole feature of Shintōism, and that it is the exclusive characteristic of the Yamato race. But even a superficial acquaintance with the three important documents mentioned above, the *Vedas* of Shintōism, is sufficient to convince any one that ancestor-worship occupies really a very insignificant part in the whole *Kâmi*-literature.

The word *Kâmi* itself is very comprehensive and includes much more than what mere ancestor-cult would imply. We get the following in Motoori's *Kojikiden*, Vol. I.:

"The term *Kâmi* is applied in the first place to the various deities of Heaven and Earth who are mentioned in the ancient records, as well as to their spirits which reside in the shrines where they are worshipped. Moreover, not only human beings, but birds and beasts, plants and trees, seas and mountains, and all other things whatsoever which deserve to be dreaded and revered for the extraordinary and pre-eminent powers which they possess are called *Kâmi*. They need not be eminent for surpassing nobleness, goodness or serviceableness alone. Malignant and uncanny beings are also called *Kâmi*, if only they are objects of general dread."

The following is the opinion of Aston in his *Shintō, the Way of the Gods*:

"The importance of the deification of human beings in Shintō has been grossly exaggerated both by European scholars and by modern Japanese writers.

* * * "It has comparatively little worship of human beings. In the *Kojiki*, *Nihongi*, and *Yengishiki* we meet with hardly anything of this element."

It is not correct, therefore, to regard Shintō and ancestor-worship as convertible terms. It may be remembered that Confucius' teachings also have been wrongly classed as purely positivistic or agnostic.

Even if ancestor-worship be a principal characteristic of the *Kâmi*-cult, it is equally so of the pre-Confucian and the Vedic, as we have noticed in Chapter II..

SECTION 3.

THE CULT OF WORLD-FORCES IN THE LAND OF *Kâmi*.

According to Aston, Shintō is "based much more on the conception—fragmentary, shallow and imperfect as it is —of the universe as sentient * * * It springs primarily from gratitude to, and, though in a less degree, fear of, the great natural powers on which our existence depends."

Further, "the humanisation of nature-deities is reflected in the vocabulary of Shintō. * * * The rhetorical impulse to realise in its various phases the human character of the nature-deities of Shintō has produced a number of subsidiary personages who are attached to them as wives, children, ministers, or attendants. Some of these are also nature-deities."

Harada gives the following account in his *Faith of Japan*:

"Shintō has neither founder, nor dogma, neither a creed nor system. Its name, 'the way of the gods,' was applied to a group of certain undefined beliefs, in order to disitnguish it from other religions. * * *

Shintō was at first a nature-worship to which was added later the worship of deified men. * * *

Shintō as a popular religion is divided into thirteen different sects some of which are further subdivided. * * * Practically all of them are polytheistic in belief; but the principal deities vary according to the different sects. Almost all of them worship the three deities of creation. * * * In addition to these deities, all Shintōists reverence all and every one of both major and minor deities in the shrines and temples—eight hundred myriads or numberless in the whole empire. * * * In many sects superstitions and obscene practices mingle with naïve and innocent beliefs.

There are undeniable traces of nature-worship in Japanese mythology. We find a sun-goddess, a moon-god, a mountain-god, a sea-god, an earth-god, a wind-god, etc., associated with the various phenomena of nature. It is safe to say that Naturism was the primitive faith of the Japanese. * * *

In A.D. 901 * * * the number of deities worshipped was 3,132. * * * The deities worshipped by the Japanese might be roughly grouped as (1) stellar bodies, (2) the elements of earth, air, fire and water; (3) natural phenomena; (4) prominent natural objects, as mountains, rocks, trees and caverns; (5) men; (6) animals; and (7) manufactured objects: in short, anything conspicuous or exalted. Not infrequently the people worship *Kâmi* of which they know absolutely nothing as to nature, origin or being. 'What god we know not, yet a god there dwells.' * * * Japan has always been polytheistic."

The above descriptions would show that *Kâmi*-cult or Shintō repeats almost all the characteristics we have described as common to Vedic India and pre-Confucian China and also to Folk-India and Folk-China of all ages. Probably the idea of *Ekam* or *Shângti*, *i.e.*, the One Supreme Being, was not developed by the primitive Japanese or was not transplanted on Japanese soil from the continent. It is also mentioned by Aston that the personifications in ancient Japan were rather weak—not to be compared with those characteristic of Indo-Aryan race-genius. But, otherwise, Japanese religious consciousness would appear to be similar to the Indo-Chinese.

Ancestor-cult is only one of the many items of the pluralistic god-lore common to the three peoples.

Not only in the pluralistic Cult of the Nature-Energies do we notice the existence of Hindu and Chinese characteristics among the ancient Japanese. The ordinary details of socio-religious life also point to the same unity. Says Aston:

"Dreams evidently were credited with great importance, the future being supposed to be foretold in them, and the will of the gods made known. * * *

Some of the gods dwelt here on earth, or descended hither from the Heavens and had children by human women. * * *

The gods occasionally transformed themselves into animals and at other times simple tangible objects were called gods—or at least they were called *Kâmi*. * * *

Conciliatory offerings made to the gods were of a miscellaneous nature. * * *

The people offered the things by which they themselves set most store. * * *

Conversations with the gods are detailed. * * * A number of very ancient prayers * * * consist mostly of declarations of praise and statements of offerings made, either in return for favours received or conditionally on favours being granted. * * *

Priests are spoken of in a few passages. * * * The profession soon became hereditary, according to the general tendency in Japan towards the hereditability of offices and occupations. * * *

We hear also of charms, * * * herb-quelling sabre, * * * tide-flowing jewel. * * * Divination by means of the shoulder-blade of a stag was a favourite means of ascertaining the will of the gods.''

The folk-religion and so-called superstitions of the Taoists, Confucianists, Vedists and Shintōists are thus the same. Students of Cultural Anthropology need take note of this.

Further particulars by which the Hindu becomes one with the Shintōist are being given from Aston's work:

''Some artificial inanimate objects of worship are worshipped for their own sakes as helpers of humanity. The fire-place is honoured as a deity. Potters at the present day pay respects to their bellows, which are allowed one day of rest annually and have offerings made them. The superstitious Japanese house-wife still, on the 12th day of the 2nd month, gives her needles a holiday, laying them down on their side and making them little offerings of cakes, etc. * * * At the time of the spring equinox there is a festival in India called *Śrī-panchamī*, when it is incumbent on every religious minded person to worship the implements or insignia of the vocation by which he lives.''

The most interesting point is the very name "Shintō," which means the *tō* or "way" of *shin*, *i.e.*, gods. The ancient faith of Japan is thus designated by the same term as is used to describe the ancient religion of the Celestials. The *Tō* of the Yamato is the *Tao* of the Chinese (Confucianist as well as Taoist); and both are equivalents of the *Rita* of the Hindu. All the three terms mean the same thing—the Way, the Path, the Order, the Permanent Truth, the Cosmic System. The religions of the three peoples are thus fundamentally the same and may be described by one term, *e.g.*, *Sanâtanism* or *Taoism* or *Shintōism*.

The following lines from Kumê's paper in *The Fifty Years of New Japan* may be adduced in evidence of the essential unity of Hindu, Chinese and Yamato faiths here indicated:

"Under a mystical symbol in the *Yi-king*, the Chinese 'Book of Changes,' Confucius remarks that Shintō (*i.e.* the Divine Way of Heaven) arranges the four seasons: 'The sages of yore, therefore,' says he, 'taught people according to the divine way (*Shin-tō*), and there was peace on earth. * * * Shintō in this primitive sense is, therefore, not peculiar to Japan.' 'Buddhism is a Shintō,' says Chisung, a Chinese monk, 'a Shintō with a deeper conviction.'"

Shintō as interpreted in these lines means the very thing that the Vedic *Rita* does, as we have seen in chapter II.. Asiatic religious consciousness has thus evolved everywhere the same idea of "Cosmic Order" or "Permanent Way" as the keystone of man's spiritual life. Pre-Buddhist Japan, if it is at all historically possible to use such an expression, pre-Buddhist China and pre-Buddhist India are, therefore, three expressions of a common mentality. Even without Buddhism Asia would still be one.

SECTION 4.

THE THREE-FOLD BASIS OF ASIATIC UNITY.

Asiatic Mind is, therefore, one. This unity rests on a common psychology supplying a fundamental basis. That foundation of Asiatic consciousness may be said to consist in three conceptions:

First is the conception of the *Tāo*, the *Tō*, the *Michi*, the *Rita*. The Chinese, the Japanese and the Hindus consciously as well as unconsciously govern their life-relations according to a postulate. They have a living faith that there is an Eternal Order, a *sanâtana* way, regulating the course of the diverse members of the Universe (including Nature and Man). The Cult of World-Forces is the common bed-rock of Asiatic spiritual institutions manifesting itself in and through a rich diversity.

Second is the conception of Pluralism. The Chinese, the Japanese and the Hindus are essentially pluralists in religious beliefs. Their pluralism is a corollary to their cult of the World-Forces or Nature-Powers. These eight hundred millions of human beings are thus fundamentally polytheists. It is impossible for Nature-worshippers to be sincere monotheists. They would never, in fact, care to define their exact position. Outsiders can vaguely guess that they are polytheistic from one point of view and monotheistic from another, or to use a bit subtler phraseology, *heino*theistic from the one and *pan*theistic from the other.

One of the great superstitions of the modern age has been the glorification of a so-called monotheism.

Monotheism has been awarded by scholars the place of honour in the schedule of religious systems. It is supposed to be the ideally best system. Students of comparative mythology and comparative religion have, therefore, managed to detect in their favourite Indo-Aryan lore grand conceptions of monotheistic faith. Asiatic scholars also in their anxiety to be abreast of the modern spirit have fallen an easy prey to this superstition.

Taking the cue from European students, Asiatic students have been tempted to catalogue the faiths of the Confucianists, Taoists, Vedists, Buddhists, Shaivas, Vaishnavas, Shintōists and others as monotheistic. Nothing can be farther from the truth. A preconceived theory or the imagination of closet-philosophers cannot give the lie to facts.

Not only in Asia, but all over the world, man has ever been a polytheist. Monotheism is a psychological absurdity. Both the physical organism and the nervous system of man predispose him to be a polytheist. Pluralism is the debt that every human being must pay to the flesh, the sense-organs;—it is almost a physiological necessity. Constituted as man is, he cannot afford to be a monotheist except on occasions of abstract intellectual discussion.

It is a fact that man is a pluralist in every worldly field. He is a pluralist in all his social relations—economic, political and even domestic. In governmental matters no man nowadays believes in one-man rule. The economist has declared: "There is a limit to each want, but there is no limit to the *variety* of wants." And this doctrine of variety is corroborated by the evidences of Biology and medical science. So far so that Ibsenism is now being preached from house-tops by more than one Bernard Shaw in Europe and more or less actually practised everywhere.

And people in the land of *Democratic Vistas* have been oscillating between the Scylla of "Free Love" and the Charybdis of Polygamy.

The poet has said—"A child is a plaything for an hour." As a matter of fact, not only the child, but all the greatest things loved by man and woman are playthings only "for an hour." It would be the torment of a hell to live under the perpetual domination of any one idea, any one person, any one institution.

If in all affairs that affect the most vital interests of life man has been a pluralist, how is it that in the other-worldly affairs alone he is an advocate of monism, and the more concrete monotheism? The only explanation seems to be that he is sincere in his worldly beliefs, but a hypocrite in other-worldly matters; or probably he is really interested in those things but quite indifferent with regard to these.

It may be asked—"Is there no unity underlying the psycho-physical system of human beings?" The reply is that this unity of individual personality is an abstraction, to which the Tāo, the *Rita*, the *Michi*, the Way, the One, the Eternal, the *Ekam*, *Shāngti*, Brahma, Oversoul, God and other monistic abstractions of metaphysics may be said to correspond. But, for all practical purposes, man must be treated not in the singular number but in the plural—as a composite bundle of sensations, perceptions, emotions, volitions, pleasures, pains, prejudices, superstitions, attitudes, relations, etc.. And if there is to be a system of religious ideas, beliefs or faiths, it must have to be essentially composite, pluralistic, polytheistic—with a monistic or monotheistic under-current. This is what the Confucianists, Taoists, Vedists, Upanishadists, Buddhists, Shaivas, Shintōists and others have conceived in Asia.

The third basis of Asiatic Mentality is the spirit of Toleration or the conception of "peace and good-will to all mankind." Toleration follows as a matter of course from the conception of Pluralism. This is, as it were, a 'second nature' to the polytheistic Hindus, Chinese and Japanese. It has been well-said that "monotheistic Gods are jealous gods." Polytheistic peoples, on the contrary, are habituated to accord a warm reception to every new deity into their pantheon. Jealousy, bigotry and fanaticism are not the stuff out of which the polytheistic head and heart are made. They are filled with the idea of "good in everything" and the milk of human kindness. What Socialism is in the economic sphere, what Republicanism is in the political world, that is Polytheism or the Cult of the Many in matters spiritual or religious. Each has for its motto the individualistic doctrine of *laisser faire*, non-intervention, or creation of opportunities for all.

The synthesis between the one and the many, the spirit and the matter, the transcendental and the positive, the infinite and the finite, the universal and the particular, on the one hand; and the toleration and encouragement of diversities, angularities, discrepancies and inconsistencies, on the other,—these are the outcome of this triple foundation of Asiatic consciousness. We have been led up to this by the inductive study of the facts and phenomena of the socio-religious world in India, China, and Japan.

It is this psychological groundwork that makes Asiatic Unity a philosophical *necessity* in spite of ethnological and linguistic diversities. The unity is thus more fundamental than has been hitherto recognised by historians. The intercourse between the members of the *San-goku* established by Buddhistic missionising or by commercial activity and diplomatic relations has only supplied additional connecting links. But the chief point to be noticed is that, Buddhism or no Buddhism, international relations or no international relations, the three nations of Asia have had a common mentality. That commonness is deeper than what can be supplied by actual coming and going—in fact, *absolute*, as contrasted with the *relative*, which is born of political or commercial contact. The *relative* unity may disappear through changes in the diplomatic grouping of Powers, as it has done so often in history, but the *absolute* psychological unity can perish never.

CHAPTER XI.

Sino-Japanese Buddhism and Neo-Hinduism

Section 1.

The Alleged Extinction of Buddhism in India.

The name Buddha either as that of the Great Teacher of the sixth century B.C. or as that of a God has not been much in vogue among the followers of what is called Neo-Hinduism, *i.e.*, those who accept as their Bibles the *Purânas* and *Tantras*. It has, therefore, been held among Orientalists that Buddhism whether as *Hînayânism* or as *Mahâyânism* is extinct in India, the land of its birth.

This is a very superficial and erroneous view of the actual state of things. For, taking the evolutional view of Sociology, it would appear that Buddha has been immortal in Indian consciousness both as a teacher and as a divinity. In the first place, Hinayânism, *i.e. Nirvânism* or Cessation-of-Miseryism, or the Doctrine of Renunciation or Self-sacrifice, or Philanthropy and Social Service, or Asceticism and Monasticism, is still practised by the Hindus who do not call themselves Buddhists as much as by the professed Hînayânists of Ceylon, Burma, and Siam. Secondly, Mahâyânism, which alone I have called Buddhism, as the worship of the deities named Buddha, Avalokiteswara, etc., is as great a living religion of the modern Hindus who have no Buddha in their pantheon as of the Buddhists of Tibet, Mongolia, China and Japan.

Let as apply what is known as the *philosophical method* to the elucidation of this problem. If the deities of the neo-Hindu pantheon, male and female, were catalogued and studied alongside of the "Gods of Northern Buddhism," *i.e.*, the so-called Buddhistic deities of trans-Himâlayan Asia, it would appear

1. that in many cases, the same deity exists in all the countries under different names.

2. that the purposes of invocation and the modes of worship are more or less identical.

3. that the folk-ideas associated with the deities and the efficacy of worshipping them do not practically differ among these peoples.

4. that deities which seem to be special to India, China or Japan, having no analogues in the sister countries, are new creations adapted to local conditions, but easily assimilated to the entire system in each.

5. that if the Japanese and Chinese mythologies have any claims to be called Buddhistic, so do the Paurânic and Tântric of the Indians, though they practically ignore the name of Buddha.

Besides, a *historico-comparative* study of the mythologies of the races of the *San-goku* would bring out three important factors which have contributed to the building up of each:

1. The Cult of World-Forces common to the Vedists (*Rita*ists), pre-Confucian Chinese (Tāoists) and the worshippers of *Kâmi* (Shintōists).

2. The Religion of Love and Romanticism which grew out of the first. This was born almost simultaneously in India and China as the worship of saints, *avatâras*, heroes, Nature-Powers, etc., with the help of images; and transferred to the Land of the *Kâmi* in the very first stage of its history, where it found a most congenial soil, and where the race-consciousness might have developed it independently.

3. The Religion of the Folk which was the parent of the first two has ever been active in creating, adapting, and re-interpreting local and racial myths of the three countries down to the present day.

The Gods and Goddesses of the Purânas and Tantras are the joint products of all these factors; so, too, are the Gods and Goddesses of Buddhist China and Buddhist Japan. The present-day deities of the Hindus owe their parentage to the Mahâyânic cult of mediæval Hinduism and are historically descended from the Gods of 'Northern Buddhism' in the same way as the pantheons of modern Japan and China continue the tradition of the 'Hinduism of the Buddha-cult.'

Thus, both philosophically and historically, Neo-Hinduism and Sino-Japanese Buddhism are essentially the same. The Vaishnavas, Shaivas and Shâktas of India should know the Chinese and Japanese Buddhists as co-religionists. Similarly the Sino-Japanese Buddhists should recognise the neo-Hindus of India as Buddhists.

The alleged "strangling" of Buddhism by Hindus is a fiction and cannot stand the criticism of the philosophico-historical method. The disappearance of Buddha and his host from present-day Indian consciousness belongs to the same category as that of Indra, Varuna, Soma, Pushan and other Vedic deities. And if in spite of this the Hindus have a right to be called followers of the Vedas, they have equal claims to be regarded as Buddhists (both Hinayâna and Mahâyâna).

Section 2.

The Bodhisattva-cult in China, Japan and India

(a) Ti-Tsâng

The learned historical articles on "The Bodhisattva Ti-tsâng (Jizo) in China and Japan" by M. W. De Visser in the *Ostasiatische Zeitschrift* (July, 1913 to December, 1914) supply enormous facts from which it would be obvious to students of Indology that the so-called Buddhist gods of China and Japan and the gods of neo-Hinduism in India are substantially the same. There are slight differences in name and function, in features of images and modes of worship. But people used to the mythology of the Purânas would notice a family-likeness and even analogues or identities in the Sino-Japanese Buddhistic mythology. In some cases it is not possible to trace the historical connexion —but philosophically speaking, even there the identity is obvious and indicates a common mythological development among the three peoples on more or less independent lines.

In China Ti-tsâng is described "as the compassionate priest, whose *khakkhara* shakes and opens the doors of hell, and whose precious pearl illumines the Region of Darkness."

A Korean prince of the eighth century was declared to be a manifestation of Ti-tsâng.

Visser quotes the statements of a modern Japanese author on the history of the Ti-tsâng cult in China: "From the time of the Tsin, Sung, Liang, Chin, T'sin and Chao dynasties (A.D. 265-589) the cases of those who were saved by invocating and reciting the names of Kwanyin, Ti-tsâng, Maitreya and Amitâbha were so many that they are beyond description."

The following is a picture of Ti-tsâng in the Chinese work *Yuh-lih* (Calendar of Jade): "After some pictures representing Shângti throning as judge of the dead, surrounded by his officials, and virtuous souls rewarded with heavenly joy, while the wicked are tortured by the demons of hell, we see Ti-tsâng in the robe of a priest, with the *urna* on his forehead, wearing a five-pointed crown and with a round halo behind his head. He rides on a tiger, and is escorted by his attendants, two young priests, of whom one carries his master's Khakkhara, whereas the other holds a long streamer adorned with a lotus flower. We read on the streamer: 'The Tantra-ruler of the Darkness, King Ti-tsâng the Bodhisattva.' A boy leads the tiger with a cord."

(*b*) JIZO.

The Japanese have ever been as good Purânists and Tântrists as the neo-Hindus; or, what is the same thing, the neo-Hindus have been as good Buddhists as the Japanese.

In Japan Jizo is worshipped as a deity of the roads. Jizo in one form is the "Conqueror of the armies" and an *avatâra* of an old Yamato Thunder-god. This Jizo represented on horseback is the tutelary god of warriors who used to erect his images on the battlefields and at the entrance to their castles.

Jizo in another form is the giver of easy birth. There is "the custom of placing Jizo images before the house of a newly married couple in the bridal night."

Jizo is believed to save the souls from hell and lead them to paradise. He also healed the sick and many of his images were known for curing special diseases. He is also the special protector of the children.

It is superfluous to add that the Paurânic and Tântric Hindus with their three hundred and thirty million deities would recognise in these Japanese Jizos some of the objects of their love and devotion. The cult of these gods is not a matter for mere archæological study in the great empire of the Far East. Any tourist would endorse the following remarks of Visser: "Thus we see that New Japan goes on worshipping this mighty Bodhisattva and imploring his assistance and protection in all the phases of human life. * * * The present day with all its western civilisation, sees our gentle, merciful Bodhisattva gloriously maintaining his mighty position and living in the people's heart like in the days of yore."

If this is Buddhism, it is sheer pedantry to say that Buddhism has been driven out of India "to seek Lavinian shores."

This most important Bodhisattva of China and Japan is historically none other than *Kshiti-garbha*, one of the Eight Great Bodhisattvas of Mahâyânic pantheon, for the Chinese name Ti-tsâng is the exact equivalent of the Sanskrit term. It is interesting to note that "his name is apparently seldom mentioned in Indian literature. Therefore we have to consult the Chinese Tripitaka for getting information about his nature." Further, "in the well-known Chinese work on India, entitled *Records on Western regions made under the Great Tâng dynasty* (A.D. 618-907), and composed in A.D. 646 by the famous Buddhist pilgrim Hiuen-Thsâng (A.D. 602-664) we do not read one word about Kshiti-garbha. Also, *The Traditions on the Inner Law, by one who returned from the Southern Ocean to China*, written by another famous pilgrim I-tsing (A.D. 634-713) who in A.D. 671 started from China and returned in A.D. 695 does not mention Kshiti-garbha."

It is probable, therefore, that Kshiti-garbha was not worshipped as such in India, and that the Ti-tsâng-cult as well as Jizo-cult should be regarded as independent extra-Indian developments. The only items borrowed by the Chinese and Japanese seem to be the name, and, of course, certain theological notions recorded in the *Sutras*; but the elaboration is mainly original. And yet in the complex pantheon of the neo-Hindus there are deities which are the exact duplicates of Ti-tsâng and Jizo, *i.e.*, of the primal Kshiti-garbha.

These and thousand other facts would lead to the conclusion that Mahâyânic Buddhism lives in and through the so many cults of modern Hinduism, and that this Hinduism is essentially the same as Chinese and Japanese Buddhism. The members of the Sino-Japanese pantheon are all to be found under new names in the Vaishnava, Shaiva, Shâkta and other pantheons of modern India.

(*c*) AVALOKITESWARA.

In fact, the Bodhisattva came into the Mahâyânic pantheon with all the marks of recognised Neo-Hindu deities. Thus it is not difficult to identify Avalokiteswara with a Vishnu or a Brahmâ.

In the *Journal of the Royal Asiatic Society of Great Britain and Ireland* for the year 1894, Waddell contributed a paper on the genesis and worship of the Great Bodhisattva Avalokita, the keystone of Mahâyâna Buddhism—and his *Shakti* or Energy, *i.e.*, consort, Târâ, the savioures. His literary sources of information were Tibetan, and illustrations were drawn from the lithic remains in Magadha (Bihar, India). This was one of the first attempts to study the dark period of Indian Buddhism subsequent to Hiuen Thsâng's visit (A.D. 645).

The following is taken from that paper:

"Avalokita is a purely metaphysical creation of the Indian Buddhists who in attempting to remedy the agnosticism of Buddha's idealism, endeavoured to account theistically for the causes lying beyond the finite, and so evolved the polytheistic Mahâyâna form of Buddhism. * * * The metaphysical Bodhisattva Avalokita ultimately became so expanded as to absorb most of the attributes of each of the separate Buddhist deities. His different modes were concretely represented by images of different forms and symbols; his more active qualities were relegated to female counterparts (*Saktis*), chief of whom was Târâ."

The cult of Avalokita brought with it organised worship, litanies and pompous ritual. The style of the worship was similar to that for his consort Târâ. It is divided into seven stages:

1. The Invocation.
2. Presentation of offerings.
3. Hymn.
4. Repetition of the spell.
5. and 6. Prayers for benefits present and to come.
7. Benediction.

All this is thoroughly orthodox Brâhmanic or neo-Hindu.

The introduction of Târâ into Buddhism seems to date from the sixth century. Hiuen Thsâng refers to her image in a few shrines; but "her worship must soon thereafter have developed rapidly, for her inscribed images from the 8th to the 12th centuries A.D. are numerous at old Buddhist sites* throughout India and in Magadha—the birth-place of Buddhism."

* Many have been unearthed in recent years by the archæologists of the "Varendra Research Society" in Rajshahi, Bengal.

This Târâ might be a Lakshmî or a Durgâ or a Saraswatî as the goddess of wealth, terror or wisdom or what not, according to the thousand and one manifestations of Energy.

(*d*) Moods of Divinities.

An Âdi Buddha is called *Vajrasatta* (whose essence is thunderbolt) in Sanskrit. He is the Buddha of supreme intelligence. He is worshipped in China as *Suan-tzu-lo-sa-tsui*, and in Japan as *Kongōsatta.*

Mrs. Getty gives the following account in her *Gods of Northern Buddhism*:

"He has both a 'mild' and 'ferocious' form. The mild form has usually two arms and is seated on a lotus throne which is often supported by an elephant. The ferocious form has six arms, a third eye, and a ferocious expression. Above the forehead is a skull. His colour is red. In this form he is not supported by an elephant."

Not only are the characteristics and functions of the Bodhisattvas and the Buddhas identical with those of the Paurânic and Tântric deities, but the canons of art also are the same for Mahâyânic as well as neo-Hindu Iconography. Thus the ferocious and mild forms of the Buddhist deities are repeated in the non-Mahâyanic, too. One common art-tradition* was utilised by the sculptors and painters to express the common spiritual consciousness.

---

* As the work was passing through the press the author saw in the *Modern Review* (Calcutta, October 1915) A. N. Tagore's paper on "*Sadanga* or the six limbs of Painting." It is a contribution to the psychology of Hindu Æsthetics. Vide the works of Havell and Coomâraswâmy on Hindu Architecture, Sculpture and Painting.

The following remarks about icons in *Sukra-nîti*, once quoted in a previous connexion, could be made by a *Purânist* or *Tântrist* as much as by a so-called Buddhist:

"The characteristic of an image is its power of helping forward contemplation and *Yoga*. The human maker of images should, therefore, be meditative. Besides meditation there is no other way of knowing the character of an image —even direct observation (is of no use)." Chapter IV. Section iv. 147-50.

As for the moods of the divinities corresponding to which sculptors should select the forms of the images* the following is recorded by Doctor Sukra (I.V. iv. 159-166):

"Images are of three kinds—*sâttvika*, *râjasika* and *tâmasika*.

The images of Vishnu and other gods are to be worshipped in the *sâttvika*, *râjasika* or *tâmasika* form according to needs and circumstances.

The *sâttvika* image is that which has *yoga mudrâ* or the attitude of meditation, the straight back, hands giving blessings and courage, and has the gods represented as worshipping it.

The *râjasika* image is that which sits on some *vâhana* or conveyance, is adorned with numerous ornaments, and has hands equipped with arms and weapons as well as offering courage and blessings to the devotees.

The *tâmasika* image is that which is a killer of demons by arms and weapons, which has a ferocious and vehement look and is eager for warfare."

---

*See the paper on "Some Hindu Silpa-Sâstras in their relation to South Indian Sculpture" by Hadaway in the *Ostasiatische Zeitschrift* (April-June 1914).

In *Sukra-nîti**, which is evidently neo-Hindu, there is no mention of Buddhas, Bodhisattvas or Avâlokiţesvaras. But readers of Getty's book and Waddell's paper would notice that the Mahâyânist iconography also presents the same threefold type.

It need also be added that Indian Æthetics, whether called Hindu or Buddhist, crossed the Himâlayas to enrich the art-consciousness of the Chinese. Thus in reviewing *Das Citralakshana* edited and translated by Berthold Laufer of the FieldMuseum, Chica go, Smith writes in *The Ostasiatische Zeitschrift* (January-March 1914):

"Laufer holds that the influence of Indian painting in China was not confined to Buddhist subjects, but that it extended to the composition and technique, specially, the colouring of painting in general."

And Abanindranâth Tagore in his contribution on "*Sadanga* or the Six Limbs of Indian Painting as given by Bâtsâyana (670 B.C?—200 A.D?)" in the same journal (for April-June 1914) remarks on the theory of "Six Canons of Chinese Painting" enunciated by the Celestial art-critic Hsieh Ho (5th century A.D.) as being eminently significant.

There is thus one art-inspiration governing the so-called Buddhist and the so-called Hindu, *i.e.*, all the peoples of India, China and Japan.

Section 3.

The Buddhism of China and Japan Euphemism for Shaiva-cum-Shâktaism.

A few feminine divinities are being described according to Getty's *Gods of Northern Buddhism*.

---

* *Sukra-nîti* translated from Sanskrit into English for "The Sacred Books of the Hindus Series" (Panini office) by B.K. Sarkar.

Târâ as a goddess was known to the Chinese in the 7th century, A.D. "Hiuen Thsang mentions a statue of the goddess Târâ of great height and endowed with divine penetration, and says that on the first day of each year kings, ministers and powerful men of the neighbouring countries brought flower offerings of exquisite perfume, and that the religious ceremonies lasted for eleven days with great pomp."

The Japanese Târâ "holds the lotus, and may be making 'charity' and 'argument' *mudrâ* or have the hands folded. Her colour is a whitish green. * * * She holds the blue lotus or the pomegranate which is believed as in India to drive away evil."

Ekajatâ or blue Târâ is a ferocious form of Târâ. "She has from four to twenty-four arms, and is generally standing and stepping to the right on corpses—she has the third eye, is laughing horribly, her teeth are prominent, and her protruding tongue, according to the *Sâdhana*, is forked. Her eyes are red and round. Her hips are covered by a tiger-skin, and she wears a long garland of heads. If painted, her colour is blue, and her chignon is red. She is dwarfed and corpulent. Her ornaments are snakes."

Saraswatî is worshipped by the Buddhists of China and Japan as the goddess of music and poetry. "In Japan the goddess Benten is looked upon as a manifestation of Saraswatî. Her full name is * * Great Divinity of the Reasoning Faculty. * * * The white snake is believed to be a manifestation of Saraswatî. * * The goddess is generally represented either sitting or standing on a dragon or huge snake—she has only two arms, and holds a *biwa* or Japanese lute."

Red Târâ is "the goddess of wealth and follows in the suite of the god of wealth Kuvera, but is not his consort or *Sakti*." Vasudharâ, "goddess of abundance, is the *sakti* of Kuvera, god of wealth. She is always represented with one head, but may have from two to six arms, and wears all the Bodhisattva ornaments. When she has but two arms, the left hand holds a spike of grain, while the right holds a vase, out of which pours a quantity of jewels."

If the people of Tibet, Mongolia, China, and Japan are known as Buddhists because they worship these deities, the modern Hindus who follow the Tantras and Purânas are also good Buddhists. The Shaiva-cum-Shâkta pantheon of neo-Hinduism can present duplicates of all these divinities and is in essence but an expression of Sino-Japanese Buddhism.

It is superfluous to add that the goddesses of Shiva's family, in fact, his consorts, *e.g.*, Kâlî, Durgâ, Jagad-dhâtrî, etc., are the sisters of some of the trans-Himâlayan Târâs, and that his daughter Lakshmî, the goddess of wealth, also can be identified with one of them. Besides, the Hindu Lakshmî's sister, Saraswatî, goddess of learning, is known by the same name among extra-Indian Buddhists.

Descriptions of some of the members of the Shaiva pantheon, with illustrations by painters of the modern nationalist school of Indian Art, are to be found in *The Myths of the Hindus and Buddhists* by Niveditâ and Coomâraswâmy. Niveditâ's *Studies from an Eastern Home* as well as *Kâlî the Mother* may also be consulted.

The following invocation of the Buddhist Târâ given in Waddell's paper could be made by a neo-Hindu to his Durgâ:

"Hail! O! verdant Târâ!
The Saviour of all beings!
Descend, we pray Thee, from Thy heavenly mansion, at Potala
Together with all Thy retinue of gods, titans, and deliverers!
We humbly prostrate ourselves at Thy lotus feet,
Deliver us from all distress! O Holy Mother!"

So also the presentation of offerings to the Buddhist Shakti is in the characteristic spirit of India:

"We sincerely beg Thee in all Thy divine Forms
To partake of the food now offered!
On confessing to Thee penitently their sins
The most sinful hearts, yea! even the committers of the
Ten vices and the five boundless sins,
Will obtain forgiveness and reach
Perfection of Soul—through Thee!"

In the Buddhist hymn translated by Waddell. Târâ is praised in her twenty-one forms as:—(1) supremely courageous, (2) of white moon brightness, (3) golden coloured, (4) grand hair piled, (5) *H'ung* shouter, (6) best three-world worker, (7) suppresser of strife, (8) giver of supreme power, (9) best bestower, (10) Dispeller of grief, (11) Cherisher of the poor, (12) brightly glorious, (13) of universal mature deeds, (14) with the frowning brows, (15) giver of prosperity, (16) subduer of passion, (17) supplier of happiness, (18) excessively vast, (19) dispeller of distress, (20) advent of spiritual power, (21) completely perfect.

Such forms are known to the Purânists and Tântrists also about their own *Shaktis* (Goddesses of Energy). The hymns also are identical.

Just as Buddhist divinities may be said to have been receiving worship as Shaiva deities in modern India, so also the Shaiva divinities may be said to have been receiving the worship of the Sino-Japanese Buddhists.

The great masses of gods and goddesses in Japanese Buddhism regarded as the manifestations of the supreme original divinity are thus described by Okakura:

" Fudo, the immovable, the god of Samâdhi, stands for the terrible form of Shiva. * * * He has the gleaming third eye, the trident sword and the lasso of snakes. In another form, as Kojin, * * * he wears a garland of skulls, armlets of snakes, and the tiger-skin of meditation.

His feminine counterpart appears as Aizen, of the mighty bow, lion-crowned and awful, the God of Love —but love in its strong form, whose fire of purity is death and who slays the beloved that he may attain the highest. * * *

The Indian idea of Kâlî is also represented by Kariteimo, the mother-queen of Heaven. * * * Saraswatî as Benten, with her *vinâ* (lute), which quells the waves; Kompira or the Gandharva, the eagle-headed, sacred to mariners; Kichijoten or Lakshmî, who confers fortune and love; Taigensui, the commander-in-chief (Kârtikeya) who bestows the banner of victory; Shoden, the elephant-headed Ganesh, Breaker of the Path, to whom the first salutations are paid in all village worship * * * —all these suggest the direct adoption of Hindu deities."

Trans-Himâlayan Buddhism is really an euphemism for Shaiva-cum-Shâktaism.

SECTION 4.

NEO-HINDUISM IN TRANS-HIMÂLAYAN ASIA.

There are other goddesses in Buddhist China and Japan besides Saraswatî and Târâ whose names are identical with those of the Paurânic and Tântric deities of India.

Among the deities worshipped by the Buddhists of China and Japan under the same name as by the Hindus of India may be mentioned—

(1) Nâgas and Garudas
(2) Kuvera and Lokapâlas.
(3) Mahâkâla.
(4) Mârîchî.
(5) Hâritî.

Thus not only is Shaivaism Buddhistic or Mahâyânic but other Indian isms also are equally so. In other words, the Chinese and Japanese Buddhists are Hindus of the Paurânic and Tântric sects.

The following is taken from Getty:

"In China Yen-lo-wang (Yama) is not regent of the Buddhist hells, he is a subordinate under Ti-tsâng and the fifth of the ten kings of hell, who reign over ten courts of judgment. They are represented in Chinese temples, standing when in the presence of Ti-tsâng, and surrounded by representations of the torments of the different hells." He is believed to be assisted by his sister who judges the women, while he judges the men.

"In Japan Emma-O (*Yama*) is regent and holds the same position as Yama in India. In both China and Japan the representations of Yama are practically alike, a middle aged man with a fierce expression and a beard. On his head is a judge's cap, and he is dressed in flowing garments with the feet always covered. He is seated with the legs locked and in his right hand is the mace of office."

The twelve Japanese gods alleged to have been painted by the celebrated Kōbō Daishi are:

(1) Bôten—(Brahmâ) attended by (2) the white bird *Ha Kuga* or swan. (3) Khaten—(Agni, Fire god). (4) Ishanna—(name of Rudra or Siva). (5) Thaishak—(Indra —a Vedic deity). (6) Futen. (7) Vishamon (Kuvera—Lord of wealth) whose consort is Kichijoten (Goddess of Fortune). (8) Emma (Yama)—riding on a buffalo, and bearing the great staff of death, surmounted by two heads. (9) Nitten (Suryya the Sun-god). (10) Getten (the Moon-god). (11) Suiten (the God of waters on a tortoise). (12) Shoden (Ganesha).

Neo-Hinduism must be said to be flourishing as much in Buddhist China and Japan as in modern India; or modern Hindus are Mahâyânists still like the Chinese and Japanese.

The following picture of what may be regarded as Japanese Vaishnavism is furnished by Okakura:

"A wave of religious emotion passed over Japan in the Fujiwara epoch (A.D. 900-1200), and intoxicated with frantic love, men and women deserted the cities and villages in crowds to follow Kuya or Ipen, dancing and singing the name of Amida as they went. Masquerades came into vogue, representing angels descending from Heaven with lotus dais, in order to welcome and bear upward the departing soul. Ladies would spend a lifetime in weaving or embroidering the image of Divine Mercy, out of threads extracted from the lotus stem. Such was the new movement, which * * closely paralleled in China in the beginning of the Tâng dynasty * * * has never died, and to this day two-thirds of the people belong to the Jōdō sect, which corresponds to the Vaishnâvism of India.

Both Genshin, the formulator of the creed, and Genku, who carried it to its culmination, pleaded that human nature was weak, and try as it might, could not accomplish entire self-conquest and direct attainment of the Divine in this life. It was rather by the mercy of the Amida Buddha and his emanation Kwannon that one could alone be saved."

SECTION 5.

MODERN HINDUISM.

Haraprasâd Sâstri was probably the first to bring to the notice of scholars that mediæval Buddhism exists even now among the lower orders of the Bengalee people. The worship of the god Dharma is according to him nothing but the Mahâyânic cult elaborated in the *Sunya Purâna* of Râmâi Pandit. The doctrine of *Sunya* or void, *i.e.*, Nothingness, was a principal theory of one of the forms of mediæval Buddhism, and, though generally associated with the name of Nâgârjuna, may be traced back to Aswaghosha according to Vidhusekhara Sâstrī's communication in the Journal of the Royal Asiatic Society (London, 1914). H.P. Sâstri's contributions to the *Journal* of the Asiatic Society of Bengal (No. 1, 1895), and *Proceedings* of the Society (for December, 1898), supply interesting facts about Buddhism in modern Bengal.

Dines Chandra Sen in his *History of Bengali Literature* also refers to Buddhist elements in the literature and life of Bengal from the tenth to the seventeenth century. His remarks on the absorption of Buddhism by Vaishnavas who have followed Chaitanya the Reformer

(A.D. 1483-1533) are also relevant to the present topic. And in Nagendranâth Vasu's *Modern Buddhism*, one can see the various forms under which Buddhism is maintaining its existence even at the present day in some of the border districts between Bengal and Orissa.

Another work by a Hindu scholar may also be mentioned. Haridâs Pâlit's *Âdyer Gambhirâ*, written in Bengali language, deals with a folk-festival of the Shivaites in northern Bengal. In this he has presented a historic treatment of the stages and processes in the evolution of the neo-Hindu Shiva-cult out of the Mahâyânic and pre-Sâkyan (*i.e.* Vedic) elements. The modern Shiva is descended as much from the primitive Rudra as from the Yoga-Tântric Avalokiteswara, and has assimilated, besides, the characteristics of various popular deities. In fact, all the three factors mentioned in Section 1 have contributed to the making of Shiva and His host.

Conclusions of these and other Indian scholars have been incorporated with my forthcoming* work *The Folk-Element in Hindu Culture*. It is unnecessary to summarise what has been said there; but the titles of some of the chapters may be mentioned here:

Chapter VI. Popular Buddhism in Hindu Bengal.

Chapter X. Buddhist and Jaina Elements in Modern Hinduism.

Chapter XI. National Festivals of the 7th century A.D.

Section 1. The Age of Religious Eclecticism

2. Two festivities witnessed by Hiuen Thsâng

(a) The Festival at Kanauj

(b) The Festival at Allahabad

* In the press in England (Longmans Green & Co.)

If the religious beliefs and practices of all classes of the so-called Hindus were scrutinised, it would be found that, historically speaking, the foundations of every sect of the present-day Purânists and Tântrists are to be sought in that romantic religion of love, which expressed itself simultaneously in Mahâyânism and also in the isms of the so-called Brâhmanic order. And as has been pointed out in the preceding sections, philosophically, also, neo-Hinduism and Sino-Japanese Buddhism are the same. For if the Jōdō Sect of

Japan be regarded as Buddhistic, the Vaishnava sects of India which are equal advocates of *Bhakti* or love and devotion are all Buddhists. If it is good Buddhism in China and Japan to worship a god of war, a patron-saint of children, a protector of roads, and so forth, the Hindus or Brâhmanists of India who worship Kârtika the warrior-god, and Kâlî the goddess of terror, Mother Sîtalâ the defender from smallpox, Mother Sasthî the protector of offsprings, and a thousand others, are equally Buddhists.

Regarding the Sino-Japanese Buddhism, therefore, the following brilliant suggestion of Sister Niveditâ in her introduction to Okakura's *Ideals of the East* may be taken as scientifically established:

"Rather must we regard it as the name given to the vast synthesis known as Hinduism, when received by a foreign consciousness. For Mr. Okakura, in dealing with the subject of Japanese art in the ninth century, makes it abundantly clear that the whole mythology of the East, and not merely the personal doctrine of the Buddha, was the subject of interchange. Not the Buddhaising but the *Indianising* of the Mongolian mind, was the process actually at work—much as if Christianity should receive in some strange land the name of Franciscanism, from its first missionaries."

Are the Chinese and Japanese, then, Hindus? The answer is "yes." But at once the difficulty arises as to the answer to the question—"What is Hinduism?" Whatever it is, it is not the name of a religion. Strictly speaking, it is a convenient ethnological term adopted by foreigners to understand certain races of men, just as 'Barbarian' or *Mlechchha* or *Yavana* is used by certain Asiatic peoples to describe the European and other foreign races.

The people of India themselves know their faiths to be Vaishnavism, Sauraism, Shaivaism, Shâktaism, Brâhmaism, Âryaism and other isms according to the cult or principal tenet. The term Hindu is not to be found in any Sanskrit work, ethnological, political or religious. If thus 'Hinduism' cannot be the name for the religion of the Indians, it is *prima facie* absurd that it should be the name for the identical religions of the sons of Han and the Yamato race.

Should, therefore, the religions of the three peoples be all known by the name of Buddhism? *i.e.*, Should the people of India import from China and Japan back to its native land the name so popular there still? Evidently the answer must be in the affirmative. In spite of the ambiguity associated with the term as with Christianity (as explained in a previous chapter), Buddhism seems to be the most acceptable name.

But the term Buddhism also is objectionable, since it pins down the thoughts and feelings of people to a certain historic person or suggests the exclusive sway of a certain deity. This would be quite out of keeping with the spirit of Asia. The mentality of the three peoples has grown through the ages, evolving fresh personalities and deities in almost every generation. It is the historic birth-right of every Asian to create his own god, his own saint, and his own *avatâra*.

In matters spiritual every individual in Asia has ever chosen his or her love with his or her own eyes. Freedom of conscience leading even to seemingly anarchic individualism is the characteristic of the Far East; it has given birth to an incalculably varied godlore and saintlore. No personal name is thus adequate to express the ever-growing religious consciousness of the people in *San-goku*.

Both the terms, Hinduism and Buddhism, are unfortunate, and should, if possible, be abandoned. But in these days when age-long historic tradition has solidified and "polarised" the terms, and national superstitions have grown up around them it is out of the question to do so. Besides, neither would the so-called Hindus of India probably like to be known as Buddhists because this would involve exclusive faith in a certain deity; nor the so-called Buddhists of China and Japan as Hindus, because this would be confounding their nationality.

It is clear, however, that for scientific purposes, *e.g.*, for cultural anthropology and comparative religion, the eight hundred millions of human beings in the Far East should be considered as professing the same faith. And if following the example of Christianity which under one abstract name embraces a thousand and one denominations, sects, cults, orders, or churches, we are called upon to select a term that would embrace the Ti-tsângists, the Jizoists, the Shivaists and thousand other ists of China, Japan and India, I venture to think that such a name is to be found in Tāoism, Shintōism or Sanâtanism, *i.e.*, the religion of the eternal way, *michi* or *mârga*. And the metaphysics of that great *ism* of mankind is Monism in Pluralism.

CHAPTER XII.

Epilogue:

The Study of Asiatic Sociology

I began with the hypothesis: "What pass for Buddhism in the lands of Confucius and Shintō cult are but varieties of the same faith that is known as Tântric and Paurânic Hinduism in modern *Tienchu* (Heaven) or *Tenjiku*, the land of Sâkya the Buddha."

Indications of the affinity as well as the methods of investigation have been presented in the foregoing pages. For a complete verification of the hypothesis one has only to make a parallel and comparative study of Sino-Japanese Buddhism and modern Hinduism through their historic landmarks.

It would be necessary to have recourse to the "philosophical method" of inquiry. This would involve (1) an analysis of the concepts underlying the mythology, ceremonials, superstitions, pilgrimages, etc., of Sino-Japanese Buddhism, and (2) an analysis of the concepts underlying the mythology, ceremonials, superstitions, pilgrimages, etc., of those who regulate their socio-religious life according to the teachings of the *Purânas* and *Tantras*. The two analyses will yield the same results and establish a common psychological basis of the three peoples.

Tantra-studies in English are few. Avalon's translation of *Mahâ-nirvâna Tantra* from Sanskrit, *Hymns to the Goddess* and *Principles of Tantra* (*Tantra-tattva*) are recent works. According to "The Prabuddha Bhârata" (or "The Awakened India"), a journal conducted by the Vivek-ânandists, "educated minds in the East as well as in the West will be, ere long, disabused of all that mass of prejudice that they have allowed to gather round the name of Tantra. * * * Tântrikism, in its real sense, is nothing but the Vedic religion struggling with wonderful success to reassert itself amidst all those new problems of religious life and discipline which later historical events and developments thrust upon it."

Secondly, it would be necessary to have recourse to the "historical method" of inquiry. This would involve

(1) a study of the growth, modification and development through the ages, of the mythology, superstitions, etc., of Sino-Japanese Buddhists. Visser's exhaustive study of Ti-tsâng (Jizo), epoch by epoch, down to the twentieth century, and Getty's *Gods of Northern Buddhism* are instances of this method.

(2) a study of the growth, modification and development, through the ages, of the mythology, superstitions, etc., of the Vaishnavas, Shâktas, Jainas, Shaivas, and other sects of India. Sir R.G. Bhândârkâr's *Vaishnavism, Shaivaism and Minor Religious Systems* in the Encyclopædia of Indo-Aryan Research (Strassburg), and Pâlit's treatment of Shaivaism in *Âdyer Gambhîrâ* are instances of this method.

The historical studies will yield the result that the pluralistic or polytheistic faiths of Buddhist China and Japan as well as of Hindu India are but divergent streams descended from the same fountain. The brilliant period of the mighty Tângs (A.D. 618-905) in Chinese history,—synchronous with the Nârâ Period (A.D. 710-794) and Kyoto Period (A.D. 782-1182) of Japanese, and the epoch of Imperialism continuing both in Southern and Northern

India all the traditions of the Vikramâdityan Renaissance;—which was signalised by the propagandism and literary activity of such synthetic philosopher-saints as Hiuen Thsâng (A.D. 602-664), Kōbō Daishi (A.D. 774-835) and Sankar-âchârya (A.D. 788-850),—was the most important age for the inauguration of that common fountain of love, faith and hope, out of which the Hwângho and the Yângtse, the Yōdō and the Sumidâ, the Narmadâ and the Godâvarî, and the Indus and the Ganges have been regularly fed for over one millennium. It is not the purpose of this work to trace the history of that practical idealism, romantic positivism and assimilative eclecticism, which have been the inspiration of eight hundred million souls during the last thousand years. I stop just at the threshold of the great Asiatic Unity.

INDEX

WORKS RELATING TO INDIA AND HINDU CULTURE

SCIENCE

1. Comparative Electro-Physiology, (Longmans 15s). Prof. J. C. Bose, D. Sc., (London).
2. Plant Response (Longmans £1-1s). Prof. J. C. Bose, D. Sc.. (London).
3. Researches on the Irritability of Plants (Longmans 7s-6d). Prof. J. C. Bose, D. Sc.
4. Response in the Living and Non-Living (Longmans 10s). Prof. J.C. Bose, D. Sc., (London).
5. History of Hindu Chemistry 2 vols. (Bengal Chemical Works, Calcutta). Prof. P. C. Ray, D. Sc.
6. The Positive Sciences of the Ancient Hindus (Longmans 12s. 6d.). Prof. B. N. Seal, Ph. D.
7. Indian Medicinal Plants with 1,300 Plates (Panini Office, Allahabad £16). Lt. Col-Kirtikar, Major Basu, Prof. Chatterji.
8. Medicine of Ancient India Pt. I. Osteology (Oxford). Dr. Hœrnle.
9. History of Aryan Medical Science (Macmillan). Gondal.
10. Materia Medica of the Hindus (Calcutta). Dutt.

THE POETICAL WORKS OF SIR RABINDRANATH TAGORE (THE NOBEL-PRIZE-MAN, 1913-14)

1. Gîtânjali or Song-offerings (Macmillan 4s. 6d.).
2. The Gardener (Lyrics of Love and Life) (Macmillan 4s.6d..
3. The Crescent Moon (Child-Poems) (Macmillan 4s. 6d.).
4. Chitrâ (a play—an allegory of love's meaning) (Macmillan 2s. 6d).
5. The Post Office (a play) (Macmillan 2s. 6d.).
6. The King of the Dark Chamber (a Play) Macmillan 4s. 6d.).
7. Rabindranath Tagore the Man and his Poetry (Dodd Mead & Co., New York, $1.50). Roy.
8. Tagore (London). Rhys.

MENTAL AND MORAL PHILOSOPHY

1. Vaishnavism and Christianity, (Calcutta). Prof B. N. Seal.
2. Science of Religion (Udbodhana Office, Calcutta) Swâmi Vivekânanda.
3. Epochs of Civilisation (Luzac, London 5s. 4d.). P. N. Bose, F.G.S.
4. The New Essays in Criticism (Literary) (Calcutta). Prof. Seal.
5. Science of Emotions (Benares) Prof. Bhagavân Das
6. Hindu Philosophy of Conduct (Madras 6s. 8d). Prof. Rangacharya.
7. Essays in National Idealism (Indian Review Office). Coomâraswâmy.
8. India : Her Cult and Education (Panini Office). Prof. P. N. Mookerji.
9. Krishna and the Gîtâ (Calcutta, 3s. 4d.) Tattwabhushana.
10. Sâdhanâ or the Realisation of life (Macmillan 5 s). Tagore.
11. Science of History and the Hope of Mankind. (Longmans 2s. 6d.). Prof. B. K. Sarkar.
12. Science of Peace (Benares). Prof. Bhagavân Das.
13. Chhândogya Upanishad (Panini Office, 16s). Vasu.
14. Yoga Philosophy (Panini Office, 7s). Vasu.
15. Vedânta Philosophy (Panini Office, £1). Vasu.
16. Vaisesikha Philosophy (Panini Office, 9s-4.). Sinha.
17. Sâmkhya Philosophy (Panini Office, £1). Sinha.
18. Nyâya Philosophy (Panini Office 8s). Prof. Vidyâbhushana.
19. Psychical Research and Man's Survival (Modern Review Office, Calcutta 6d) Prof. Haldar.
20. Introduction to the Science of Education (Longmans 3s. 6d.). Prof. B. K. Sarkâr.
21. Philosophy of Brâhmoism (Calcutta, 3s. 4d.). Tattwabhushana.
22. Vedânta, its relation to Modern Thought (Calcutta. 3s. 4d.) Tattwabhushana.
23. Jnâna Yoga (Udbodhana Office, Calcutta). Swâmi Vivekânanda
24. Bhakti Yoga (Udbodhana Office, Calcutta). Swâmi Vivekânanda.
25. Râja Yoga (Udbodhana Office, Calcutta). Swâmi Vivekânanda.
26. Karma Yoga (Udbodhana Office, Calcutta). Swâmi Vivekânanda.
27. Hatha Yoga (Panini Office, 2s). Vasu.
28. Philosophical and Literary Essays (Nava-vidhâna Office, Calcutta). Prof. B. N. Sen.
29. Chinese Religion through Hindu Eyes—A study in the tendencies of Asiatic Mentality (Commercial Press Shanghai 6s.). Prof. B. K. Sarkar.
30. Addresses Literary and Academic (Calcutta). Sir Asutosh Mookerji. Late Vice-Chancellor.
31. A Few Thoughts on Education (Calcutta 3s. 4d.) Sir G. D. Banerji. Late Vice-Chancellor.
32. Hindu Realism (Indian Press, Allahabad). Chatterji.
33. The Pedagogy of the Hindus and the Message of India (Panini Office 6d). B. K. Sarkar

34. Education in Baroda. T.R. Pândyâ Ph.D. (Columbia).
35. Religion and Dharma (Longmans). Niveditâ.
36. Aspects of the Vedânta (Ind. Rev. 1s).

ECONOMICS AND POLITICS.

1. Essays on Indian Economics. (Indian Review Office, Madras 2s. 8d). Justice Ranade.
2. Poverty and Un-British Rule in India (London). Naoroji.
3. Economic History of British India (London 2. vols.). Dutt.
4. The Economics of British India. (Calcutta 4s.). Prof. J. N. Sarkar.
5. Indian Economics (Macmillan 3s 6d). Prof. Banerji.
6. Introduction to Indian Economics (Calcutta). Prof. Mookerji.
7. Indian Industrial and Economic Problems (Poona, 1s 4d). Prof. Kale.
8. Agricultural Industries in India (Indian Review Office, Madras 1s4d). Sayani.
9. The Swadeshi (One's-own-Country or Home-Industry) Movement (Ind. Rev. 1s. 4d.).
10. Recent Indian Finance (Indian Review Office, Madras). Wacha.
11. The Imperial Gazetteer of India. (London). Vol. on Economics. Vol. on Administration.
12. The Foundations of Indian Economics (Longmans). Prof. Mukerjee.
13. Indian National Congress. (Indian Review Office, Madras 4s). Natesan.
14. Indians of South Africa (Indian Review Office. Madras 1s. 4d.). Polak.
15. Report and Speeches of the Social Conference. (Leader Office, Allahabad) Chintamani.
16. The Position of Indian Women (London). Mahârâni Baroda.
17. Political Speeches of Publicists: (Indian Review Office): (*a*) Hon. Naoroji, (2s. 8d.). (*b*) Hon. Banerji. (*c*) Hon. Gokhale. (4s). (*d*) Sir Mehta (*e*) Hon. Malaviya (*f*) Mr. Lalmohan Ghosh (*g*) Mr. Joshi (*h*) Mr. Pâl (*i*) Sir Râshbehari Ghosh, (1s).
18. The Congress Diary. (Bee Press, Calcutta, 1s)
19. Reports of Indian Industrial Conference. (R. N. Mudholkar, Amraoti, C.P. India)
20. The Growth of Currency Organisations in India (Higginbotham, Madras 6s) Dhari.
21. Lives of Eminent Indians (Indian Review Office). 50 booklets 4d. each.
22. History of Indian National Evolution (Indian Review Office 2s. 8d). Majumdar.
23. Romesh Dutt (Dent. London 3s. 6d.). Gupta.
24. Telang (Indian Review, 1s. 4d.). Naik.

ANCIENT HINDU POLITICAL SCIENCE

1. The Artha-sâstra of Kautilya (Mysore). Translated by Shamasastri from Sanskrit
2. The Niti-sâstra of Kâmandaka (Calcutta). Translated by Dutt from Sanskrit.
3. The Niti-sâstra of Sukrâchâryya (Panini Office 8s.). " B. K. Sarkar from Sanskrit.
4. Studies in Ancient Hindu Polity (Longmans 3s 6d.). Naren Law.
5. Science of Social Organisation based on Sanskrit *Manu Samhitâ.* Bhagavan Das.
6. Abul Fazl's *Ayeen Akbari.* Gladwin.
7. Warfare in Ancient India (Ind. Rev. 6d). Jagannathaswami.

CLASSICAL SANSKRIT LITERATURE IN ENGLISH VERSE

1. The Hero and the Nymph (Modern Review Office, Calcutta 1s). Aurobinda Ghosh.
2. Lays of Ancient Ind. R. C. Dutt.
3. Nala and Damayanti (Panini Office 2s.). Milman.
4. Indian Ballads (Panini Office 2s). Waterfield.
5. Idylls from the Sanskrit (Panini office 2s. 8d.). Griffith.
6. Scenes from the Râmâyana (Panini Office). Griffith.
7. Specimens of Old Indian Poetry (Panini Office 2s.). Griffith.
8. Shakuntalâ, an Indian Drama by Kâlidâsa (Dent and Sons, London 1s.). Prof. Ryder
9. Meghaduta or "Cloud-Messenger" of Kâlidâsa (Panini Office 1s.). Sarkar
10. Uttara-charitam, a Drama (Harvard Oriental Series). Belvalkar.
11. History of Sanskrit Literature (Reprint, Panini Office 7s). Maxmuller.
12. History of Sanskrit Literature (London). Macdonell.
13. History of Indian Literature (London). Weber.

CULTURE-HISTORY

1. Essay on the Architecture of the Hindus (Royal Asiatic Society). Râm Râz.
2. Selected Examples of Indian Art (Luzac & Co., London). Coomâraswâmy.
3. The Arts and Crafts of India and Ceylon (Foulis, London, 5s.). Coomâraswâmy.
4. South Indian Bronzes (Luzac £1). O. C. Gangoly.
5. Hindu Iconography (Madras £1). Gopinath Rao.
6. Hindu Music (London). Strongways.
7. Indian Sculpture and Painting (London). Havell.
8. Indian Architecture (London). Havell.
9. History of Fine Art in India and Ceylon (Clarendon Press, Oxford). Vincent Smith.

10. The Folk-Element in Hindu Culture. A contribution to Socio-religious Studies in Hindu Folk-Institutions (Longmans) B. K. Sarkar and H. K. Rakshit.

11. The Positive Background of Hindu Sociology. (Panini Office 9s. 6d). B. K. Sarkar.

12. The Fundamental Unity of India (Longmans 3s. 6d). Mookerji.

13. Modern Buddhism in Orissa (Probsthain, London). N. N. Vasu.

14. Pânini. His Place in Sanskrit Literature (Reprint, Panini Office 6s. 8d.). Goldstucker.

15. *The Ashtâdhyâyî of Pânini.* The greatest work on Sanskrit Linguistics (Panini Office. pp. 1,700. £3). Translated from the Sanskrit text of the sixth century B.C. by Vasu.

16. Orissa and Her Remains (Calcutta). M. Ganguly.

17. The Songs of India (Luzac 1s.). Inayat Khân.

18. The Orion (Bombay). Tilak.

19. Indian Mythology (Luzac) Fausboll.

20. Indo-Aryans 2 vols (Stanford, London). Mitra.

21. History of Mediæval Indian Logic (Calcutta University) Prof. Vidyâbhushana.

22. Mediaeval Sinhalese Art (London) Coomâraswâmy.

23. Indian Artistic Anatomy (Luzac). A. N. Tagore.

24. Ajantâ Paintings (Luzac £4. 4s). Herringham.

25. Bronzes from Ceylon (Oxford). Coomâraswâmy.

26. Study of Indian Music (Longmans). Clements.

VERNACULAR LITERATURE IN ENGLISH.

1. The Abbey of Bliss (a novel by Bankim Chatterji, containing the national song, *Bande Mâtaram*, Calcutta 2s. 8d.). Translated by Sen Gupta from Bengali
2. Poems of Kabir (Macmillan 4s. 6d.). Translated by Tagore from Hindi.
3. Vidyâpati (Love-poems, London). Translated by Coomâraswâmy.
4. The Râmâyana of Tulsidâs. (Government Press, Allahabad). Translated by Growse (fm Hindi).
5. The Poems of Tukârâm. (Christian Literature Society, Madras). Translated by Fraser and Marathe (from Marathi).
6. Tiruvâsagam of Mânikka Vâsagar. (Clarendon Press, Oxford). Translated by Pope (from Tâmil)
7. The Passing of Spring—a prose-poem on the mysteries of life (Macmillan), Translated from the Bengali of Mrs. Das. with introduction by Tagore.
8. Culture of Devotion (Calcutta). Translated by Sen from Aswini Dutt's Bengali.
9. History of Bengali Language and Literature (Calcutta University 13s. 4d.) Sen.

HISTORY.

1. Imperial Gazetteer of India (London). Descriptive Volume, Historical Volume.
2. Early History of India (Clarendon Press, Oxford). Vincent Smith.
3. Ancient India (History of Southern India). (Luzac). S. K. Aiyangar.
4. A Peep into the Early History of India (Bombay). Sir Bhândârkâr.
5. The Early History of the Dekkan (Bombay). Sir Bhândârkâr
6. History of Indian Shipping and Maritime Activity (Longmans 7s. 6d). Prof. Mookerji.
7. The Cambridge History of India (5 vols. £3-10.)
8. History of India (Ghadiali Pole, Baroda 7s. 6d.) Dalal.
9. History of Aurangzib (Luzac & Co., London 9s. 4d). Prof. J. N. Sarkar.
10. Anecdotes of Aurangzib and Historical Essays (Luzac 2s). Prof. J. N. Sarkar.
11. History of the Saracens. (London). Ameer Ali.
12. Promotion of Learning in India, by Muhammadan Rulers (Longmans). Naren Law.
13. The Arctic Home in the Vedas. Tilak.
14. Rise of Maratha Power (Punalekar, Bombay). Ranade.
15. History of the Punjab. Abdul Latif.
16. The Mundas and their country (Calcutta, 9s) S.C. Roy.
17. The Oraons of Chota Nagpur (Calcutta) S. C. Roy.
18. History of the Reign of Shah Alam (*c* 1759-1806). Franklin. (Reprint, Panini Office 2s 8d.)
19. The Beginning of Hindu Culture as World-Power (A.D. 300-600). (Commercial Press. Shanghai, 1s.) B. K. Sarkar.
20. The Antiquities of Orissa. Mitra.
21. The Madras Presidency (Macmillan 2s 8d). Thurston.
22. The Pâlas of Bengal (Asiatic Society, Calcutta 14s) R. D. Banerji.
23. Begams of Bengal (Calcutta 1s) B. Banerji.

RELIGIOUS MOVEMENTS.

1. Vedic India (London). Ragozin.
2. Buddhist India (London). Rhys Davids.
3. Vaishnavism, Shaivaism and Minor Religious systems (Encyclopædia of Indo-Aryan Research, Strassburg) Sir Bhandarkar.

4. Sankaráchâryya, (Madras 1s) Aiyar and Tattvabhushana.
5. Life of Râmânuja (Murthy, Madras). Govindâchârya.
6. Chaitanya's Pilgrimages and Teachings (Luzac & Co., London, 2s. 8d). Prof. J. N. Sarkar.
7. The Sikh Religion (Clarendon Press Oxford). Macauliffe.
8. History of Brâhmo Samâj (Calcutta). Sâstri.
9. Works of Râmamohan (Panini Office, Allahabad).
10. Works of Swâmi Vivekânanda (Mayavati Edition).
11. Works of Râm Tirath (Delhi Edition).
12. Ârya Samâj and Swâmi Dayânanda (Longmans 3s. 6d.). Rai
13. Speeches (Calcutta). Keshab Sen.
14. Hinduism Ancient and Modern (Panini Office 4s.). Baijnâth.
15. Introduction to Hinduism (Panini Office 1s.8d.). Sen.
16. The Essentials of Hinduism (Leader Office, Allahabad 8d).
17. The Daily Practice of the Hindus (Panini Office 1s.8d.). Vasu.
18. Pranava-Vâda. The Science of the Sacred Word. (Benares). Translated from Sanskrit by Prof. Bhagavan Das.
19. The Autobiography of Maharshi Devendranath Tagore. (Macmillan 7s. 6d).
20. The Catechism of Hinduism (Panini Office).
21. Hinduism and India (Benares). Govinda Das.
22. The Master as I saw him (Life of Swâmi Vivekânanda). Nivedita (Miss Margaret Noble).
23. Râmkrishna: His Life and Teachings (Scribner, New York). Maxmuller.
24. Principles of Tantra (Luzac) Avalon.
25. Tantra of the Great Liberation—Translated from Sanskrit (Luzac). Avalon.
26. Hymns to the Goddess (Luzac). Avalon.
27. Kâli the Mother. (Udbodhana Office, Calcutta) Niveditâ.
28. Myths of Hindus and Buddhists. (Harrap, London 15s.). Niveditâ and Coomâraswâmy.
29. Hindu Psalms and Hymns (Ind. Rev. 4d.) Râmaswâmi.
30. Ten Tamil Saints (Ind. Rev. 1s.) Pillai.
31. Aggressive Hinduism (Ind. Rev. 4d.) Niveditâ.
32. Vaishnavite Reformers (Ind. Rev. 1s. 4d). Râjagopâlachariar.
33. India's Untouchable Saints (Ind. Rev. 6d.) Râmaswâmi.
34. Kashmir Shaivaism (Luzac 2s. 6d.) Chatterji.
35. Râmânuja (Ind. Rev. 1s.) Aiyangar, Rangachârya, &c.
36. Madhwa (Ind. Rev. 1s.) Aiyar and Row.
37. Buddha (Ind. Rev. 1s.) Dharmapâla.

FOLK-LORE.

1. Folk-Tales of Bengal (London) Lal Behari Day.
2. Legends of the Panjab (London) Temple.
3. Old Deccan Days (London) Frere.
4. Wide Awake Stories, Bombay (London). Steel and Temple.
5. Folk-Tales of Kashmir (London) Knowles.
6. Indian Nights' Entertainment (London) Swynnerton.
7. Indian Fairy Tales (London) Stokes.
8. The Folk-Tales of Hindusthân (Panini Office 2s. 8d.) Vasu.
9. The Adventures of Gooroo Noodle (Panini Office 1s.) Babington.
10. Legends of Vikramâditya (Panini Office, 2s. 8d). Singh.
11. Folklore of the Telugus (Madras 4d.)
12. Tales of Tennali Raman (Madras 4d.)

INTERPRETATION OF INDIAN LIFE BY FOREIGNERS.

1. The Web of Indian Life (Longmans). Sister Niveditâ. (Miss Margaret Noble.)
2. Studies from an Eastern Home (Longmans). " "
3. Foot Falls of Indian History (Longmans 7s. 6d.). " "
4. Cradle-Tales of Hinduism (Longmans 5s). " "
5. Indian Study of Love and Death (Longmans 2s. 4.d.). " "
6. Civic Ideals (Longmans). " "
7. New India (London). Cotton.
8. Impressions about India (London). Keir Hardie.
9. The New Spirit in India (London). Nevinson.
10. The National Awakening in India (London). Hon. Ramsay Macdonald, M.P.
11. Essays on Indian Art, Industry and Education (Indian Review Madras 2s.) Havell.
12. My Indian Reminiscences (Indian Review 2s). Deussen.
13. India (Laurie, London). Piere Loti.